# BODIES OF EVIDENCE

# BODIES OF EVIDENCE

## Reconstructing History through Skeletal Analysis

*Edited by*

**Anne L. Grauer**
*Department of Sociology and Anthropology*
*Loyola University of Chicago*
*Chicago, Illinois*

**WILEY-LISS**
**A JOHN WILEY & SONS, INC., PUBLICATION**
New York • Chichester • Brisbane • Toronto • Singapore

**Address All Inquiries to the Publisher**
**Wiley-Liss, Inc., 605 Third Avenue, New York, NY 10158-0012**

The text of this book is printed on acid-free paper

Library of Congress Cataloging-in-Publication Data

Bodies of evidence : reconstructing history through skeletal analysis
/ edited by Anne L. Grauer
    p. cm.
  Includes bibliographical references and index.
  ISBN 0-471-04153-X (alk. paper). — ISBN (invalid) 0-471-04279-X
(pbk. : alk. paper)
   1. Human skeleton—Analysis. 2. Human remains (Archaeology)—
North America. 3. Excavations (Archaeology)—North America.
4. Paleopathology—North America. 5. Cemeteries—North America.
6. North America—Antiquities. I. Grauer, Anne L., 1958–  .
GN70.B63 1995
573—dc20
                                              94-44503

# Contents

PART III: RECONSTRUCTING PATTERNS OF HEALTH AND DISEASE

# Contributors

**Robert L. Blakely**, Department of Anthropology, Georgia State University, Atlanta, GA 30303-3083

**Gerald Boyce**, Department of Anthropology, McMaster University, Belleville, Ontario, Canada

**Joseph Craig**, Hanson Engineers Incorporated, 1525 S. 6th St., Springfield, IL 62703

**Thomas A. J. Crist**, John Milner Associates, 1216 Arch St., Philadelphia, PA 19107 and Temple University, Department of Anthropology, Philadelphia, PA

**Lynne Goldstein**, Department of Anthropology, University of Wisconsin–Milwaukee, Milwaukee, WI 53201

**Anne L. Grauer**, Department of Sociology and Anthropology, Loyola University of Chicago, Chicago, IL 60626

**Judith M. Harrington**, Department of Anthropology, Georgia State University, Atlanta, GA 30303-3083

**D. Ann Herring**, Department of Anthropology, McMaster University, Hamilton, Ontario, Canada L8S 4L9

**Rosanne L. Higgins**, Department of Anthropology, State University of New York–Buffalo, Buffalo, New York 14261

**Dale L. Hutchinson**, Department of Anthropology, East Carolina University, Greenville, NC 27858

**M. Anne Katzenberg**, Department of Archaeology, University of Calgary, Calgary, Alberta, Canada T2N 1N4

**Clark Spencer Larsen**, Department of Anthropology and Research Laboratories of Anthropology, University of North Carolina, Chapel Hill, NC 27599 and Department of Anthropology, American Museum of Natural History, New York, NY 10024

**John P. McCarthy**, Senior Research Archaeologist, Institute for Minnesota Archaeology, Minneapolis, MN

**Elizabeth M. McNamara**, Department of Sociology and Anthropology, Loyola

University of Chicago, Chicago, IL 60626

**Randall W. Moir**, Department of Anthropology, Southern Methodist University, TX

**Elizabeth A. Murray**, Department of Biology, College of Mount St. Joseph, Cincinnati, OH 45233

**Stephen P. Nawrocki**, Department of Biology, University of Indianapolis, Indianapolis, IN 46227-3697

**Anthony J. Perzigian**, Department of Biology, University of Cincinnati, Cincinnati, OH

**Susan Pfeiffer**, School of Human Biology, University of Guelph, Ontario, Canada N1G 2W1

**Daniel G. Roberts**, Director, Cultural Resources Department, John Milner Associates, Inc., 309 North Matlack Street, Westchester, PA 19380

**Jerome C. Rose**, Department of Anthropology, University of Arkansas, Fayetteville, AK, 72701

**Katherine F. Russell**, Department of Anthropology, Kent State University, Kent, OH 44242

**Shelly R. Saunders**, Department of Anthropology, McMaster University, Hamilton, Ontario, Canada L8S 4L9

**Margaret J. Schoeninger**, Department of Anthropology, University of Wisconsin, Madison, WI 53706

**Leslie E. Sering**, Department of Sociology and Anthropology, Purdue University, W. Lafayette, IN 47907

**Joyce E. Sirianni**, Department of Anthropology, State University of New York–Buffalo, Buffalo, New York 14261

**Richard C. Sutter**, Department of Anthropology, University of Missouri, Columbia, MO 65211

**Douglas H. Ubelaker**, Department of Anthropology, National Museum of Natural History, Smithsonian Institution, Washington D.C. 20560

**Matthew A. Williamson**, Department of Sociology and Anthropology, Purdue University, W. Lafayette, IN 47907

**Frank Winchell**, 1923 S. Cheyenne, Tulsa, OK 74119

# Preface

The idea for this book stems from a simple unexpected question posed to me by a student several years ago. "How," the student inquired, "could analyzing human remains from historic cemeteries be so difficult when you have so many historic documents to help you?" I hardly knew how to answer. It became obvious to me, however, that many people, students and professionals alike, are under the impression that excavating and analyzing historic non-Native American populations was either less of a challenge than exploring the lives of the earliest inhabitants of the New World, or more likely to provide scientific "truth." Neither, of course, is the case.

With an increasing number of historic non-Native American remains being excavated due to urban development or changes in the use of land, has come an increasing complexity in the excavation and analysis of these remains. Some of this increased complexity arises from the political and ethical situations encountered by researchers. Other aspects of the complexity are due to the overwhelmingly erratic nature of human record keeping, which comprises most of the historical documentation available. Yet another complicating factor is the rapid pace of change and the use of new technologies within the fields of paleopathology and paleodemography. The goal of this book is to explore these complexities and provide insight into the potential for skeletal analysis to elucidate history.

The contributions to this book are intended to serve several purposes. First, this book is designed to provide both professionals and nonprofessionals with a glimpse into the problems faced by researchers embarking on the excavation and/or analysis of historic human remains. Politics, for instance, have played an enormous role in many excavations. Chapter 1, by Lynne Goldstein and Chapter 2, by Daniel Roberts and John McCarthy, carefully outline some of the considerations, delicate situations and powerful repercussions that occur when excavations take place under public scrutiny. Other types of challenges are addressed by Douglas Ubelaker (Chapter 3) and Steven Nawrocki (Chapter 4). These chapters outline the possible variations in human preservation and emphasize the need for vigilant excavation techniques. Similarly, the contributions made by virtually all the authors in Parts II and III of this book take a problem-oriented approach towards understanding the demographic patterns, or patterns of health and disease, in a particular historic population. Each chapter attempts to juggle the desire to utilize as much documentary and skeletal evidence as possible with the need to continually examine the inherent biases of each source of information.

Another goal of this book is to highlight the importance of theory in the excavation and analysis of human remains. In all aspects of excavation and analysis a variety of theoretical foundations serve as the starting point for research. Contributors to Part II, for instance, consistently grapple with the theories designed to help us understand patterns of human demography. The issue as to whether the archaeological population under investigation is a reasonable representation of the greater population living at that time is a recurring theme in the chapters by Shelly Saunders, Ann Herring, and Gerald Boyce (Chapter 5), Anne Grauer and Elizabeth McNamara (Chapter 6), Judith Harrington and Robert Blakely (Chapter 7), and Rosanne Higgins and Joyce Sirianni (Chapter 8). Similarly, contributors to Part III repeatedly question the validity of the techniques they have chosen to use and the application of various techniques to the population under investigation. While Clark Larsen et al. (Chapter 9), Frank Winchell, Jerome Rose, and Randall Moir (Chapter 10), and Elizabeth Murray and Anthony Perzigian (Chapter 11) attempt to utilize many different available techniques to gain insight into the patterns of health and disease of their particular populations, Richard Sutter (Chapter 12), Thomas Crist (Chapter 13), and Anne Katzenberg and Susan Pfeiffer (Chapter 14) apply specific techniques to skeletal populations in order to reach their conclusions. In all instances, the authors are forced to consider the problems inherent to their chosen techniques along with the array of potential biases inherent to the archaeological population and the accompanying historical documentation.

Yet another goal of this book is to provide students and professionals (both within and outside the fields of archaeology and skeletal biology) with an accessible source of information. It is apparent as you read through the chapters that some authors have chosen to simplify their language and provide a basic understanding of the problems and potential within our field. This method of communication is rarely found in journals or reference books. Other authors have provided more detailed and complex accounts of their research in order to highlight the need for expertise and precision in various aspects of analysis. Both approaches are critical to the health and development of our discipline, and both techniques will, hopefully, serve the novice and the expert well.

Anne L. Grauer

# Acknowledgments

I wish to extend my warmest thanks and appreciation to the contributors to this book for their cooperation and patience. I am indebted to my colleagues Dr. J. Calcagno and Dr. K. Johnson for sharing their expertise. Thanks also goes to my laboratory assistants Debra Brown, Chris Engle, Cinthia Leman, Alexia Sabor, Julie Smentek, Paula Tomczak, and Patrick Waldron for providing feedback for many of the chapters, and to Elizabeth McNamara for helping me bring the final version together. I am grateful to Karen Chase, our department secretary, for her seemingly endless skills, and to Loyola University for providing necessary resources. I also wish to acknowledge the support and encouragement that I received from William Curtis, editor, and David Ades, assistant editor, at Wiley-Liss. Support for this effort and the inclusion of undergraduates into scientific research has been in part supported by NSF Grant No. SBR-9350256.

Anne L. Grauer

# BODIES OF EVIDENCE

# PART I
## Issues and Considerations

# 1 Politics, Law, Pragmatics, and Human Burial Excavations: An Example from Northern California

LYNNE GOLDSTEIN

## WHAT CAN WE LEARN FROM BOOKS?

When I was asked to prepare this chapter on the political and legal aspects of burial excavation, it occurred to me that probably no topic in archaeology has received as much attention in the past few years. In particular, I thought about the new laws that have been written, as well as the repeated concern expressed for proper ethical behavior on the part of archaeologists. Archaeologists have been told, and have been telling themselves again and again that, as anthropologists, we must take into account the feelings, beliefs, interests, and concerns of the people we are studying. Given this perspective, I wondered if we were now teaching students how to behave ethically and responsibly.

I examined more than 12 basic archaeology textbooks, ranging from the most common to the more obscure. The books usually include a discussion about Native Americans or other indigenous groups and their concerns about graves and sacred objects, as well as statements indicating that one must operate with sensitivity. What I did not find, however, were many discussions placing the issues of permissions and claims to the past in a broader context. Rarely did an author mention that one needs permission to conduct archaeological research, or that the excavation of burials often requires permission from a number of different people, or groups of people, and a number of different offices. I was especially struck by the fact that landowners and stakeholders other than native groups were not mentioned in the textbooks. For instance, *Australian Field Archaeology: A Guide to Techniques,* edited by Graham Connah (1983), discusses the notion of permission at some length. Even in this

*Bodies of Evidence*, Edited by Anne L. Grauer.
ISBN 0-471-04153-X  © 1995 John Wiley & Sons, Inc.

excellent handbook, however, the focus is placed upon getting permission from the aborigines, not from landowners or other possible stakeholders. The problems of negotiating with government bureaucracies are never mentioned in this or any other text, except for an occasional reference to problems of getting permission in a foreign country.

Given the results of this cursory research, I concluded that a discussion of the political and legal aspects of burial excavation might be helpful if presented by means of examples. The details of laws and regulations can be found in a good library, but advice on the pragmatics of excavating burials today is apparently more difficult to find. While much of the advice below may appear elementary, or simply to fall within the realm of common sense, my experience leads me to believe that no one can be too cautious or too thorough when planning an archaeological excavation of a historical cemetery.

## BACKGROUND

Over the past few years there has been a lot of media attention concerning the excavation of burials and cemeteries in the United States. Whereas much of this attention has been focused on Native American burial sites, a number of new discoveries in surprising locations or circumstances have also been featured. These include the previously unknown African American cemetery discovered in New York City (Harrington, 1993), the African American Baptist Church cemetery in Philadelphia (Parrington & Roberts, 1984), and the colonial cemetery in Maryland, which yielded lead coffins (Valvo, 1991).

The excavation of a cemetery, especially a historic cemetery, brings out curiosity and strong emotion. No matter what the particular case, the excavation is rarely ignored by the public. Further, it is likely that someone related (or claiming to be related) to the individuals being excavated will step forward. If ever an archaeologist needed to be aware of the political and legal realities and ramifications of a situation, the excavation of a historic cemetery is the time.

A variety of scholars have examined the public's interest in the past and the nature of that interest (e.g., Hodder, 1990; Lowenthal, 1985; Merriman, 1989). For the purposes of this chapter, the very fact that the public holds an interest in the past is all that is important. The archaeologist can generally do little to control public involvement, and when work is ongoing, knowing the nature of the public's interest is not always of much help. What one needs to know is how to cope, how to excavate in a responsible manner, and how to respectfully address and include the myriad of people who hold an interest or a stake in what you are doing.

## THE FORT ROSS EXCAVATION

The example of a historical cemetery excavation used here is my own work at the Russian Orthodox cemetery at Fort Ross, Sonoma County, California. The Russian fort and settlement was founded on the Pacific coast in 1812 and was occupied until 1841. The site is now part of the Fort Ross State Historic Park, operated by the California Department of Parks and Recreation (hereafter referred to as DPR). The settlement of Fort Ross was associated with Russian expansion of the Pacific maritime fur trade. The Russian colonies in North America (in Alaska, northern California, and very briefly in Hawaii) were established to gain access to productive sea otter territories and to provide other trade and agricultural items. Fort Ross was the southernmost Russian colony in North America.

The Fort Ross cemetery excavations, conducted over a three year period from 1990 through 1992, are unusual from a number of perspectives: 1) the work was not part of a contract project—the site was not in jeopardy or endangered; 2) prior to beginning excavations, we attempted to get permission from all groups that might be represented or have an interest in the cemetery; 3) the excavators were coming from out of state, a somewhat unusual (and not entirely accepted) occurrence in California; and 4) each individual would be reburied in the grave from which they had been excavated.

How we had come to be at Fort Ross was also unusual. In 1989, Sannie Osborn, one of my Ph.D. students and a native Californian, proposed for her dissertation research a study of mortuary practices in a frontier setting—specifically, Fort Ross. What happens to prescribed customs of funerary behavior when members of a society are removed from the familiar surroundings of family, friends, and church, and relocated to a frontier outpost such as the Russian colony at Fort Ross? Osborn's dissertation would use archival materials to explore how well written records reflected information garnered from the archaeological investigation. No one, however, was certain about the precise location of the cemetery, its extent, or who specifically was buried there. My own interests focused on the cemetery organization and the potential impact of colonialism as viewed from mortuary practices.

Prior to officially proposing excavation of the cemetery, we talked with and gained the support of a number of individuals, including an ethnohistorian in the then-Soviet Union, as well as members of the Russian Orthodox clergy, and DPR employees. We outlined our plan and explained our goals. Once we had discussed the project with a number of individuals, we began the official process of requesting permission and permits. I cannot overemphasize the importance of laying this groundwork *before* officially requesting permission to excavate. By operating in this way we were not treated as strangers when the request to excavate was made. It also allowed us to determine how our work might benefit the many groups involved. Was there something they wanted to know, or could our research assist them in resolving issues related to their own work?

Currently, most historic cemeteries are excavated because of development and other impending threats. Our work at Fort Ross was unusual because the cemetery was not directly threatened. We had time to insure that we proceeded in a proper manner. We were told, however, that the project was the first noncontract cemetery excavation in California in close to 20 years. Our proposal was not routine and represented a rarely considered option. Consequently, while using the Fort Ross excavation as an example may not provide advice that is practical in all situations, it may be useful to those negotiating the political mazes associated with many burial excavations today, regardless of sociopolitical context.

For all of our work, we followed several common-sense, but critical, principles: 1) be inclusive (both in the sense of from whom you ask permission and in participation in the project); 2) don't lie (lying always causes problems, since you have to remember precisely what you told each party); and 3) keep your promises (people have to be able to believe and trust you).

I have chosen to organize this chapter topically. Under each topic heading, I have indicated the basic question to be answered; in parentheses is the "twist" to the question, which can often be the cause of logistic, political, and practical problems. It is our experience that the wise archaeologist will pay more attention to the potential consequences of the "twist" than to the question itself.

## LEGALLY EXCAVATING CEMETERIES

### What Laws are Relevant to This Project (and What Other Laws May Suddenly Apply)?

If a cemetery excavation is being undertaken because a development, highway, or other project is planned, the specific laws are probably familiar to the archaeologist. These laws have perhaps led to his or her presence in the project. However, many of the recent laws requiring archaeological work at historic cemeteries (cf. Price, 1991) in the path of construction are less widely known by the public and officials. The recent nature of these laws may require that the archaeologist, and others, convince the contractor that the work is necessary and that it must be done by a professional archaeologist. In other words, archaeologists may find themselves dealing with suspicious and potentially hostile audiences.

It is also the case that most states allow, at least theoretically, the excavation of cemeteries for other purposes, assuming that the proper permits and the permission of potentially affected parties have been obtained. Archaeologists attempting such an endeavor will need to be as familiar as possible with local and state laws in order to circumvent future problems and avoid alienating participating groups.

On the basis of my own experience, I would offer the following advice: since you're probably not an attorney, do the best you can in following the law; ask for help and advice; be flexible; make a lot of friends; and try not to lose your temper while you are being firm about your rights! In the case of Fort Ross, the DPR outlined the laws and steps required for excavation of the cemetery. After we had permission, we thought that all legal hurdles were completed. This was a premature assumption on our part.

The cemetery area at Fort Ross is adjacent to Highway 1. During the first week of excavation, we attempted to tie our excavations to a USGS benchmark located approximately 100 meters down the road. Our first violation of the law occurred when we failed to wear orange vests and hardhats, as required by California law when participating in highway work (we didn't realize we were conducting highway work).

Having solved this problem with the help of the Fort Ross maintenance crew, we were stopped by a CalTrans (California Transportation Authority) supervisor, who informed us that we would have to cease operations unless we could produce an encroachment permit. He claimed that traversing state land with surveying equipment required such a permit, and further, we were not allowed to be on Highway 1 with surveying equipment without a permit.

I began by asking how one received such a permit. I was told that we would have to go to San Francisco, a three-hour drive away. Having decided that simple compliance was not going to be easy, I explained that we were moving from state land to state land, and that this was a DPR-sponsored, and therefore a state-sponsored project.

The CalTrans official was unimpressed. After some discussion, he claimed that he would have us reported and cited. Having grown up in the Chicago area, I immediately assumed he wanted a bribe, but rather than offering my driver's license with a $50 bill wrapped around it, I did the following: 1) I asked that he talk with the personnel at the park office before he "turned us in"; 2) I made my students move as quickly as possible to complete the surveying work before he returned; 3) I called the Regional DPR office and asked why they had not informed me of this law (they had never heard of the encroachment permit); and 4) I talked with everyone on the park staff who might know this CalTrans fellow. The last measure was most effective. One park employee talked with the individual and apparently settled the permit issue. I was told never to be on the highway without orange vests and hardhats, but otherwise heard nothing more about encroachment permits. We later went out of our way to befriend the CalTrans official. It was he who helped us get permission to profile the road cut so we could determine whether highway construction had destroyed part of the cemetery.

It is unlikely that any researcher can learn every law that may or may not apply to a particular situation. You can try, nonetheless, to familiarize yourself with the laws clearly pertaining to your project. It is also wise to cover yourself and make sure that you have as many local friends as possible.


## GETTING PERMISSION

### From Whom Do I Need to Get Permission (and Who Thinks I Need Their Permission)?

Archaeologists have been used to going to landowners or federal and state agencies and asking their permission to proceed with excavations. Now, however, we must also be concerned with other real or potential stakeholders.

For most archaeologists excavating a historic cemetery, getting permission may not be difficult, since the project is usually required because of development. However, given the number of individuals and/or groups who now make claims on remains in any cemetery, it is in the best interest of the archaeologist to determine as many potential stakeholders as possible and ask their permission to excavate. It is in this area that we operated on the principle of inclusiveness—if in doubt, include the group among those whose permission we need.

Following our principles, it took a total of 18 months to get permission to excavate the Fort Ross cemetery. We needed to get explicit permission from the County Coroner, two different branches of the Russian Orthodox Church, the Kashaya Pomo, the Bodega Miwok, the California Native American Heritage Commission, Alaska Native organizations, and several different offices within the DPR. Our strategy in getting permission was to arrange a single gathering with as many of the parties as possible in one room. At the meeting, we attempted to clearly state what we wanted to do, why we wished to do it, and how we thought the project might benefit the various groups represented at the table. There are several aspects to this approach that are important to emphasize:

1. We had previously talked with all of the representatives about our plans and had received input concerning their interests in the project.
2. We asked for advice on how best to proceed with the project, so that everyone felt that they were involved from the beginning. We did not present a formal plan expecting everyone to approve.
3. During the meeting, we again asked each group what they might like to see as a result of the project. Were there specific aspects of interest to them, and did they have questions that our work might be able to address?
4. Everyone met together so that all groups were aware of what was discussed with each group.
5. Since it is notoriously difficult to get written confirmation from groups of stakeholders, I prepared a summary of our meeting and sent it to all relevant parties, even those who were unable to attend. I also included self-addressed postcards so participants could object to my summary or provide additional questions.
6. After the meeting, once comments were received, we went about completing the formal permit application.

While it is important to understand the intricacies of permission and permits, it is also important in these negotiations and discussions that the archaeologist be very clear about what he or she expects beyond answers to research questions. In other words, in order for the project to be successful, it must be clear to all that the archaeologist (even if working on the basis of a research design written by others) is in charge of field and laboratory work and strategies. While he or she may ask for advice and may need permission, approvals, and reviews, there can be no micro-management of the project by others.

One final issue is of critical importance in the matter of gaining permissions: don't make promises you can't keep. One of the Native American groups potentially represented in the cemetery stated that they did not want us to excavate any of their people. If we found someone from their tribe, we were to rebury the individual immediately, without study. We pointed out that although we would like to honor such a request, it was most unlikely that we could identify a grave as belonging to that tribe until we had excavated and analyzed it. We did, however, agree that once we knew or suspected that any burial belonged to the tribe, we would notify the appropriate representatives immediately, discuss the particulars of the situation with them, and follow their instruction. This alternative was acceptable. It allowed us to proceed in a reasonable manner, rather than putting us in the position of making promises that we knew could not be kept.

## FUNDING

### Who Might Fund the Project (and What Strings May Be Attached)?

Even in situations where funding is coming from the agency or firm responsible for the development, there is rarely sufficient money to complete the project. For historic cemeteries, it makes sense to request at least some funding from groups who have an interest in the site. Churches, interest groups, and other organizations are logical candidates. While such groups are the most likely targets for funding requests, it is very likely that the researcher will find that there are strings attached to these grants, since the groups have intense interest in the site and are generally not in the business of providing funding for research.

What kind of strings might be attached? Perhaps you will be asked to provide a number of favors for the group. Perhaps you will be encouraged to make certain conclusions or interpretations over others. Or perhaps members of the group will expect to contribute to the excavation and analysis. Our experience at Fort Ross suggests that requests for outside funding work best when the money is directly associated with a specific portion of the project. This portion ought to be one in which the funding group is most interested. The group, however, should be distantly removed from the excavations themselves.

One of the reasons that the Russian Orthodox Church granted permission to excavate the cemetery at Fort Ross is that they thought that the cemetery and the individuals interred within were not receiving sufficient recognition and respect. To a number of individuals of Russian descent in the area, the fact that the precise cemetery location was unknown and unadorned was a crime. The Church felt strongly that the cemetery should be reconstructed, so proper respect could be paid. Reconstruction meant that each grave should be marked with a cross.

We did not ask the Church for funds to excavate the cemetery, to analyze the remains, or to rebury the remains. The Church gave their permission for each aspect of the work, and they were active participants in many portions of the project, but they were only asked to fund the reconstruction of the site. That is, they raised the money to construct and erect the crosses on each grave site. They also made plans to install a large plaque commemorating the site and the archaeological work. This was the portion of the project that was critical to the Church. The archaeological role was simply to indicate the proper locations for each cross, and consult on the appropriateness of particular cross styles.

Whether or not to ask affected groups for money requires judgement on the part of the archaeologist. We need to be aware that such requests are substantially different than most of the grants we request and receive. Recognize all the strings in advance and get them in writing, even if you have to do the writing yourself.

## KEEPING PERMISSION

**What Kinds of Information Should be Shared, When Should It be Shared, and With Whom Should It be Shared (or, Who Needs to Know What You're Doing and What You've Done)?**

To a great extent, keeping permission is a matter of keeping people informed, completely and honestly. My advice on this matter is simple: keep everyone informed and make certain that everyone is receiving the same information, whether requested or not. For the Fort Ross work, I developed the following course of action:

1. A list was prepared of all individuals/groups who should be kept informed of the progress of the work.
2. The list was approved by all of the parties. I continued to ask whether someone else should be added to the list.
3. All parties were told what they could expect from me and when they could expect it. In our case, we presented an outline of the project along with a timetable. We also indicated when we would send progress reports.
4. Individuals and groups were invited to visit, call, and ask questions. We invited groups to dinner while we were in the field, and we regularly called if something unusual came up or was discovered.
5. Reports with pictures were sent out. The exact same reports were sent to everyone. All reports were posted at the same time so that, to the extent possible, no one received a report before anyone else.
6. Every effort was made to communicate, even when our efforts seemed unappreciated. I made regular calls in addition to my reports, and each time I sent out information, I included a self-addressed, stamped postcard so that the individual or group could respond with questions, problems, or comments.
7. I gave public lectures on my work and encouraged local publicity. This helped demonstrate the importance and significance of the work, and provided an opportunity for the parties to share the limelight if they attended the talks or were interviewed by the media.

I urge archaeologists to be prepared to be surprised during this course of action, because it will seem as though no one cares what you are doing. Few parties will respond to your reports and even fewer will send back their cards. Convince yourself that this is good. In these situations, it is often the case that you hear from people only when they are upset or want something. By keeping everyone equally informed, however, you have met your responsibilities.

## DEALING WITH THE UNEXPECTED

### What Might Happen Unexpectedly (and What Do I Do When It Does Happen)?

The saying that if anything can go wrong, it will, is certainly true of many excavations, and seems to be particularly true with cemeteries. The trick to coping with emergencies or problems is to expect things to go wrong and to remain flexible.

The degree of rapport established between the archaeologist and various individuals and groups will help determine how well you can react to the unexpected. You never know which of your new friends will be of assistance, but one of my general rules of thumb is to seek out friendships with maintenance personnel because they are pragmatic and are adept at solving problems.

The first year we excavated at Fort Ross, we learned that no one in the DPR regional office expected us to find much in the way of artifacts, besides a few crosses and nails. I assumed the lack of specific discussion and concern about artifact treatment and curation was because the responsibility for materials during the excavation and analysis was mine, and that I was considered a competent professional. I simply had no idea that the issue had not been discussed because no one thought we would find valuable artifacts. This assumption on their part left them quite surprised and concerned when a number of different kinds of items were found in the excavations. DPR officials were particularly concerned about the preservation of a number of cloth fragments we had excavated. Rather than ask whether or not arrangements had been made for the cloth, or whether I knew how to deal with such artifact types, someone in the DPR sent a request for assistance to a conservator in another state (I do not know how this individual was selected). The individual did not know the specific situation at Fort Ross, nor did she know me. In response to the request, she faxed a memo indicating how to treat the cloth, then added: "FIELD ARCHAEOLOGISTS MUST TAKE IMMEDIATE PRECAUTIONS!! Arsenic was used at this time for embalming and archaeologists may be in danger." Because the warning was from an "expert," this memo triggered the California toxic waste laws. We were visited by people from the regional DPR office, who stated that they had to conduct tests for arsenic, and that they might have to consider the entire cemetery a toxic waste dump.

I responded to this shocking news as follows: 1) I pointed out that research indicated that it was against Russian Orthodox canon to use any form of embalming; 2) I asked from where would the Russians at Fort Ross have gotten arsenic?; and 3) if in the unlikely event that arsenic was used, its concentration would be minimal, since preservation of the bodies was poor. DPR officials were sympathetic but unconvinced by my responses. The warning had been "official" and they had no choice but to operate on the assumption that arsenic was present until proven otherwise. We were told that because it seemed unlikely that the danger was great (or perhaps it was just that we had already been exposed and it was too late), we could continue with our excavations. We were required to wear gloves and gas masks while working in the graves. If we chose not to comply, the excavation would be shut down until further notice.

We carefully followed the orders. We also took our own soil samples and conducted our own tests; our samples included a greater number of control samples outside the cemetery, since our geologist was aware that arsenic occurs naturally in these soils. As expected, no high levels of arsenic were detected in any samples and we were allowed to proceed the next year.

The toxic waste episode was only one of many unexpected situations during the Fort Ross project. In every case, we found that remaining flexible, patient, and calm always helped. We delighted in the humor and absurdity of many of our situations when we were amongst ourselves. We were keenly aware that grandstanding to the DPR or other officials would have gained us nothing.

## THE PUBLIC

### How Does One Deal with the Press and the Public (and Who Is Considered the Public or a Key Figure in the Project)?

No matter where you are digging or what the context, you must assume that the excavation of graves will bring out the press and the general public. For cemetery excavations in public places, it is common to have one or more people designated as tour guide/press secretary. There is neither the time nor space here for a detailed discussion of how to deal with the press or the general public, except to summarize a few of the procedures and lessons I have learned:

1. In addition to a spokesperson or tour guide, have a general public "shpiel" prepared. Make sure that all members of the excavation understand what is and is not to be discussed publicly.

2. Do not let members of the press or general public take pictures of burials without your express permission and understanding of how the photographs or videotape will be used. At Fort Ross, although the Church did not object to pictures, such a decision may well have changed if a close-up of a skull with a questionable headline had appeared in the local newspaper. Explain that restrictions are made out of respect for the dead, and recommend alternate scenes or items for photographs.

3. Make sure that every visitor to the site is escorted, including those visitors you know. In terms of safety and public relations, you never know what people are likely to do or where they are likely to go.

4. In the case of parks or other agencies, it may be very important to an official's career, the agency organization, or an individual's self-esteem to be recognized

as the official news source or representative. While the archaeologist in charge need not hide completely, all press coverage (whenever possible) should go through the appropriate channels, and it may be useful to have an agency representative as the official spokesperson.

5. When you are excavating in a very public setting, a crew tends to band together against the "Other." This type of behavior becomes an important way to build and maintain morale, but there is a trap. The Other in this setting is anyone who is not out at the site working every day. To my crew, for example, anyone who wasn't there daily was considered "the public" or a "tourist." Much to my dismay and embarrassment, several DPR employees overheard this reference by the crew and became insulted. They pointed out to me that they were the ones who lived in California, and that it was their park—how could they be the visitors, or worse, tourists?

Explanations of group dynamics ultimately worked, but the insult had been made and the feelings were hurt. As foolish as this example may sound, it had an impact on our work and was something for which we had to compensate.

Consider the implications of your actions and statements: would you want to hear or see whatever it is you said or did on the front page of the newspaper or on television? This advice is useful whether or not the press is present, since local gossip can be more damaging or more helpful than press coverage.

## DIFFERING AGENDAS

### How Does One Clarify an Agenda for the Project (and Make Sure that You are Aware of All of the Other Agendas)?

How one states and clarifies one's own agenda has been discussed in the section on getting permission. Since it is important to realize that everyone has an agenda, it is useful to ask all parties "What do you hope to gain from the project?" Once the archaeologist knows what others expect, it is much easier to accommodate, avoid, argue against, and deal with differing goals. Carefully consider whether an agenda has an affect on your project.

The Fort Ross cemetery project provides a range of examples of differing types of agendas and interests, and a few of these examples will make it easier to demonstrate that a particular agenda may or may not be important for consideration.

1. DPR historical archaeologists were interested in the project in general terms. They anticipated an increased knowledge of the period through artifacts that might be found in context. Their interests provided many fruitful discussions and interesting background data, but did not otherwise affect our work.

2. The California Native American Heritage Commission initially expressed concern about the project. They gave their support after the native Californian

groups agreed to the project. The Commission's agenda was to reaffirm their position and to make sure that they were players in the project. They reviewed our plans and the approvals obtained from native groups.

3. The gift shop at the Fort Ross Interpretive Center was particularly interested in the artifacts found at the cemetery. A cross found in a grave in 1972 had been cast and duplicated. It was one of the most popular items in the gift shop. They were interested in artifacts that could be cast for subsequent sale.

4. The Church, as mentioned previously, was interested in reconstructing the cemetery. They gave their support to the project in order to achieve this goal. Other than specific requests associated with reburial ceremonies and cemetery reconstruction, the Church's agenda did not interfere with the project.

5. The Kashaya Pomo's interest in the project was limited. They were interested in any features that might represent a Pomo burial. When it became clear that we were unlikely to find any Pomo burials, interest in the project waned. The only request by the Pomo was that we try to confirm several stories that they had been taught as children. If we could provide answers, archaeological interpretation would add to the Pomo stories.

6. The DPR also found the project appealing. It provided good press and a significantly better interpretation of the cemetery and site. Addressing their agenda was not difficult, and it enhanced our work.

7. One of the DPR archaeologists had a personal agenda. He wanted to demonstrate that he could coordinate a complex cemetery project with sensitivity and respect. While one might see such an agenda as self-serving, this is an unnecessarily dark view. The archaeologist helped to demonstrate that many different groups, with many different goals, can work together. Not only is this an honorable agenda, we were the direct beneficiaries at little cost.

In the following two cases, participants in the project had agendas that were not helpful or useful and which had to be curtailed.

8. Very early in the project, one of the priests involved made it clear that he wanted to be more than an advisor and consultant. He attempted to undermine my direction by spreading rumors. He was confronted and told that his behavior would not be tolerated.

9. A DPR employee, who was one of the archaeologists in charge of interpretation for the state, was interested in the project because of previous work he had conducted at Fort Ross. After our field season he asked to see the artifacts "on his own time." Because this request seemed odd, we resisted. A short time later, the individual was arrested and convicted of stealing a large number of artifacts from the DPR's collections.

Researchers often worry about the agendas of others. I would argue that this is often a useless activity since even hidden agendas are not necessarily threatening. As long as interests do not interfere with the running or outcome of the project, they should be of little concern. An investigator can usually sense when someone's actions appear dubious, or if personal goals will adversely affect the research. Through quick and decisive action, enlisting the assistance of others, and keeping a clear paper trail, these hurdles can be overcome.

## PROJECT RESPONSIBILITIES

### Who Is Responsible for What (and What Do You Have to Do Even if It Isn't Really Your Responsibility)?

When you have finally received permission to excavate, the office(s) or people giving you permission will undoubtedly make it clear that you have certain tasks to perform and that other tasks are someone else's responsibility. While this may be technically true, ultimate responsibility for the project must rest with the researcher.

As an example, in the process of discovering and excavating the cemetery at Fort Ross, we had to remove a 12-foot wooden cross that had been erected by one branch of the Russian Orthodox Church. The Church used the cross in their annual Memorial Day services and were promised by the DPR that the cross would be reerected before the next Memorial Day. Unfortunately, before the cross could be replaced, Park personnel changed and the promise was forgotten. I called in November to remind the DPR of its promise and in April of the next year I called to ask whether the cross had been erected. Of course it had not. I called Church officials and the district DPR maintenance office to contract for some convict labor. I ended up flying to California to make sure that the cross was repaired and reerected.

Another example of the need to uphold responsibilities concerned promises made to the Russian Orthodox Church about reburial and reconstruction of the cemetery. The Church, the Alaskan natives, and the California natives were told that reburials would take place as the bones were analyzed and that the cemetery would be reconstructed as soon as possible. I was told that neither of these jobs were my responsibility. The DPR would tell me when the reburials were scheduled. I would make certain that the remains were ready and that the proper location for each individual to be reburied would be marked.

At the time that the first reburial was scheduled, the State of California was beginning a series of budget cuts, resulting in reorganization within the DPR and other agencies. I was told to arrange for the reburials; no assistance was offered. Rather than refuse to participate in a task that was not officially my responsibility, I made the arrangements with both branches of the Russian Orthodox Church, notified the California and Alaska natives, the coroner, and other interested parties, and planned the events. I had members of my crew excavate the graves that were to have remains placed in them. Crew members were also on hand to backfill the graves after the ceremonies were completed. Russian Orthodox canon requires that each individual must be buried with a cross. We made certain that each individual had a cross, even though no one provided crosses for the occasion. We went to a great deal of trouble to make certain that the ceremonies occurred, and that both branches of the Church were able to conduct services over an equal number of burials.

It would have been easy to have stood back from the situation and said that reburials were not my responsibility. The Church, however, had supported what we were doing and expected the individuals in the cemetery to receive proper treatment and respect. If the State had not done its job, the Church would have been angry not only with State officials, but also with me—all positive actions can easily be undone by one negative action. It is for this reason that the principal investigator must know all the agreements and formal and informal promises that have been made, and must make sure, to the best of his or her abilities, that these agreements are carried out.

I relate these stories not to show myself as a heroine or "good guy." I know that the State of California would have eventually carried out its responsibilities, and there are numerous sensitive and responsible archaeologists working for the DPR. I think, however, that it is likely that a number of individuals would have been angry and disappointed by the time the State fulfilled its promises.

It was no one's job to focus on all aspects of this project. As principal investigator, nonetheless, it was my job to make sure that I did the best job I could, and that the people with whom I worked were satisfied with what had been done. It was my job to anticipate and organize, to act as ombudsman for all of the affected parties, regardless of what my "official" responsibilities might have happened to include.

## CONCLUSIONS

After hearing about the Fort Ross project, and especially the fact that the bone preservation was poor, the first question that everyone asks is whether the project ended up being worthwhile. Although we would have been delighted if bone preservation had been better and the soil easier to excavate, we learned a tremendous amount from the project, both archaeologically and politically. The yield in terms of archaeological knowledge is beyond the scope of this paper, but it is significant. The political and legal knowledge gained from the project is undeniably of equal significance. I would summarize the lessons to be learned from this project as follows:

- Be inclusive.
- Keep your promises (and perhaps the promises of others).
- Be aware of your environment, both in terms of the consequences of your actions, and the expectations of others.
- Be generous with what you've learned.
- Be flexible.
- Take full responsibility for your actions.

In another context, I (Goldstein & Kintigh, 1990, Goldstein, 1992) have argued for the importance of trust and mutual respect between parties. Leone and Preucel (1992) present a similar view from the perspective of Habermas' theory of communicative action. Only when we treat others and other cultures with respect, sensitivity, and tolerance, can we expect and demand the same in return. This is true for all research and interaction, whether archaeological or political, historic or prehistoric, Native American or European.

# REFERENCES

Connah G (1983). Australian Field Archaeology: A Guide to Techniques. Canberra: Australian Institute of Aboriginal Studies.

Goldstein L (1992). The Potential for future relationships between archaeologists and Native Americans. In Wandsnider L (ed.), Quandaries and Quests: Visions of Archaeology's Future. Center for Archaeological Investigations, Occasional Paper No. 20, pp. 59–71. Carbondale: Southern Illinois University Press.

Goldstein L, Kintigh K (1990). Ethics and the reburial controversy. American Antiquity 55(3):585–591.

Harrington, SPM (1993). Bones and bureaucrats. Archaeology 46(2):2838.

Hodder I (1990). Archaeology and the post-modern. Anthropology Today 6(5):13–15.

Leone M, Preucel R (1992). Archaeology in a democratic society. In Wandsnider L (ed.) Quandaries and Quests: Visions of Archaeology's Future. Center for Archaeological Investigations, Occasional Paper No. 20, pp. 115–135. Carbondale: Southern Illinois University Press.

Lowenthal D (1985). The Past is a Foreign Country. Cambridge: Cambridge University Press.

Merriman N (1989). Heritage from the other side of the glass case. Anthropology Today 5(2):13–15.

Parrington M, Roberts DG (1984). The First African Baptist Church Cemetery. Archaeology 37(6):26–32.

Price HM III (1991). Disputing the Dead: U.S. Law on Aboriginal Remains and Grave Goods. Columbia: University of Missouri Press.

Valvo DK (1991). Who's in the coffins? Archaeology 44(6):20.

# 2 Descendant Community Partnering in the Archaeological and Bioanthropological Investigation of African-American Skeletal Populations: Two Interrelated Case Studies from Philadelphia

DANIEL G. ROBERTS and JOHN P. McCARTHY

## INTRODUCTION

The decades of the 1970s and especially the 1980s have witnessed a fundamental, yet painfully difficult, change in the way that anthropologists, particularly archaeologists and physical anthropologists, go about their business. Two currents have come together to make many anthropologists realize that they, as scientists, no longer can, nor should, stake an exclusive claim to data. First, and most importantly, various Native American tribal groups in several parts of the United States began to assert claims to cultural property and, especially, to human remains associated with their ancestors, seeking repatriation from museum collections and reburial. In addition, many of these communities have sought input into and oversight of the scientific investigation of ancestral skeletal remains to ensure their culturally appropriate and respectful treatment. Second, at about the same time, a segment of the archaeological community began to emerge that was strongly influenced by French structuralism, critical theory, and various neo-Marxist critiques of capitalist society (e.g., Hodder, 1982; Saitta, 1983; Leone, 1984; Miller & Tilley, 1984; Spriggs, 1984; McGuire & Paynter, 1991). These "postprocessual" archaeologists, and others

*Bodies of Evidence*, Edited by Anne L. Grauer.
ISBN 0-471-04153-X © 1995 John Wiley & Sons, Inc.

(e.g., Silberman, 1989; Trigger, 1989), have noted that archaeology is a product of contemporary society and that our conception of the past is firmly rooted in present values, attitudes, and politics. Consequently, archaeology, as currently constituted, is seen to support existing, largely Eurocentric structures that benefit the socially and politically dominant segments of society. In response, these researchers have argued for what one has termed "an actively instrumental archaeology" that is self-consciously socially progressive (Tilley, 1989, p. 110). As part of such an archaeology, the claims of minorities and other socially repressed groups to their own archaeology and history have been recognized as legitimate in "unearthing and objectifying alternative viewpoints and social dispositions, contributing to social change" (Hodder, 1984, p. 31).

From these two trends it is possible to develop a new concept that recognizes that data generated by and about people, whether relating to their past, present, or future, belong to a wider audience, not solely to the scientists who undertake the bulk of the data-gathering and interpretative processes. Further, scientific pursuits, in and of themselves, may not be sufficient reasons to gather and interpret data, nor necessarily are the data-preservation initiatives mandated by the National Historic Preservation Act (NHPA), under which most excavations of historic cemeteries and other archaeological sites are conducted in the United States today. Spiritual, political, social, cultural, and perhaps even emotional factors are equally important in decision-making processes regarding the appropriate treatment of data relating to human beings. The wider inclusion and participation of contemporary descendant communities, here considered to be partnering, is central to such a concept. While many anthropologists have been remarkably resistant to this new partnering concept, it appears that their ranks may rapidly be dwindling.

This chapter discusses the partnering of the scientific team and the affected descendant community in the excavation and bioanthropological investigation of two interrelated 19th century African-American skeletal populations in Philadelphia associated with the First African Baptist Church (FABC). The processes involved in bringing the descendant African-American community into the decision-making and data-gathering processes are also discussed. The nature of scientific/descendant community partnering and the authors' beliefs as researchers working with descendant communities are offered, along with the implications of these beliefs.


## NATIVE AMERICANS AND NAGPRA

Because anthropologists were so slow to embrace a concept of scientific/descendant community partnering, the 1980s were characterized by considerable conflict between, on the one side, archaeologists and physical anthropologists, and on the other side, various Native American tribal groups. Early warnings of this coming conflict were sounded in the professional archaeological literature beginning at least as far back as the early 1970s (e.g., Sprague, 1973; Johnson, 1974). More recently, many archaeologists (e.g., Cheek & Keel, 1984; Ferguson, 1984; Zimmerman, 1985,

1990a, 1990b; Kintigh, 1990; Goldstein & Kintigh, 1990; Klesert & Powell, 1993) have begun to recognize, if not formalize, the new partnering concept, as have several popular writers (e.g., Preston, 1989; Craig, 1990; Neiburger, 1990). Regrettably, however, a significant body of literature, scientific and lay alike, has also arisen that has served only to perpetuate the conflict (e.g., Buikstra, 1981; Turner, 1986; Peerman, 1990; Marshall, 1991; Mihesuah, 1991; Meighan, 1992; Deloria, 1973, 1992). To the Native Americans in this latter group, all scientists are unworthy of their trust, while to the scientists, the saying that "the only good Indian is a dead Indian who hasn't been reburied" sadly has been overheard more than once at professional conferences.

The net result of the more than 20-year "territorial struggle" over cultural data is that Congress has enacted the Native American Graves Protection and Repatriation Act (NAGPRA) and has amended the National Historic Preservation Act (NHPA) to better take into account the desires of Native American tribal groups. NAGPRA, of course, addresses only concerns centering on the reburial and repatriation of human skeletal remains and associated grave goods of groups that demonstrably are Native American in origin. It addresses no other living cultural group, nor does it address any issues other than reburial and repatriation. As such, NAGPRA really is a very circumscribed bill that, regrettably, is also ethnocentric in its focus. In reality, NAGPRA is little more than a legislative response to a politically active "squeaky wheel," i.e., the disenfranchised Native American tribal groups that were successful in demanding its passage and implementation (see Lovis, 1990 for a brief discussion of NAGPRA). Frankly, had the anthropological community been more responsive to Native American concerns early on, the passage and implementation of NAGPRA may have been wholly unnecessary.

NAGPRA really misses two major points. First, and most obvious, it grants no recognition or legal clout to any group other than Native Americans. Second, and most importantly, it focuses only on human burials and associated grave goods, and fails to consider other aspects of human culture that may be of equal or more importance in the collective consciousness of various communities. The next version of NAGPRA (and there surely will be one, particularly if the anthropological community continues to dig in its heels, as it did with the Native American tribal groups in the 1980s), will, most likely and quite appropriately, be exclusionary to no American cultural or subcultural group, nor most, if not all, aspects of cultural expression.

## AFRICAN-AMERICAN PARTNERING

The African-American community is presently the most conspicuous group not represented by NAGPRA. Anthropological interest in African American cultural traditions, particularly those as revealed by archaeology, has increased dramatically in the continental United States in recent years (e.g., Geismar, 1982; Gradwohl & Osborn, 1984; Rose, 1985; Wheaton et al., 1990; Bower, 1991; Singleton, 1991a,

1991b; Ferguson, 1991, 1992; Joseph et al., 1993), and this trend is sure to continue. Indeed, the African American Archaeology Network, with its twice-yearly newsletter *African American Archaeology*, has recently been established as a subgroup of the Society for Historical Archaeology, and its membership is rapidly growing (Thomas Wheaton, personal communication, 1993).

With the increased scholarly attention paid to sites associated with African-Americans, particularly by archaeologists and physical anthropologists, partnering with groups and individuals representing affected African-American descendant communities has begun to be embraced by some members of the scientific community who study African-Americans. Recent events in New York City surrounding the African Burial Ground discovered in lower Manhattan (Banks, 1992; Diehl, 1992; Laura, 1992; Muhammed, 1992; Panagos, 1992; Taylor, 1992; Harrington, 1993; Federal Steering Committee for the African Burial Ground, 1993; Weathers n.d.); Dallas, with the Freedman's Cemetery (Belkin, 1990; Ver Berkmoes, 1991; Anonymous, 1991); and Newark, with the Trinity Episcopal Church Cemetery (Walker, 1993; Larini, 1994) have emphatically brought to the fore the appropriateness of including affected African-American descendant communities in the decision-making and data-gathering processes when the object of scientific inquiry (in these cases, ancestral remains) arouses sufficient social, political, spiritual, and/or inspirational interest. From a scientific viewpoint, this is considered most appropriate, because African-American perspectives, both scientific and nonscientific alike, often are quite different from the largely Eurocentric perspectives of anthropological scientists and, accordingly, can well inform the types of research questions scientists are asking of their data (Blakey, 1990, pp. 38–39; Singleton, 1991b, p. 10). From a nonscientific point of view, this is also considered most appropriate since nonscientific values of the affected descendant African-American communities (e.g., social, political, religious, and/or spiritual values) are equally as important and legitimate as scientific values and, in many instances, are more so. Put simply, the partnering concept states that "we simply must shake the view that we alone control the past" (Zimmerman, 1990a, p. 64). Concomitant with this, of course, is the reality that we as scientists may need to willingly relinquish some, perhaps all, of that control. Indeed, in some cases partnering with affected descendant communities may result in the decision that no scientific inquiry will be conducted at all, and we must be prepared willingly to accept such a decision.

It needs to be made clear at this point that the concept of "partnering," as envisioned here, is not to be confused with the concept of "community involvement." The latter simply involves consultation by the scientific team with the affected descendant community in a unidirectional manner, and is most frequently characterized by presentations of a scientifically justified course of action to that community only after critical decisions have been made. Partnering, on the other hand, requires the proactive participation of the affected descendant community during the decision-making process, so that the resultant course of action benefits both the scientific and nonscientific concerns and perspectives of all interested parties. As such, the concept of community involvement should be viewed only as the beginning of a true partnering process.

## THE FIRST AFRICAN BAPTIST CHURCH CEMETERIES

Prior to the extensive media attention that was brought to bear on the African Burial Ground, the Freedman's Cemetery, and the Trinity Episcopal Church Cemetery, two African-American cemeteries were excavated in Center City Philadelphia with the full cooperation of, and partnering with, the local descendant African-American community. The excavation of both cemeteries was necessary as a means to mitigate adverse effects arising from two planned construction projects. Both cemeteries were related to the First African Baptist Church (FABC), still in existence in Philadelphia, and the cemeteries were located two blocks apart, along the south side of the former Vine Street, now the Vine Expressway. The Eighth and Vine FABC Cemetery was used for burial purposes between circa 1825 and 1841, while the Tenth and Vine FABC Cemetery was used slightly earlier, between circa 1810 and 1822. The Eighth and Vine FABC Cemetery project was undertaken first (for the Redevelopment Authority of the City of Philadelphia) and largely completed without the knowledge of the existence of the Tenth and Vine FABC Cemetery; several publications and reports chronicle the results of this investigation (Parrington & Roberts, 1984, 1990; Roberts, 1984; Blakey, 1986; Parrington et al., 1986; Parrington & Wideman, 1986; Angel et al., 1987; Parrington, 1987; Kelly & Angel, 1989; Aufderheide & Wittmers, 1989; Parrington et al., 1989; Rankin-Hill, 1990; Eriksen & Stix, 1991). The Tenth and Vine FABC Cemetery was excavated in 1990 and, due to budgetary constraints of the lead agency (the Pennsylvania Department of Transportation), funds to complete the analysis were not made available until the fall of 1992. As a result, no final reports or publications have as yet been produced, although several presented papers have reported on the Tenth and Vine FABC Cemetery in a preliminary fashion (Crist & Ward, 1990; McCarthy, 1990; Crist et al., 1992).

### Historical Summary of the First African Baptist Church

The First African Baptist Church was formed as an offshoot of the First Baptist Church of Philadelphia by 13 African-American church members and was admitted to the Philadelphia Baptist Association in October 1809 (First Baptist Church, 1806–1813). The congregation purchased a property on Tenth Street near Winter Street (south of Vine Street) in 1810 (Philadelphia County, 1810). By 1816, the FABC had split into two congregations, with only one of the groups continuing to be recognized by the Philadelphia Baptist Association, that being the group in possession of the meeting house at the Tenth and Winter Streets property. The second group met at a site on Thirteenth Street between Race and Vine. Although separate congregations, both continued to be referred to as the "First African Baptist Church" (Philadelphia Baptist Association, 1813, 1816).

In 1822, both the Tenth and Winter Streets church and the Thirteenth Street church members lost their respective properties at sheriff's sales (Philadelphia County, 1822). At the time of sale, the Tenth Street property was described as measuring 68 by 120 feet, and included a frame structure. While it is not known how soon after its purchase the Tenth Street property was first used as a cemetery, Philadelphia Board of Health records document burials at the Church's property in 1821 and 1822 (McCarthy et al., 1987). The descendants of the Tenth Street congregation still meet for worship today at 16th and Christian Streets in Philadelphia.

By 1824, the Thirteenth Street congregation apparently was occupying a small frame building on three lots at Smith's Alley, near the corner of Eighth and Vine. The pastor at this time is recorded as the Reverend Henry Simmons, who also apparently owned at least one of the three lots at this location (Carey & Lea, 1824, pp. 56–57). Philadelphia Board of Health records reveal that burials were also made on one of the three lots, at least between 1825 and 1842. This lot measured approximately 18 by 80 feet (Philadelphia County, 1825). Prior to the last recorded burial in 1842, however, several attempts had been made to close the burial ground due to concerns for public health (Philadelphia Board of Health, 1838, 1841). Reverend Simmons died in 1848, and it appears that the Eighth Street FABC began to dissolve after his death. Finally, in 1851, Reverend Simmons' widow sold off the Eighth Street property, despite legal action by the remnant congregation (Philadelphia County, 1851), and the association of the Eighth Street property with the FABC was ended.

To summarize, burials at the Tenth Street property may have been made as early as 1810, and apparently ceased in 1822 when the property was sold. At the Eighth Street property, burials appear not to have been made much before 1825, and continued until at least 1842. Thus, the excavation of the two cemeteries has afforded a unique perspective on a nearly continuous record of African American burial customs, demography, and health for more than three decades in early nineteenth century Philadelphia.

### The Eighth and Vine FABC Cemetery

Discovery of the Eighth and Vine FABC Cemetery occurred on November 18, 1980, during the course of archaeological monitoring of a large subsurface cut in association with construction of the Philadelphia Commuter Rail Tunnel. The monitoring was undertaken by John Milner Associates, Inc. under contract to the City of Philadelphia, Department of Public Property. On that morning, an examination of wood fragments protruding from the east slope of the tunnel cut near the southwest corner of Eighth and Vine Streets resulted in the identification of the head end of a wooden coffin approximately five feet below existing grade. Upon this identification, the exposed portion of the coffin was immediately protected with plastic sheeting and sand, and representatives of the City notified.

Consultation with the resident engineer resulted in an immediate decision to avoid any further construction disturbance in the area of the exposed remains. Fortunately, this was a practical decision, since the exposed east face of the tunnel cut at this location represented the easternmost encroachment of the cut. Indeed, the east face of the cut actually encroached further than called for in construction plans. As a result, the cemetery had not previously been identified by archival means, since it lay outside the original study corridor. A search of the historic documentary evidence was immediately initiated so as to identify, accurately locate, and date the cemetery.

Continued discussions with representatives of the City produced a consensus of opinion that the exposed portion of the site required immediate protection against potential looting and periodic slope erosion. Initial protection was provided in the form of plywood and plastic sheeting covered with earth fill. In order to further protect the site and allow excavation of the tunnel cut to continue to its full depth, concrete was subsequently poured over the earth fill. This was accomplished by the end of November, 1980 and, although not suspected at the time, the site was to remain in that protected state for the next 2½ years.

Despite several discussions with representatives of the City following the protection of the site, the City decided that it had no further responsibility with regard to the cemetery abutting the tunnel cut. The City's position was that the cemetery lay almost entirely outside its right-of-way and, accordingly, it had no further responsibility for the cemetery other than to maintain its integrity beneath the concrete and earth covering.

In November of 1981, another major project in Center City Philadelphia came to bear on the Eighth and Vine FABC Cemetery. At that time, John Milner Associates, Inc. began archaeological documentary research in association with another large-scale transportation project in Center City Philadelphia, the Vine Expressway Improvements Project. This research, undertaken as part of an Environmental Impact Statement (EIS) for the Pennsylvania Department of Transportation and the Federal Highway Administration, studied and documented archaeological and historical resources associated with several alternatives for improving traffic flow along Vine Street, a major east–west corridor through Philadelphia. Since two of the alternatives appeared to involve the parcel where the Eighth and Vine FABC Cemetery was located, further documentation of the cemetery was undertaken. As a result of that documentation, the Eighth and Vine FABC Cemetery was found to be eligible for the National Register of Historic Places by the Pennsylvania Bureau for Historic Preservation on September 24, 1982. Shortly thereafter, it was determined that the construction project would have an adverse effect on a portion of the cemetery, and that data recovery was the prudent course for the mitigation of those adverse effects.

Concurrently with these findings relative to the Vine Expressway EIS, however, another set of circumstances occurred that would significantly affect the Eighth and Vine FABC Cemetery. In December, 1982, the Redevelopment Authority of the City of Philadelphia, the owner of the parcel where the majority of the cemetery was located, began negotiations with a private developer to convey the property to him so that a large office building could be developed. Because this proposed development was on a more accelerated time schedule than the Vine Expressway Improvements Project, and because Federal action was involved in the planned development, the Redevelopment Authority decided to initiate proceedings with regard to the archaeological resources present at the site. Governed by the terms of a Memorandum of Agreement dated August 1, 1983 between the Advisory Council on Historic Preservation, the Federal Highway Administration, the Redevelopment Authority of the City of Philadelphia, and the Pennsylvania Bureau for Historic Preservation, excavation of the Eighth and Vine FABC Cemetery was begun in the summer of 1983. During two field seasons of excavation (1983 and 1984), just under 150 individual African American remains were archaeologically excavated.

*Partnering with the Descendant Community in the Eighth and Vine FABC Cemetery Project.*   Descendant community interest prior to and during the fieldwork portion of the Eighth and Vine FABC Cemetery project was considerable, which led to the beginnings of a long-term partnering relationship between the community and the scientific team. As a result of this positive interest, the project was characterized by a decided lack of dissent throughout its course. A significant portion of the project research design encouraged the direct involvement of the Afro-American Historical and Cultural Museum (AAHCM), located three blocks from the site at Seventh and Arch Streets. Initially, the direct participation of several AAHCM staff members was planned but, unfortunately, constraints associated with museum responsibilities did not ultimately allow for such direct participation. Instead, it was decided that AAHCM staff would conduct periodic tours of the site for interested members of the community. Advertisements of the availability of such tours were placed in the *Philadelphia Inquirer* and *Philadelphia Tribune* (a Center City African-American newspaper) and approximately one dozen tours were subsequently conducted by the museum staff. An elevated wooden platform was constructed at the site so that safe and unobstructed viewing of the excavation proceedings could by enjoyed by the public during these organized tours.

In addition, although not formally advertised, off-street visitors were encouraged to view the excavation proceedings at their convenience, and it quickly became common knowledge in Center City Philadelphia that an interesting and educational excavation was underway nearby. Detailed handouts outlining the history of the site and excavation strategy were made available to all interested people, whether visiting the site on their own or as part of an organized tour, and impromptu lectures were provided by field personnel on an as-warranted basis. It is estimated that 3000-4000 people benefitted from this on-site educational program, either in an impromptu off-the-street fashion, or as part of the organized AAHCM tours.

Another significant area of community partnering centered on the present-day pastor, parishioners, and elders of the First African Baptist Church, still in existence at 16th and Christian Streets in Philadelphia. The church was apprised early on of the research design planned for the investigation, and considerable interest in the scientific findings was generated among the church members. Although no direct research involvement by church members resulted, much information pertaining to the early history of the church was provided by them. In addition, periodic briefings regarding the progress of the excavation and research were provided to church members by the scientific team.

Perhaps most importantly, however, members of the contemporary First African Baptist Church became directly involved in the reburial of the human remains from the FABC Cemetery. From the outset of the project, the research design proactively advocated the reburial of the remains after sufficient time had been allowed for their scientific study. Accordingly, representatives of the First African Baptist Church, the Redevelopment Authority of the City of Philadelphia, and Eden Cemetery, a historically African-American cemetery located in nearby Delaware County, Pennsylvania, made arrangements for the timely reburial of the remains. These arrangements included provision for the reinterment of the remains in plain cardboard containers within five large concrete burial vaults that had been arranged side-by-side in a large communal grave pit.

The reburial ceremony took place in the afternoon of July 22, 1987 at Eden Cemetery, after slightly less than 3 years of scientific study. Attended by approximately two dozen people, the ceremony consisted of a very brief Christian ritual at graveside conducted by the Reverend Elvis Turner, pastor of the First African Baptist Church, followed by the recitation of the Lord's Prayer by all in attendance. This, in turn, was followed by a symbolic sprinkling of earth on the remains, the closing of the concrete vaults, and the backfilling of the grave. Today, a simple marker proclaims the final resting place in Eden Cemetery of the nineteenth century members of the Eighth and Vine First African Baptist Church.

It should finally be noted that, perhaps in no small part due to the successful partnering with Philadelphia's African-American community, media attention generated by Eighth and Vine FABC Cemetery excavation was entirely favorable. Several dozen newspaper articles, radio interviews, and televised news stories were produced during the life of the project, and none was unfavorable. Most significantly, an important documentary video was also made that chronicled the investigation. Entitled *Ground Truth: Archaeology in the City* and produced by Richard Robinson, a Philadelphia filmmaker, the video was released in 1988 by Silverwood Films. Narrated by the Reverend Paul Washington, a prominent African-American Philadelphian, the video subsequently has been well-received both nationally and internationally.

## The Tenth and Vine FABC Cemetery

The block bounded by Ninth, Tenth, Vine, and Winter Streets was designated Block 20 during the initial cultural resources assessment of the Vine Expressway (Roberts et al., 1982). As a result of this study, several blocks were recommended eligible for the National Register of Historic Places. Based on a review of historic maps and census records, two nineteenth century working-class communities were documented as formerly existing on Block 20. Both Java Place, primarily occupied by Irish immigrants, and Liberty Court, primarily home to African Americans, were courtyard communities of small "band-box" houses squeezed in behind the larger residences that faced the street. Archaeological resources potentially associated with these communities were identified as having the ability to document aspects of ethnic and working-class enclaves in nineteenth century Philadelphia. A Memorandum of Agreement dated September 6, 1983 among the Advisory Council on Historic Preservation, the Federal Highway Administration, the Pennsylvania Department of Transportation, and the Pennsylvania Bureau for Historic Preservation included archaeological testing at Block 20 to confirm the presence and significance of archaeological resources associated with the Java Place and Liberty Court communities and, as appropriate, excavations to recover representative data from each community. The archaeological testing, conducted in 1984, confirmed the presence of archaeological resources associated with the nineteenth century working-class occupation of Block 20 (McCarthy, 1984). Subsequent archaeological data recovery investigation of the southern portion of the block, focusing on the neighborhood of Liberty Court, took place during the summer of 1985 (McCarthy et al., 1987).

Unexpectedly, the 1985 excavation of Liberty Court encountered a pit containing the fragmentary skeletal remains of five individuals. This gravepit, measuring approximately 4½ feet square, was situated in a small yard area at the rear of one of the houses fronting on Liberty Court. Careful examination of deed records revealed that Liberty Court had been erected over a portion of the property along Tenth Street owned by the FABC between 1810 and 1822. In addition, Philadelphia Board of Health records confirmed the use of the FABC property for the burial of at least seven people in 1821 and 1822 (McCarthy et al., 1987). Accordingly, it appeared that the gravepit represented the reinterment of burials associated with the FABC's ownership of the property between 1810 and 1822 that were exposed during the later construction of Liberty Court. The scope of the investigation in the southern portion of Block 20 immediately expanded to address the potential for the presence of additional burials. However, these five individuals were the only human remains revealed and excavated in the portion of the block investigated in 1985.

The northern portion of Block 20, including the bulk of the former FABC property along Tenth Street, had been sealed under the east-bound traffic lanes of Vine Street when the street was widened over this portion of the block in the 1940s. Thousands of vehicles used Vine Street daily; accordingly, this area was not available for archaeological study during the 1985 excavation.

As plans for the Vine Expressway were finalized, it became clear that the northern portion of Block 20 would be affected by the construction of the depressed expressway, requiring excavation to a depth of 30 feet below existing street grade. A plan was formulated to archaeologically examine the remainder of the Tenth and Vine Streets FABC property and recover any human remains present. Based on the research conducted in 1985, there appeared to be potential for the presence of at least two additional burials. A 30-day period was included in the Vine Expressway construction schedule to accommodate the archaeological fieldwork.

At the beginning of April 1990, a service road, constructed over the southern portion of the block, was opened to divert traffic from Vine Street. The investigation of the Tenth and Vine FABC property began with the mechanical removal of the street paving covering the site. Grave shaft outlines were identified immediately under the Vine Street roadbed, and several burials were covered by only a thin mantle of soil. It quickly became evident that a relatively large number of burials was present at the site.

A field team of over 30 was mobilized, and the excavation was conducted on a 12-hour, 7 day-a-week schedule to complete the investigation of the site within the 30-day allowance in the construction schedule. Graves were encountered to a depth of approximately 6 feet below street grade. Excavation continued to a minimum of 10 feet below grade to insure the recovery of all human remains. In all, 97 graves were identified in the field and completely excavated. While not all contained intact human skeletal remains, the remains of approximately 85 individuals were recovered. At the time of this writing, bioanthropological analysis is nearing completion and a detailed report on the project is in preparation.

*Partnering with the Descendant Community in the Tenth and Vine FABC Cemetery Project.*    Partnering between the scientific team and the descendant community in the investigation of the Tenth and Vine FABC Cemetery built on and expanded the relationships established during the Eighth and Vine FABC Cemetery project and, again, a decided lack of dissent was evident. When the initial burials were identified during the 1985 Block 20 investigation, the pastor of the First African Baptist Church, the Reverend Elvis Turner, was immediately informed of the discovery, and he visited the site.

Consultation with the FABC congregation and the AAHCM continued during the full excavation of the cemetery site in 1990. Church leaders and interested congregation members were kept fully informed as the project progressed in the field, and the staff of the AAHCM was also briefed on the project. Due to the total inaccessibility of the Tenth and Vine Streets FABC Cemetery in a heavily protected construction site in the middle of an active highway, however, it unfortunately was not possible to establish a formal public interpretation or tour program during the field investigations in a manner similar to that developed for the Eighth and Vine FABC Cemetery. However, an informal tour was given to a group of congregation members, and Reverend Turner visited the site several times during the excavation.

The field investigations were followed by public programs organized by and presented at the AAHCM in February 1991 and September 1993 and at the Atwater-Kent Museum, the history museum of the City of Philadelphia, in December 1993. The initial presentation at the AAHCM provided an overview of the Tenth and Vine FABC Cemetery excavation and anticipated analyses as part of a program on death and funeral practices in the African-American community. The 1993 programs presented the preliminary results of the Tenth and Vine FABC project, focusing on the bioanthropological analyses. An enthusiastic group of 40 to 50 people attended each of these programs, including many members of the FABC congregation. Questions and discussions following each presentation brought the congregation's intense interest in its history into focus for the wider community.

A detailed presentation of project goals, methods, and preliminary results was made to members of the FABC congregation in June 1993, and included illustrated presentations on the history of the FABC, results of ongoing bioanthropological studies, and burial practices at the FABC cemeteries. Of equal if not more importance in the presentation was a homecoming service to honor the spirits of the ancestral members of the FABC that included opening and closing devotional presentations by Rev. Dr. William J. Harvey, III, Executive Secretary of the Foreign Mission Board of the National Baptist Convention, ancestral rhythms and verse presented by a member of the research team and an African musical ensemble, and a traditional African shrine dedication, also performed by a member of the research team. The scientific presentation and devotional ceremony was attended by nearly 100 members of the FABC and other members of the Philadelphia community, and was well-received by all in attendance.

While the FABC congregation does not include individuals with professional training or expertise in history or anthropology, the scientific team has developed and continues to maintain close communication with interested congregation members, building on ongoing consultations and public presentations. Team members have also elicited oral history remembrances and other cultural information from church members, particularly regarding attitudes and practices surrounding death and mourning. These data have been of particular value in developing interpretive frameworks for the project, and have given project researchers fresh insights into African-American culture and cultural meanings of immeasurable value to the project.

Finally, church leaders and congregation members are actively participating in the development of plans for the reinterment of the Tenth and Vine FABC Cemetery population, scheduled for the spring of 1995, after approximately 2 years of scientific study. It is expected that the reinterment will take place at Eden Cemetery, where the Eighth and Vine FABC Cemetery population was reinterred in 1987, and that a suitable ceremony will take place to mark the event.

## CONCLUDING SUMMARY

In summary, the partnering programs for both the Eighth and Vine and the Tenth and Vine FABC Cemetery investigations proved to be appropriate for the time and place at which they were enacted. Although "partnering" largely portrays the character of both programs, neither was fully "inclusionary" in nature, since neither African-American scholars nor members of Philadelphia's African-American community assumed leadership positions on the project (although several African Americans did assume key research roles on one or both of the projects). As it happened, neither the members of the First African Baptist Church nor the broader African-American community in Philadelphia assumed a decidedly proactive stance in either project at all. Rather, while a certain intellectual curiosity towards both projects was a constant, there was neither the outpouring of emotion nor cries for empowerment that recently has characterized the African Burial Ground project in New York, and to a lesser extent the Freedman's Cemetery project in Dallas and the Trinity Episcopal Church Cemetery in Newark. Although descendant community interest and participation in the Eighth and Vine FABC Cemetery project can most accurately be characterized as passive, and in the Tenth and Vine FABC Cemetery project as slightly more active, neither project elicited forceful proactive involvement from either the members of the FABC congregation or the broader local community.

In spite of this passivity, however, it is equally accurate to characterize the evolution of the two projects as one of an increasing strengthening of the ties between members of the church and the scientific team. The congregation's intense interest in the Church's history served as a unifying focus of the investigations. While at the onset of excavations at Eighth and Vine in 1983 the project team members primarily viewed what they were about to embark on as a purely scientific endeavor, by the time the Tenth and Vine excavations began in 1990, the nonscientific values of both projects had come into clear focus, even though the members of the church did not force the issue. This led to an increasingly heightened awareness among the church members about the scientific value of studying their ancestral remains, and a concomitant awareness on the part of the scientific team regarding those nonscientific values held to be important by the members of the church. By the time that the homecoming ceremony for the Tenth and Vine remains was held in the summer of 1993, the melding of scientific and nonscientific values had become relatively complete.

The successes of the partnering programs associated with the two FABC Cemetery projects, however, can be viewed as little more than a relatively isolated modest beginning in making such programs commonplace in all projects where ancestral remains are to be the object of scientific inquiry. In Philadelphia, neither the wishes of the descendant community nor the responses of the scientists were in the least forceful—indeed, most of the scientific "responses" were, instead, proactive initiatives, including the proposal for appropriate reburial after study. Because of the recent community-initiated successes at New York's African Burial Ground and Dallas' Freedman's Cemetery, as well as the enactment of NAGPRA, it is likely that the relative passivity experienced in Philadelphia will no longer be the norm, particularly as scientific inquiry may affect contemporary disenfranchised communities, most certainly including African Americans. Accordingly, it is well past time for the anthropological community at large to enthusiastically embrace the emerging practice of partnering if the conflicts of the past are to be avoided in the future. Scientific inquiry simply is not the only, nor even necessarily the primary, value that human remains and their associated artifacts embody. Indeed, as Klesert and Powell (1993, p. 352) have boldly yet correctly pointed out, the wishes of living descendant populations, not the wishes of the scientists, should be accorded a position of primacy with regard to the treatment of ancestral remains, even if those wishes result in the decision that no scientific study of excavated human remains will be conducted. As anthropologists, we must recognize that one of our primary responsibilities is to living communities, and if such living communities derive more meaning from treatments of ancestral remains that involve no scientific study, then we must be willing not only to accept, but also to proactively foster, such nonscientific treatment. To continue to insist that what science can inform is all-important, even in the face of rejection from affected descendant communities, is nothing short of inappropriate and professionally irresponsible. However, if an effective and inclusionary partnering program can be developed, such a program can only be to the benefit of all by providing for the emergence of a clear picture of the past within a framework of its relevance to the present.

# REFERENCES

Angel JL, Kelley JO, Parrington M, Pinter S (1987). Life stresses of the free black community as represented by the First African Baptist Church, 8th and Vine Streets, Philadelphia, 1823–1841. Am J of Phys Anthropol 74:213–229.

Anonymous (1991). Citizens monitor Freedman's. North Central, Newsletter of the Texas State Department of Highways and Public Transportation 4(1):1–4.

Aufderheide AC, Wittmers LE (1989). Human bone and lead content from the First African Baptist Church cemetery. Paper presented at the 58th annual meeting of the American Association of Physical Anthropologists, San Diego, California.

Banks WS (1992). Precious bones and ancestral spirits. Ground Truth 1(3):18.

Belkin L (1990). Unearthing of freed-slave cemetery may put Dallas road project on hold. New York Times, August 13:A12.

Blakey ML (1986). Fetal and childhood health in late 18th and early 19th century afro-americans: enamel hypoplasia and hypocalcification in the FABC skeletal population. Am J of Phys Anthropol 72:179.

Blakey ML (1990). American nationality and ethnicity in the depicted past. In Gathercole P, Lowenthal D (eds.), The Politics of the Past, pp. 38–48. London: Unwin Hyman.

Bower, BA (1991). Material culture in Boston: The black experience. In McGuire RH, Paynter R (eds.), The Archaeology of Inequality, pp. 55–63. Oxford: Basil Blackwell.

Buikstra J (1981). A specialist in ancient cemetery studies looks at the reburial issue. Early Man 3(3):26–27.

Carey HC, Lea I (1824). Philadelphia in 1824, or a brief account of the various institutions and public objects in this metropolis: being a complete guide for strangers and an [sic] useful compendium for the inhabitant. Philadelphia: Carey and Lea.

Cheek AL, Keel BC (1984). Value conflicts in osteo-archaeology. In Green EL (ed.), Ethics and Values in Archaeology, pp. 194–207. New York: The Free Press.

Craig B (1990). Bones of contention: The controversy over digging up human remains in parks. National Parks 64:7–8.

Crist TAJ, Ward JA (1990). The archaeology and osteology of the 10th street First African Baptist Church cemetery, Philadelphia. Paper presented at the annual meeting of the Council for Northeast Historical Archaeology, Kingston, Ontario.

Crist TAJ, McCarthy JP, Roberts DG (1992). Comparative archeology and osteology of the First African Baptist Church cemeteries: Observations regarding the formation of Philadelphia's early nineteenth century African-American community. Paper presented at the 25th annual meeting of the Society for Historical Archaeology, Kingston, Jamaica.

Deloria V Jr. (1973). God is Red. New York: Delta Books.

Deloria V Jr. (1992). Indians, archaeologists, and the future. American Antiquity 57(4):595–598.

Diehl LR (1992). Skeletons in the closet: uncovering the rich history of the slaves of New York. New York 25(39):78–86.

Eriksen MF, Stix AI (1991). Histological examination of age of the First African Baptist Church adults. Am J of Phys Anthropol 85:247–252.

Federal Steering Committee for the African Burial Ground (1993). Memorialization of the African Burial Ground. Recommendations Report to the U.S. Congress, August 6, 1993.

Ferguson L (1991). Struggling with pots in colonial South Carolina. In McGuire RH, Paynter R (eds.), The Archaeology of Inequality, pp. 28–39. Oxford: Basil Blackwell.

Ferguson L (1992). Uncommon Ground: Archaeology and Early African America, 1650–1800. Washington: Smithsonian Institution Press.

Ferguson TJ (1984). Archaeological ethics and values in a tribal cultural resource management program at the pueblo of Zuni. In Green EL (ed.), Ethics and Values in Archaeology, pp. 224–235. New York: The Free Press.

First Baptist Church (1806–1813). First Baptist Church minute book No. 7, from August 8th 1806 until November 8th 1813. Ms. on file, First Baptist Church, Philadelphia.

Geismar JH (1982). The Archeology of Social Disintegration in Skunk Hollow. New York: Academic Press.

Goldstein L, Kintigh K (1990). Ethics and the reburial controversy. American Antiquity 55(3):585–591.

Gradwohl DM, Osborn NM (1984). Exploring Buried Buxton: Archaeology of an Abandoned Iowa Coal Mining Town with a Large Black Population. Ames: Iowa State University Press.

Harrington SPM (1993). Bones and bureaucrats: New York's great cemetery imbroglio. Archaeology 46(2):28–38.

Hodder I (ed.) (1982). Symbolic and Structural Archaeology. Cambridge: Cambridge University Press.

Hodder I (1984). Archaeology in 1984. Antiquity 58:25–32.

Johnson E (1974). Professional responsibilities and the American Indian. American Antiquity 38(2):129–130.

Joseph JW, Reed MB, Marsh DC (1993). And They Went Down into the Water: Archaeological Data Recovery of the Riverfront Augusta Site, 9RI165. Report prepared for the City of Augusta Office of Economic Development. Stone Mountain, GA: New South Associates, Inc.

Kelley JO, Angel JL (1989). The First African Baptist Church Cemetery: Bioarcheology, Demography, and Acculturation of Early Nineteenth Century Philadelphia Blacks (Volume III, Osteological Analysis). Report prepared for the Redevelopment Authority of the City of Philadelphia. Washington: Smithsonian Institution.

Kintigh K (1990). A perspective on reburial and repatriation. Society for American Archaeology Bulletin 8(2):6–7.

Klesert AL, Powell S (1993). A perspective on ethics and the reburial controversy. American Antiquity 58(2):348–354.

Larini R (1994). Compromise sought on cemetery excavation stalling Jersey arts center. Newark Star-Ledger, January 9.

Laura E (1992). Honoring the dead: a bridge between two worlds. Ground Truth 1(1):7–8.

Leone M (1984). Interpreting ideology in historical archaeology: using the rules of perspective in the William Paca Garden in Annapolis, Maryland. In Miller D, Tilley C (eds.), Ideology, Power, and Prehistory, pp. 25–35. Cambridge: Cambridge University Press.

Lovis WA (1990). How far will it go?: A look at S. 1980 and other repatriation legislation. Society for American Archaeology Bulletin 8(2):8–10.

Marshall BK (1991). Native American grave sites at risk. The Progressive 55(1):14.

McCarthy JP (1984). Vine Street Expressway, L.R. 67045: Phase II Archeological Investigations in the Block Bounded by Ninth, Tenth, Vine, and Winter Streets, Philadelphia, Pennsylvania. Report prepared for Michael Baker, Jr., Inc. and the Pennsylvania Department of Transportation. West Chester, PA: John Milner Associates, Inc.

McCarthy JP (1990). African American acculturation as reflected in the cemeteries of the First African Baptist Church, Philadelphia: population dynamics and social stress in the early nineteenth century. Paper presented at the annual meeting of the Council for Northeast Historical Archaeology, Kingston, Ontario.

McCarthy JP, Tidlow EM, Cress G, Pinter S, Wagner DP (1987). Vine Street Expressway, L.R. 67045: Archeological Data Recovery in the Block Bounded by Ninth, Tenth, Vine, and Winter Streets, Philadelphia, Pennsylvania. Report prepared for Michael Baker, Jr., Inc. and the Pennsylvania Department of Transportation. West Chester, PA: John Milner Associates, Inc.

McGuire RH, Paynter R (eds.) (1991). The Archaeology of Inequality. Oxford: Basil Blackwell.

Meighan CW (1992). Some scholar's views on reburial. American Antiquity 57(4):704–710.

Mihesuah DA (1991). Depositing and desecration of Indian property and possessions. National Forum: Phi Kappa Phi Journal 71(2):15–17.

Miller D, Tilley C (eds.) (1984). Ideology, Power, and Prehistory. Cambridge: Cambridge University Press.

Muhammed AA (1992). Let us not marginalize ourselves, let us get involved. Ground Truth 1(2):8.

Neiburger EJ (1990). Profiting from reburial. Nature 344:297.

Panagos N (1992). Unearthing of African-American burial ground highlights primary economic role of these early New Yorkers. The Lubin Letter 11(3):1–4.

Parrington M (1987). Cemetery archaeology in the urban environment: A case study from Philadelphia. In Staski E (ed.), Living in Cities: Current Research in Urban Archaeology, Special Publication Series No. 5, pp. 56–64. Ann Arbor: Society for Historical Archaeology.

Parrington M, Roberts DG (1984). The First African Baptist Church cemetery: An archaeological glimpse of Philadelphia's nineteenth century free black community. Archaeology 37(6):26–32.

Parrington M, Roberts DG (1990). Demographic, cultural, and bioanthropological aspects of a nineteenth-century free black population in Philadelphia, Pennsylvania. In Buikstra JE (ed.), A Life in Science: Papers in Honor of J. Lawrence Angel, Scientific Papers No. 6, pp. 138–170. Kampsville, IL: Center for American Archeology.

Parrington M, Pinter S, Struthers TL (1986). Occupations and health amongst early nineteenth century black Philadelphians. MASCA Journal 8(1):37–41.

Parrington M, Roberts DG, Pinter S, Wideman JC (1989). The First African Baptist Church Cemetery: Bioarcheology, Demography, and Acculturation of Early Nineteenth Century Philadelphia Blacks (Volumes I and II). Report prepared for the Redevelopment Authority of the City of Philadelphia. Philadelphia: John Milner Associates, Inc.

Parrington M, Wideman JC (1986). The archaeology of a black Philadelphia cemetery: acculturation in an urban setting. Expedition 28(1):59–62.

Peerman D (1990). Bare-bones imbroglio: repatriating Indian remains and sacred artifacts. Christian Century 107:935–937.

Philadelphia Baptist Association (1813). Philadelphia Baptist Association minutes. Ms. on file, Philadelphia Baptist Association, Philadelphia.

Philadelphia Baptist Association (1816). Philadelphia Baptist Association minutes. Ms. on file, Philadelphia Baptist Association, Philadelphia.

Philadelphia Board of Health (1838). Health office minutes. Ms. on file, City Archives, Philadelphia.

Philadelphia Board of Health (1841). Health office minutes. Ms. on file, City Archives, Philadelphia.

Philadelphia County (1810). Deed between James and Rachel Ash and Edward Simmons, David Jackson, and William Vinson (Trustees of the First African Congregation in the City & Vicinity of Ph.). Philadelphia County Deed Book IC 23:293.

Philadelphia County (1822). Sheriff's deed between Caleb North and Richard Peters. Philadelphia County Sheriff's Deed Book D:69.

Philadelphia County (1825). Philadelphia County, Manuscript Survey, 3rd Survey District, October 14, 1825.

Philadelphia County (1851). Deed between Martha Simmons and John Murray. Philadelphia County Deed Book GWC 107:103.

Preston DJ (1989). Skeletons in our museum's closets. Harper's Magazine, February:66–75.

Rankin-Hill LM (1990). Afro-American Biohistory: Theoretical and Methodological Considerations. Unpublished Ph.D. dissertation. Department of Anthropology, University of Massachusetts, Amherst.

Roberts, DG (1984). Management and community aspects of the excavation of a sensitive urban archaeological resource: An example from Philadelphia. American Archeology 4(3):235–240.

Roberts DG, Cosans BJ, Barrett D (1982). Archeological Resources Technical Basis Report Supporting the Environmental Impact Statement for Vine Street Improvements, Philadelphia, Pennsylvania. Report prepared for Gannett, Fleming, Corddry, and Carpenter, Inc. and the Pennsylvania Department of Transportation. West Chester, PA: John Milner Associates, Inc.

Rose JC (ed.) (1985). Gone to a Better Land: A Biohistory of a Rural Black Cemetery in the Post-Reconstruction South. Fayetteville: Arkansas Archaeological Survey, Research Series No. 25.

Saitta D (1983). The poverty of philosophy in archaeology. In Moore JA, Keene AS (eds.), Archaeological Hammers and Theories, pp. 299–304. New York: Academic Press.

Silberman NA (1989). Between Past and Present: Archaeology, Ideology, and Nationalism in the Modern Middle East. New York: Henry Holt and Company.

Singleton TA (1991a). The archaeology of slave life. In Campbell EPC Jr., Rice KS (eds.), Before Freedom Came: African-American Life in the Antebellum South, pp. 155–175. Richmond: The Museum of the Confederacy, and Charlottesville: the University Press of Virginia.

Singleton TA (1991b). Editor's notes. African American Archaeology, Newsletter of the African American Archaeology Network 4:1.

Sprague R (1973). American Indians and American archaeology. American Antiquity 39(1):1–2.

Spriggs M (ed.) (1984). Marxist Perspectives in Archaeology. Cambridge: Cambridge University Press.

Taylor R (1992). Looking at our history: The discovery of the Negro cemetery. Ground Truth 1(1):3–4, 8.

Tilley C (1989). Archaeology as socio-political action in the present. In Pinsky V, Wylie A (eds.), Critical Traditions in Contemporary Archaeology: Essays in the Philosophy, History and Socio-Politics of Archaeology, pp. 104–116. Cambridge: Cambridge University Press.

Trigger, BG (1989). A History of Archaeological Thought. Cambridge: Cambridge University Press.

Turner II CG (1986). What is lost with skeletal reburial? I. adaptation. Quarterly Review of Archaeology 7(1):1–3.

Ver Berkmoes R (1991). Dignity at last. American Medical News, January 14, 29–33.

Walker ST (1993). Newark council, arts center discuss gravesite. Newark Star-Ledger, December 22:30.

Weathers NR (n.d.). The African Burial Ground of 1712. New York: Manhattan Borough President's Office.

Wheaton TR Jr., Reed MB, Elliott RS, Frank MS, Raymer LE (1990). James City, North Carolina: Archeological and Historical Study of an African American Urban Village. Stone Mountain, GA: New South Associates, Inc.

Zimmerman LJ (1985). A perspective on the reburial issue from South Dakota. In Quick PM (ed.), Proceedings, Conference on Reburial Issues, pp. 1–4 (appendix). Chicago: Newberry Library.

Zimmerman LJ (1990a). Made radical by my own: An archaeologist learns to accept reburial. In Layton R (ed.), Conflict in the Archaeology of Living Traditions, pp. 60–67. London: Unwin Hyman.

Zimmerman LJ (1990b). Human bones as symbols of power: Aboriginal American belief systems toward bones and "grave-robbing" archaeologists. In Layton R (ed.), pp. 211–216. Conflict in the Archaeology of Living Traditions. London: Unwin Hyman.

# 3  Historic Cemetery Analysis: Practical Considerations

DOUGLAS H. UBELAKER

## INTRODUCTION

Recent years have witnessed a surge of interest in the excavation and analysis of mortuary sites in the New World. To a large extent this interest stems from urban growth and renewal projects. New construction, both in suburban areas and within city cores, inevitably invades the vestiges of earlier human activity. The disturbed archaeological features are usually the remains of old dwellings, roads, and other structures. Increasingly, however, these archaeological features include the remains of the people themselves—old cemeteries that with time have been forgotten or overgrown (see, e.g., Pfeiffer et al., 1992; Winchell et al., 1992). The role of physical anthropologists has subsequently become critical to archaeological reconstruction.

Recent political developments within the United States regarding the excavation, curation, and analysis of American Indian human remains has had an impact on skeletal analyses (Ubelaker & Grant, 1989). Increasing criticism from Native American Indian groups, coupled with the passage of federal laws requiring that these groups decide the fate of collections of American Indian human remains, may have affected attitudes of American physical anthropologists. The predominately negative attitudes toward the study of human remains expressed by many contemporary American Indians has created a controversial environment for such analysis. Many scientists may welcome the opportunity to do their work in a more amiable environment, and turn to the analysis of historic-period remains. Although professional flight from the study of precontact American Indian remains is by no means complete, it may have contributed substantially to the clear interest in historic-period cemetery analysis of non-American Indian origin.

This shift of interest also reflects a growing awareness of the inadequacy of the historic written record on many biological matters and the need for verification of the information that is written. Although historic records frequently offer general state-

*Bodies of Evidence*, Edited by Anne L. Grauer.
ISBN 0-471-04153-X   © 1995 John Wiley & Sons, Inc.

ments about disease and life expectancy, such information may be difficult to interpret because of the observer's lack of knowledge about disease process and diagnosis. Much historical information may be biased by preconceptions or politics, or may be missing altogether.

Modern scientists learn about the past through the careful excavation, curation, and analysis of human remains. They often learn much more about the people being studied than the traditional determinations of age at death, ancestry, sex, and living stature. Histological techniques are now available to sharpen estimates of age at death and assist in the interpretation of pathological lesions. Chemical analysis offers information concerning diet and disease. Dental analysis may reveal problems regarding patterns of physiological stress suffered during the growth years. Modern DNA analysis may even reveal the genetic relationships of individuals within the sample.

The goal of this chapter is to highlight several issues that might be encountered in the excavation of historic remains and to provide useful approaches toward analysis. Although these recommendations will likely prove useful in many of the situations encountered by archaeologists and physical anthropologists, they do not represent all the situations and problems that might arise in the field. There is no "cook book" on how to properly recover and analyze historic remains. Each situation presents its own unique problems and calls for logical and thorough research strategies.

## THE EXCAVATION: LEGAL, POLITICAL, AND TIMELY CONSIDERATIONS

When human remains are discovered, medical–legal authorities should first be notified. These might include the Medical Examiner's Office, local law enforcement agencies, the State Attorney General's Office, and the State Archaeologist. Once it is determined that the remains are human, but not of modern forensic interest, administrative authorities usually decide how to proceed. In most cases, they may need to be educated about the historic value of the material and what can be learned from careful excavation and analysis (see Goldstein, this volume). Local, state, and federal laws may also shape decisions on the procedures to follow. Many states have passed laws detailing procedures to follow when human remains are encountered. Although the language of these laws varies considerably, in general, they require that when human remains are discovered, excavation ceases and appropriate authorities are notified. If the State Medical Examiner determines that the remains are old, then many states require the State Archaeologist or other authority to assess their ancestry. If they are determined to be of American Indian origin, the law may name an advisory board or committee to assess what Indian group should be notified. Procedures vary with each state (Ubelaker & Grant, 1989), so excavators must be informed of applicable laws in their areas.

If historic remains can be linked to existing groups, then representatives from those groups must be contacted. The strength of the link between the living and the deceased are, not surprisingly, often related to the antiquity of the remains. The link, however, can be equally shaped by historical, religious, and/or political concerns of the group. At the early stages of planning, the role of the anthropologist should be to inform all concerned about the discovery, educate them about what can be learned from careful scientific excavation and analysis, and recommend a plan to follow. Medical examiners, administrative officials, urban planners, construction supervisors, private landowners, and local representatives and descendants all potentially play a role in the decision-making process (see, e.g., Goldstein & Roberts, this volume).

An excavation plan should be devised to retrieve the maximum amount of information possible with the resources provided. Factors that significantly affect planning might include: time limits imposed by others on excavation and analysis; availability of monetary resources, personnel, and equipment; historical information available relevant to the site; the extent of destruction prior to excavation; and the political, environmental, and historical context of the discovery. If historical records (including oral history) are available, they need to be studied carefully. Information may be available on individual grave contents, depth, or orientation that may affect excavation plans. Historical records may also enhance the ultimate success of the excavation.

For example in 1992, I was contacted by the Colonial Williamsburg Foundation in Williamsburg, Virginia to study a skull reputed to belong to Colonel Alexander Scammell, a Revolutionary War soldier who was wounded at the Battle of Yorktown and transferred to Williamsburg for medical attention. Upon his death he was allegedly buried along with 157 fellow soldiers in a cemetery in the west garden of the Governor's Palace. Records indicated that the cemetery had been previously excavated in 1930 and the 158 skeletons had been studied by Ales Hrdlicka of the Smithsonian Institution. For unknown reasons, one of the skulls was removed and stored in the facilities at Williamsburg. Oral history refers to the skull as that of Col. Scammell. To determine if the skeleton was that of Col. Scammell, and to reunite the skull with the rest of the skeleton, an excavation was planned. A careful search of the 1930 records revealed information that pinpointed the exact location and even orientation of the grave from which the skull had been disinterred. This information facilitated excavation and allowed discovery of the rest of the remains with comparatively minimal effort. Analysis later determined that this individual was most likely too short to be Col. Scammell.

Examples of instances where archaeological excavation has enriched otherwise limited historic information are plentiful. A recent example occurred when the vestry of Christ Episcopal Church of Brandy Station, Virginia requested the archaeological investigation of the ruins of St. James Episcopal Church in Virginia in order to learn about the history of the church, determine if both civilian and military burials were associated with the structure, and gather data to determine if the site was eligible for inclusion on the National Register of Historic Places (Owsley et al., 1992). The Church had been destroyed during the Civil War. No photographs, sketches, or detailed descriptions existed of the facility. Some records, however, offered information about the general location of the cemetery and its relationship to the building. Through detailed excavation supplementary information was provided to the extremely limited written record (Owsley et al., 1992).

## NEW EXCAVATION TECHNIQUES

Although careful archaeological excavation is the ultimate tool needed to recover information from historic cemeteries, new technology is available to help locate individual graves and plan excavation. Ground-penetrating radar (GPR) is one such technique. GPR transmits broad-bandwidth radar waves to detect subsurface structures (Ubelaker, 1989). The technology has been used over both land and water to detect human remains and associated structures. Since the success of the technique depends upon structural contrasts within the ground's subsurface matrix, soil type, as well as the size and depth of the remains, are important factors to consider.

Another potentially useful detection method involves the utilization of electromagnetic devices, such as a proton magnetometer, to measure soil resistivity (Ubelaker, 1989). This technique is especially useful in detecting grave pits. The initial act of digging a grave disturbs the preexisting electromagnetic properties of normal soil in a manner that can be detected years after the event. Using a proton magnetometer provides the most useful results when the soil has been minimally disturbed or is uniform outside of the individual graves.

In some situations dogs may provide clues. Dogs have long been sources of accidental discoveries in human forensic cases as well as useful in exposing historic cemeteries. Specially trained "cadaver" dogs are available to smell out decomposing modern forensic cases. Many of the dog teams report impressive results with modern material. It is not clear that such dogs would routinely be useful with most historic-period cemeteries, but in cases of exceptional preservation, they may be employed to provide additional indicators.

A low-technology approach advocated by many is the metal probe. The probe consists of a long rod with a metal sphere (frequently a ball bearing) attached to the end that enters the soil and a horizontal handle on the opposite end. The probe is slowly inserted into the soil to search for a detectable change in soil resistance. Change in soil resistance is often associated with a grave pit. Preliminary testing in nearby areas with known sterile soil should be conducted to familiarize the operator with the normal soil compaction. Using a metal probe has been scorned by some archaeologists since the technique is a low-cost favorite of nonprofessional excavators. In the hands of a professional, however, it offers yet another tool to rapidly and economically help locate individual graves or define the extent of a mortuary site.

King et al. (1993) provide an example of the application of different types of survey techniques in the excavation of a historic period cemetery. Prior to excavation, a proton magnetometer and ground-penetrating radar system were employed to assess subsurface features in a historic cemetery in southern Maryland. The cemetery is associated with the Plains Plantation in St. Mary's County, Maryland. Twelve slab stones located on the surface suggest that this family cemetery was in use between 1720 and 1835.

The site was first cleared of plant growth, surface rocks and debris. Two survey techniques (GPR and proton magnetometry) were employed using a grid system. The results were compared. Detailed test excavations then allowed the examination of the subsurface features that were indicated by the geophysical surveys. Ultimately, 20 grave shafts and 10 brick foundations were identified through a combination of geophysical survey and excavation. The radar survey identified 12 suspicious areas. Testing revealed that six of these included graves (one with three graves) but six had no recognizable archaeological features.

The proton magnetometer suggested that four areas of the site might be of archaeological interest. Excavation revealed graves in two of these areas and brick foundation pads in another. One of the indicated areas contained no features of archaeological interest. Additional features were identified through archaeological interpretation that were not detected by the magnetic survey.

In assessing the results of the different techniques employed, the authors suggest that the failure of the proton magnetometer to detect many features was due to the presence of a considerable quantity of magnetic material scattered throughout the site. This material included refuse and numerous large metal objects. Although the GPR system was not entirely successful in locating subsurface features either, the Maryland experiment suggests that it offers an important tool in historic site/cemetery excavation if used as part of archaeological interpretation.

## PRESERVATION FACTORS

Archaeologists have long recognized that preservation varies between sites. This is particularly true when comparisons are made between pre-European contact sites and historic-period mortuary sites. These latter sites often yield a tremendous variety of artifacts and materials such as glass, metal, stone, bone, wood, fabric, and even paper. Since the skill and experience necessary to analyze particular materials often falls beyond the abilities of a single archaeologist, these materials must be conserved and analyzed by the appropriate specialists in order to ensure that proper care and conclusions are obtained.

The extent of human preservation can also vary significantly in historic mortuary sites (see Nawrocki, this volume). At one extreme, only traces of bone and teeth fragments within faint pit outlines may remain. In especially favorable environments, however, preservation can be remarkable and even approximate that found in recent forensic cases.

Recent analysis of historic remains from Pittsburgh, Pennsylvania offers examples of such variability. In the mid-1980's highway construction in downtown Pittsburgh removed old asphalt in preparation for new construction. The area under construction was in the vicinity of the former Voegtly Evangelical Church, founded in 1833 and disbanded around 1861. The church and cemetery was used by the German–Swiss immigrant population, who worked primarily as mill workers and farmers. The cemetery was supposedly moved after the church closed and the area had subsequently been paved. However, when the asphalt was removed during the new construction, careful archaeological excavation revealed the remains of over 700 individuals in a pattern suggesting age and status segregation.

Analysis of the remains, currently in progress at the Smithsonian Institution, reveals considerable variability in preservation. Many of the individuals, especially young infants, are very poorly preserved, with only small bone fragments surviving. In others, the preservation is rather extraordinary with not only bone and teeth surviving with limited erosion, but traces of hair, wood, and other normally perishable materials being recovered.

Bass (1984) offers an example of remarkably complete preservation, even after 113 years of interment. In December 1977, Bass was notified by authorities in Tennessee that a family cemetery had been disturbed, revealing what appeared to be decomposing human remains. The remains were lacking the cranium and mandible, and were located on top of and partially within a cast-iron coffin. Bass (1984) reports on the nearly complete preservation of soft tissue and clothing, and the presence of a strong odor. He noted that pink flesh was still present in association with a femur, and the intestines were still recognizable. Given the excellent preservation of the normally perishable remains, Bass assumed that a recently deceased individual had been deposited in this old grave, and estimated the time since death to be between six and 12 months.

Later, more careful analysis revealed evidence of embalming fluids and fragments of the missing cranium and mandible. The remains turned out to be those of Lt. Col. W. M. Shy. Shy had suffered a gunshot wound to the head in the Battle of Nashville during the Civil War at the age of 26, thus explaining the fragmented cranium. As Bass (1984, p. 139) notes "my estimate of length of time since death had been off by 112 years!"

Clearly, a variety of often unpredictable factors can influence the extent of preservation. Prominent among these factors are postmortem treatment (embalming, etc.) of the body, exposure to scavenging birds and mammals, the extent of exposure to insects and other arthropods, depth of burial, type and extent of clothing, type of coffin, soil pH and consistency, the amount of ground water, and the season of burial (see Nawrocki, this volume, for a detailed discussion of taphonomic processes). In my experience, cast-iron coffins provide outstanding preservation, while decomposition of individuals placed in simple wooden boxes (which normally decompose rapidly) is slower in dry or well-drained soils.

Extreme environments often lead to remarkable preservation as well. Dry environments, in particular, allow for soft tissue desiccation and natural mummification. Extremely wet environments can lead to the formation of adipocere, a soap-like substance that is very durable. The tannic acid produced in peat bogs, or bog-like environments, also contributes to superb preservation. The environmental context within which human remains have been found is thus critical to the analysis of the material.

## RECOVERING SOFT AND HARD TISSUES

Since historic cemeteries can provide a wealth of skeletal and material artifacts in varying states of decomposition, excavation must proceed with the goal of carefully exposing important features while simultaneously protecting them from undue damage. This often requires the removal and examination of soil and other overburden without movement of the human remains and associated artifacts. Grave pit outlines, for example, provide useful information. Although larger equipment, such as shovels and rakes, can be useful to clear the ground surface in preparation for excavation, it is preferable to remain cautious about their use. By proceeding slowly with small tools, pit sizes and shapes can be documented even before bones or artifacts are encountered. A grave pit outline can usually be identified by differences in soil color and consistency. Trowels, grapefruit knives, bamboo sticks, and small brushes allow for slow and careful soil removal.

Recovery of small materials (such as wood or pebbles) within the pit fill may also provide useful information on the burial procedure or conditions prior to the burial. Bones and artifacts should be left *in situ* until their position has been thoroughly documented. Abundant photographs, notes, and drawings should be recorded for permanent documentation. Since memories fade quickly, all notes should be clearly labeled so they can be deciphered by anyone (not just the excavator or note-taker).

Archaeological materials need to be exposed long enough for documentation, but not so long as to risk being damaged by exposure to the sun or trampling. The sun can rapidly dry out exposed remains, causing fractures and other alterations. Before complete removal, a bone or artifact should be fully exposed and then gently dislodged from its soil matrix. Obviously, removal should proceed as cautiously as excavation, minimizing fragmentation. All materials removed should be placed in clearly labeled containers. Since bones often contain considerable moisture, containers, labels, and written documentation must be moisture resistant.

In those instances when a great amount of soft tissue preservation is detected, it is desirable to treat the individual as though it were a modern forensic case and perform a modified autopsy. Frequently, the expertise needed for such an examination is greater than that provided by any one specialist. In these instances, a team of experts should be called. Such a team might include a forensic pathologist, a physical anthropologist (preferably a forensic anthropologist who may have experience studying soft tissue), a clothing specialist to help interpret garments as they are removed, and other experts as the situation warrants. Careful dissection of the soft tissues may detect cause of death and even allow toxicological tests on the recovered tissues.

The type of complete preservation calling for an autopsy is unusual in historic cemeteries. More frequently, some desiccated soft tissue remains clinging to the bones along with hair and decomposed clothing. A specialist in hair and fiber analysis can offer a great deal of valuable information. In particular, hair offers information on the ancestry of the individual, as well as cultural factors of hair treatment. Samples should be placed in clean sealed containers. Care should be taken to avoid contamination, particularly from the hair of the participants.

Radiography can also be an important component of analysis. Excavation of prominent historic individuals, or those who may have suffered gunshot wounds or other related trauma, may require the use of a portable radiography unit to document the positions of radiodense materials prior to movement. Even in cases where individuals can be moved relatively intact for examination elsewhere, it may be important to document metal position, since small fragments can shake loose or otherwise migrate during travel. It is important to note, however, that historic burials frequently contain metal fragments from a variety of sources, since corrosion and fragmentation of elements of the enclosing containers is common.

Analysis of historic remains should follow standard procedures of data collecting, with adequate radiography and photography. If remains will not be permanently curated, then analysis should be as thorough and exhaustive as possible. The forensic anthropology data bank (Moore-Jansen & Jantz, 1989) and the Chicago Field Museum data collection standards (Buikstra & Ubelaker, in press) offer recommendations for data collection in such circumstances.

An example of the need for the team approach and meticulous record keeping occurred in October of 1991, when I participated in the exhumation and analysis of Dr. Carl Weiss, the 29-year-old ear, nose, and throat specialist from Baton Rouge, Louisiana who stood accused of shooting former Governor Huey Long on September 8, 1935. Eye witnesses suggest that Weiss was shot many times by Long's bodyguards after having shot Long at close range (Zinman, 1993).

In order to verify these accounts, a team of experts was formed to analyze the human remains. Our team consisted of a forensic pathologist, a firearms specialist, and myself as the anthropologist. Careful dissection, guided by radiographs that documented the positions of bullet and bone fragments, allowed the recovery of even the smallest fragments. This enabled the researchers to later reconstruct the affected bones and reveal the direction of the bullet trajectories. Radiographs taken at the exhumation site, using a portable unit, documented the original positions of the bone and bullet fragments and proved that their positions had not changed during the transfer to the autopsy facility.

Microanalysis of the recovered bullet fragments provided considerable information about the bullet characteristics and the type of substances they impacted. A minimum of 23 distinct gunshot trajectories were identified. Since three of them were located in the arms and hands, the projectiles could also have impacted other areas of the body. Thus a minimum of 20 projectiles were stated to be involved (Ubelaker & Scammell, 1992). Although the entrance sites were from all directions, 50% were clearly from the back. This finding contrasts with testimony by Long's bodyguards, who indicated Weiss was not shot in the back.

An issue in the historical controversy surrounding the deaths of Long and Weiss, and thus a focus of our investigation, was whether or not Weiss had struck Long with his fist. Some have argued that if Weiss struck Long, he likely was not the assassin. Before his death, Long reportedly attributed a cut lip to "where he hit me." Careful radiological and microscopic analysis of Weiss' hand bones revealed small longitudinal fractures of the diaphyses of the metacarpals. However, the presence of similar small fractures on the metatarsals of the feet suggested that the lesions had a postmortem taphonomic origin.

An examination of the dentition also provided intrigue. A curious black metallic stain was noted on the inside surfaces of most teeth and the outside surfaces of the anterior lower teeth. Analysis revealed that the black substance had a mercury composition. Black stains without the metallic sheen were also present in an irregular pattern on many other bones of the skeleton. Analysis revealed these to be sulfuric in origin, apparently products of body decomposition.

To test the possibility that the black oral stains could represent mercury ingested by Dr. Weiss during life, fragments of hair and toenails were analyzed. Mercury ingested during life would have been distributed throughout the body, and thus would be detected in those portions of hair and toenail that were forming at the time of death. The basal portions of those materials revealed no mercury. The only logical conclusion was that the mercury originated from the postmortem breakdown of the amalgam fillings in the teeth.

With the help of a team of experts, questions concerning the assassination of Huey Long were answered and unusual findings were systematically explored. No one person was qualified to complete this detailed and complex analysis, and careful planning, excavation and recording procedures allowed for the success of this project.

## RECOVERING INSECT REMAINS

In some contexts, insect remains associated with historic burials offer clues to mortuary procedures. During the 1960's, rising river-water levels, due to dam construction, forced the salvage excavation of various mortuary sites in the vicinity of Mobridge South Dakota (Bass et al., 1971). One of these sites was the historic Leavenworth site, visited by Lewis and Clark and shelled by Col. Henry Leavenworth in 1823. Others include the protohistoric Rygh (39CA4) site, Nordvold sites (39C031, 39C032, 39C033), Mobridge site (39WW1), and the Larson site (39WW2).

During the excavation of many of the burials, excavators were careful to collect soil samples. In the field, workers noted that not only was the bone well preserved, but associated insect remains were present as well (Gilbert & Bass, 1967). Most of the preserved insect remains consisted of fly puparia, the chitinous exoskeleton of pupating calliphorid or sarcophagid flies. Since the flies are not active during the winter months, the preserved puparia allow the burials to be seasonally dated (Gilbert & Bass, 1967).

At some sites, beetle remains were also found. Analysis revealed them to be from the genus *Trox*, a beetle representing one of the last arthropods in the chain of succession to be attracted to decomposing flesh. Trox is known to arrive only when the remains are mostly decomposed and consisting of desiccated flesh and hair (Vaurie, 1955). In addition, analysis revealed that the fly pupal cases were open, indicating the adult flies had emerged. Since adult fly parts were not found, we reasoned that the adults must have emerged prior to burial. The pupal cases not only offered information on seasonality, but also on the length of time the body was kept above ground prior to burial (Ubelaker & Willey, 1978). Furthermore, frequencies of the late-arriving Trox beetle appeared to decrease at sites dated to be more recent. The insect remains suggested that the Indian group changed their mortuary customs through time, shortening the interval between death and burial. This interpretation has been corroborated by various ethnographic accounts.

## SAFETY CONCERNS

Concern for health while working with human remains is an important issue. At this time, most pathologists and anthropologists conducting autopsies or working with fresh cadavers assume a very defensive posture. The safest attitude is to assume that any single individual could be infected with transmittable infectious disease. Protection is critical. Such protection involves a surgical mask, eye protection, complete disposable body clothing, and disposable gloves that will not tear.

Much of the fear in working with recently deceased individuals centers on the possibility of acquiring the human immunodeficiency virus that can cause acquired immunodeficiency syndrome (AIDS). The fear is justified, since, in 1993, 1,500,000 Americans were estimated to be HIV positive and 350,000 Americans were estimated to have died from AIDS by the end of 1993 (Ling et al., 1993). It is possible to test human remains for the presence of AIDS or other diseases prior to removal and study. Unfortunately, most testing requires time, which is usually not available in most archaeological projects. Ling et al. (1993) report that two rapid assays have been tested by the FDA to detect HIV-1 antibodies. These are the Cambridge latex agglutination assay and the SUDS assay from the Murex Corporation, Norcross, Georgia. In their independent testing on body fluid samples from modern autopsies, Ling et al. (1993) found the SUDS assay to be effective and easy to use and interpret. Perhaps more fortunately, most studies suggest that soon after death bodies become safe to work with, presenting virtually no risk of contracting AIDS. With archaeological material, there is no reason to believe the virus can be contracted.

Clearly, risk of acquiring disease from human remains decreases rapidly with time and decomposition and loss of soft tissue. I am not aware of a single archaeologist or physical anthropologist who has contracted an infectious disease from handling human remains. Some concern, however, may be warranted with tuberculosis, since the organism has a reputation of being especially hardy. The potential presence of arsenic may also warrant concern during the disinterment of historic skeletons. Arsenic was used for embalming and as a preservative for museum collections.

The greatest risk in excavating and studying historic burials is common infection from cuts or scratches sustained from accidents during excavation and analysis. The only prevention is adequate protection, especially through the use of gloves, coupled with proper care if a cut is sustained.

In certain closed environments additional protection may be warranted. In 1990, I collaborated with officials in Ecuador on the excavation and study of the central ossuary within the church of the Convento de San Francisco in Quito Ecuador. The Convento was founded in 1535 and continues to function as a Franciscan Catholic church and monastery (Teran, 1988). Archaeological exploration revealed three chambers in a subterranean location beneath the floor of the church. Large quantities of human remains were present in all three chambers, with some believed to date from the foundation of the church. The remains were mixed with soil and decayed wood and clothing. In that deep, humid environment, considerable mold and fungus was also present. Not knowing what modern pathogens could be present, the excavators took the precaution of not only wearing gloves and protective clothing, but also wore respirators to maximize protection against possible airborne organisms.

The exhumation of human remains calls for common sense. Gloves should be worn at all times in the field and laboratory, and additional precaution should be taken (such as a mask, eye protection, and gowns) when soft tissue has been preserved. If an error is made, it should be on the side of overprotection.

## CONCLUSION

Historic mortuary sites offer new challenges and exciting new possibilities to supplement the existing written record. As research increases in this area, tools for detection, excavation, and analysis are becoming more numerous and more sophisticated. Clearly, the study of historic-period human remains produces important new information about the history and people of the local areas being investigated. Eventually, such research should allow an overview of the nature of human adaptation in the historic period and assessment of the biological correlates of immigration and population displacement.

## REFERENCES

Bass WM (1984). Time interval since death, a difficult decision. In Rathbun TA and Buikstra RE (eds.), Human Identification: Case Studies in Forensic Anthropology, pp. 136–147. Springfield, IL: Charles C. Thomas.

Bass WM, Evans DR, Jantz RL (1971). The Leavenworth Site Cemetery: Archaeology and Physical Anthropology. University of Kansas Publications in Anthropology, No. 2. Lawrence. KS: University of Kansas.

Buikstra JE, Ubelaker DH, (in press). Standards for Data Collection From Human Skeletal Remains, Proceedings of a Seminar at The Field Museum of Natural History. Fayetteville, AR: Arkansas Archeological Survey Press.

Gilbert BM, Bass WM (1967). Seasonal dating of burials from the presence of fly pupae. American Antiquity, 32(4):534–535.

King JA, Bevan BW, Hurry RJ (1993). The reliability of geophysical surveys at historic-period cemeteries: An example from the Plains Cemetery, Mechanicsville, Maryland. Historical Archaeology, 27(4):4–16.

Ling L, Constantine NT, Zhang X, Smialek JE (1993). Determination of human immunodeficiency virus antibody status in forensic autopsy cases using a rapid and simple FDA-licensed assay. Journal of Forensic Sciences, 38(4):798–805.

Moore-Jansen P, Jantz RL (1989). Data Collection Procedures for Forensic Skeletal Material: Report of Investigations, No. 48. Knoxville, TN: The University of Tennessee.

Owsley DW (1990). The skeletal biology of North American historical populations. In Buikstra JE (ed.), A Life in Science: Papers in Honor of J. Lawrence Angel, pp. 171–190. Chicago, IL: Center for American Archaeology.

Owsley DW, Krakker JK, Jacobs M, Mann RW (1992). The History and Archaeology of Saint James Episcopal Church, Brandy Station, Virginia. Fredericksburg, VA: Bookcrafters.

Pfeiffer S, Dudar JC, Austin S (1992). Prospect Hill: Skeletal remains from a 19th-Century Methodist cemetery, Newmarket, Ontario. Northeast Historical Archaeology, 18:29–48.

Teran P (1988). Estudio de Investigacion Arqueologia, Convento de San Francisco de Quito, Sitio: OPQSR-2. Report presented to Instituto de Cooperacion Ibero Americana de Espana, Quito, Ecuador.

Ubelaker DH (1989). Human Skeletal Remains: Excavation, Analysis, Interpretation. Washington, DC: Taraxacum.

Ubelaker DH, Grant LG (1989). Human skeletal remains: preservation or reburial? J. of Phys. Anthropol. 32:249–287.

Ubelaker DH, Scammell H (1992). Bones, A Forensic Detective's Casebook. New York: HarperCollins.

Ubelaker DH, Willey P (1978). Complexity in Arikara mortuary practice. Plains Anthropologist, 23(79):69–74.

Vaurie P (1955). A revision of the genus *Trox* in North America (Coleoptera, Scarabaeidae). Bulletin of the American Museum of Natural History, 106(1).

Winchell F, Rose JC, Moir RW (1992). Bioanthropological Investigation of Nineteenth Century Burials at Site 41DT105. Dallas, TX: Southern Methodist University.

Zinman D (1993). The Day Huey Long Was Shot. Jackson, MI: University Press of Mississippi.

# 4 Taphonomic Processes in Historic Cemeteries

STEPHEN P. NAWROCKI

## INTRODUCTION

Even though they study bones, paleontologists, archaeologists, and physical anthropologists are equally interested in the living organisms that contributed those bones to the geological record. The goal of these researchers is to learn something of the population of organisms that once inhabited a particular ecosystem. Yet the data on which we base our studies of dead and extinct organisms is usually limited because we are only able to obtain a sample of those that were once alive. After, during, and even before death, numerous processes begin to bias or skew the sample, altering or removing individuals from possible future study. In essence, the assemblages of bones examined by scientists represent scattered "fallout" from the ecosystem and may or may not accurately mimic the characteristics of the living community.

The study of the processes that cause sampling bias or differential preservation in bone or fossil assemblages is known as "taphonomy." Literally meaning "the laws of burial" (from the Greek *tafo* = burial, *nomos* = laws), taphonomy was initially proposed before the middle of this century yet was not established as an organized field of scientific study until the 1970's (Dodson, 1980; Gifford, 1981; Olson, 1980). Early efforts stemmed primarily from vertebrate paleontology and paleoecology (Brain, 1981; Behrensmeyer & Hill, 1980; Shipman, 1981). Recent volumes and symposia, however, have applied these more traditional approaches to the study of human remains, exploring both archaeological (Roberts et al., 1989; Boddington et al., 1987a; Nawrocki & Bell, 1991) and forensic contexts (Haglund & Sorg, 1993; Micozzi, 1990; Haglund, 1991).

"Human taphonomy" as a specialized field of study bridges the gap that commonly exists between the field archaeologist and the physical anthropologist. A lack of continuity between these specialists, as may occur when a skeletal analysis is per-

*Bodies of Evidence*, Edited by Anne L. Grauer.
ISBN 0-471-04153-X  © 1995 John Wiley & Sons, Inc.

formed long after disinterment and by individuals not directly involved in the excavation, allows potentially important taphonomic information to slip by unnoticed. Consequently, osteological reports frequently ignore taphonomic issues and fail to recognize alternative explanations for observed phenomena. For example, in his analysis of the distribution of battle scars on the King Site material from Georgia, Mathews (1988) neglects to address exactly how one could differentiate between a perimortem sword cut and, say, a shovel or trowel mark created at the time of excavation, or by damage inflicted by farming equipment. Anthropologists have only recently begun to address these issues adequately and comprehensively, and it is becoming clear that separating perimortem and postmortem phenomena is not nearly as easy as it is frequently thought to be (Nawrocki & Clark, 1994; Nawrocki & Pless, 1993).

This Chapter examines taphonomic factors that affect the survival, recovery, and analysis of human remains in historic-period cemeteries. While few of the specifics that are presented here are new, the focus has been carefully tailored in a way that is, at least in the North American archaeological literature, rather unique in its blending of archaeological and forensic perspectives. Taphonomic variables that influence buried human remains are first categorized into a simple framework that recognizes and accommodates the special concerns of those dealing with historic cemeteries. Then a case study utilizing a late-19th-century cemetery from New York is presented to illustrate some common taphonomic effects as well as a general approach to the scientific study of postmortem processes.

## CLASSIFICATION OF TAPHONOMIC PROCESSES

Taphonomic processes can be classified and subdivided in numerous ways, depending on the level of analysis and subject matter chosen by the analyst. For example, Clark et al. (1967, pp. 115–120) define seven hierarchical categories of factors ranging from specific features of the organism's life (species range, body size) down to curatorial variables (packaging, identification) (see also Andrews & Cook, 1985, p. 689; Waldron, 1987, p. 56). Each subsequent category is generally accompanied by a loss of information, with the successive modification or complete removal of elements from the assemblage.

For simplicity, I have narrowed the scope slightly and identify three major classes of taphonomic processes and variables that are relevant to the study of human remains. *Environmental factors* are external variables, such as climate and animals. *Individual factors* are those that the subjects bring to the decomposition process themselves, such as body size and age at death. Finally, *cultural factors* are a special subset of variables that characterize human mortuary activities, such as embalming and autopsy procedures. These three general categories are not always mutually exclusive in that a variable can sometimes be classified in more than one way. For example, while the use of a coffin is certainly a cultural factor, its presence can also be treated as an environmental factor that will affect the decomposition and preservation of the remains.

The following sections examine specific taphonomic factors and their effects on bone. The discussion is by no means exhaustive, but rather addresses only a sampling of factors that are likely to be of importance in historic cemeteries. As such, detailed discussions of certain topics and theoretical concerns that are more relevant to vertebrate paleontology have been omitted. For example, an important question in paleontology is how natural processes (such as water action) create accumulations of bones (see Marshall, 1989). While there are exceptions, human cultural activities are the most important "accumulators" of human remains in historic cemeteries, being more important than any environmental factors.

## Environmental Factors

Environmental factors that affect the recovery and analysis of human bone can be subdivided into *biotic* and *abiotic* categories. Biotic factors involve the action or presence of living organisms. For example, large carnivores (bears, dogs) are known to scavenge human remains and can inflict significant damage to the bones in the process (see Haglund et al., 1988, 1989). Although this situation is unlikely to occur to remains buried in a historic cemetery, a more likely situation is physical disturbance by large burrowing rodents. Groundhog holes frequently intrude into grave-shafts, and for shallow burials significant dispersal and fracturing of bones can result. In addition, subsurface animal activity can increase water flow into the burial and thus precipitate other environmental processes.

Smaller organisms, including fungi and bacteria (Hackett, 1981; Marchiafava et al., 1974), are also involved in the decomposition and destruction of buried human remains. Necrophilous insects can invade a body and produce significant soft tissue destruction even before burial (Catts & Haskell, 1990). Insect activity may be pronounced in situations where the body is unembalmed or must be transported to a home burial site, although they can also invade the body after entombment or burial. While insects may do little damage to the bone tissue itself, disarticulation and dispersal of the remains within the coffin will result. Large maggot masses can carry and scatter ribs much like a surfboard is carried by waves. It is possible that the mysterious "tumbling" of the thoracic skeleton of some buried individuals (see Boddington, 1987; Brothwell, 1987) could result in part from the action of maggot masses.

Plant activity can have profound effects on skeletal preservation. A common practice has been to plant small bushes or trees, such as arborvitae or cedars, adjacent to burials or family plots. Many of these plants can actually grow to quite a respectable size if left untrimmed, pushing over headstones and cracking vaults in just a few decades. Below the surface, large roots can easily stave in a coffin or a skull or wind their way through the shafts of long bones, creating mechanical damage and dispersing the remains (see Willey & Heilman, 1987). Roots also secrete acidic by-products, etching the bone surfaces. Curiously, however, some of the best-preserved skeletons I have excavated were closely associated with the deep root systems of (long-dead) trees (Nawrocki, 1989). While mechanical damage was frequently evident, bones surrounded by networks of smaller rootlets were usually in good shape.

The rootlets had apparently drawn water away from the bone surfaces, helping to prevent the periodic soaking and drying that can crack even the dense outer cortical layers of long bones. In addition, the rootlets had broken up the surrounding soil, facilitating its removal and ultimately decreasing the amount of damage introduced during the excavation process.

Abiotic environmental factors include temperature, exposure to water and sunlight, soil pH, and depth below surface. Water is especially critical in the preservation equation. Its power to modify buried cultural resources was perhaps no better illustrated than in the Great Flood of 1993 in the Midwest. In July the rising floodwaters removed more than 800 caskets from the town cemetery in Hardin, Missouri, dispersing some of them 20 miles downstream (Sledzik, 1994; Smith, 1993). Even heavy concrete burial vaults were tossed about like corks. It goes without saying that the effects of this event (which is by no means unique) on archaeological and osteological analysis would be dramatic.

At the molecular level, water hydrolyzes collagen proteins into smaller polypeptide units, disrupting the protein-mineral bond and leading to more rapid degradation of the bone tissue (Von Endt & Ortner, 1984). Percolating ground water brings acids and other chemicals into the bone. Repeated freeze/thaw cycles can create fractures. Even simple evaporation, if it occurs rapidly, can be destructive. I have watched fresh, green, adult human femora from a forensic case develop deep, longitudinal fractures running the entire lengths of the shafts as they were being air-dried in a fume hood. Excavators must be careful to shade damp bones from direct sunlight to prevent warping and flaking caused by rapid and irregular drying.

Fractures are ubiquitous in excavated skeletal assemblages and are commonly the subject of misinterpretation. Unfamiliarity with taphonomic processes can result in the misdiagnosis of postmortem phenomena as perimortem trauma or pathology. The pressure of surrounding soil can distort, warp, and eventually fracture the sturdiest of bones. This process would be exacerbated when acidic conditions have demineralized the bone, making it soft (Wells, 1967). Fortunately, fractures produced by perimortem and postmortem processes can be distinguished with practice (Bonnichsen & Sorg, 1989; Villa & Mahieu, 1991; Johnson, 1985). Subtle warpage of bones, however, can be more difficult to detect and can mimic certain pathologies (e.g., anemia) or deliberate, culturally induced cranial deformation. Warpage can also throw off statistical analysis of skeletal measurements. This latter problem might not be noticed unless all fragments of the skull were present and incorporated into the reconstruction, where a lack of perfect fit or gaps between articulating fragments would indicate that distortion had occurred.

The process of soft-tissue decomposition and the resulting effects on bone position is also frequently misunderstood. For example, in an intact coffin the cranium frequently rotates backwards or sideways as the muscles and ligaments of the neck decay, leaving the mandible behind to rest on the cervical vertebrae. This position should not be interpreted as evidence that the head was separated from the torso before burial. Similarly, the femora and tibiae may be found to overlap substantially at the knees in a coffin that appears to be too short for its occupant. The erroneous conclusion would be that the legs were deliberately "broken" at the knees, disarticulated, and laid loosely on the lower thighs to avoid the costs of constructing a larger box. However, if the individual were placed with his knees flexed and pointing up, the tibiae would naturally drop down over the distal femora as the soft tissues of the joint decayed, giving the impression of thrift when none was present (Cook, 1993).

## Individual Factors

Boddington et al. (1987b, p. 4) state that " . . . the nature and rate of decay is as much a product of the buried skeleton as the burial environment." Variation in bone decomposition can be seen both within and between individuals. Different bones of the body and, for that matter, different areas of the same bone, vary in the amount and distribution of cortical (dense) to trabecular (spongy) bone and in the amount of bone exposed on external and internal surfaces. Vertebral bodies, ribs, the sternum, carpals, and tarsals are comprised primarily of spongy bone with only thin external layers of cortical bone. The shafts of long bones, on the other hand, are composed of thick layers of cortical bone, although their epiphyses are similar in form to vertebral bodies. It should be of no surprise that long bone shafts tend to resist degradation better than other elements (see Waldron, 1987). Experiments by Von Endt & Ortner (1984) suggest that surface area is an important factor influencing how quickly water can produce chemical breakdown of the collagen and mineral matrix of bone at exposed surfaces. Spongy bone, with a much larger surface area per volume than cortical bone, will thus decay much more rapidly.

Disease processes and trauma will frequently affect skeletal preservation. Osteoporosis, characterized by marked demineralization of the bone, differentially affects postmenopausal females and would, theoretically, lead to more rapid degradation of the buried remains. On the other hand, the bony osteophyte production across joint surfaces in osteoarthritis tends to have an opposite effect. I have seen vertebral columns fused by spondylitis deformans survive when the normal columns of those interred nearby had long since turned to bone meal. Both of these disease processes—osteoporosis and degenerative joint disease—are age-dependent, introducing yet another potentially important taphonomic variable to the preservation equation.

Body size differences due to age and sexual dimorphism may affect skeletal preservation. It is generally recognized that subadult remains (particularly those of infants) do not survive the ravages of time as well as adult remains because they are smaller and are only partially mineralized (Gordon & Buikstra, 1981; Walker et al., 1988; but see Saunders, 1992). By the same line of reasoning, the bones of larger, more robust adults would survive better than smaller adults, although this hypothesis has been more difficult to verify (see below).

Soft tissues play a significant role in protecting the skeleton in living individuals and may continue to do so after death. Very dry or very moist environments can delay the decay of the skin and muscles, allowing them to form a protective sheath that would insulate the bone surfaces from water, acids, and erosion. Fats will undergo hydrolysis (saponification) in moist environments, producing greasy adipocere or "grave wax" on the body surfaces (Evans, 1963; Mant, 1987). Individuals with a greater amount of adipose tissue to begin with may thus be at an advantage with respect to skeletal preservation. Studies have revealed that the soil immediately surrounding a buried body becomes more alkaline as the soft tissues decay (Rodriguez & Bass, 1985), which may ultimately affect the preservation of the bony tissues.

## Cultural Factors

Humans are unique in the animal kingdom in the complexity of their mortality-related behaviors. A plethora of cultural practices, such as postmortem preparation of the body, deliberate below-ground burial, the construction of stone vaults, the design of ritually recognized cemeteries, multiple disinterments and repeated reburials, cremations, and many more death-related activities have an immense impact on the anthropologist involved in the excavation and analysis of human skeletal remains. On the one hand, it can be argued that these practices make the study of human remains much more complex and can potentially obscure or destroy biological data. However, the simple act of burial does more to preserve bones than any other phenomenon in the natural world. Animal carcasses that come to rest on the ground surface are quickly dispersed and destroyed by environmental agents and only rarely become significant parts of the paleontological record. Thus the increased complexity of the human context brings with it a much richer archaeological and biological record from which to draw hypotheses and conclusions.

In historic cemeteries the coffin is an important contributor to the condition of the remains. The surrounding walls act as a shield to the external environment. When the top collapses the wood intimately covers the bone and can prevent direct contact with the soil and roots. Yet a coffin may be detrimental to skeletal preservation as well. Few are airtight and none stay so for long, and water may actually obtain more direct access to the body and bones because the coffin walls will maintain an airspace that can trap and hold water long after it has percolated down through the surrounding matrix. In recent years, many cemeteries have adopted the use of small concrete vaults or shells into which the coffin is dropped. In cases of disinterment it is frequently observed that the vaults are filled with water, the coffins bobbing within.

In his study of World War II victims in Germany, Mant (1987, p. 68) observed that bodies buried in coffins decayed much more rapidly than those buried without, presumably due to the presence of the airspace. In addition, the inclusion of wood shavings or straw in the base of the coffin accelerated decomposition because these layers raised the internal temperature as they composted. Clothing and burial shrouds, on the other hand, helped to preserve soft tissues, protecting from insects and assisting in adipocere formation. Metal artifacts (jewelry, coffin nails and hardware) in close association with the body may not only stain the surfaces of the bones but may also help to preserve soft tissues, fabrics, and leather (Janaway, 1987).

The effects of human activities sometimes extend well after the burial of the dead. In March of 1991, construction activities on the White River levee in Indianapolis uncovered the remains of a large box containing human bones. Documentary research by the Division of Historic Preservation and Archaeology of the Indiana Department of Natural Resources (Ellis et al., 1991) and by the University of Indianapolis (Blankman, 1994) indicates that the remains were most likely associated with any one of a number of 19th century cemeteries once located in the immediate area, which were subsequently removed or destroyed as local industries encroached on the river. The context suggests that the assemblage represents a secondary interment, with a number of individuals having been removed from their original burial locations and reinterred together in a common coffin sometime in the early part of this century. The inventory of bones clearly supports such a scenario. At least 15 individuals are present, represented by both craniodental and postcranial remains. Conspicuously absent from the assemblage, however, are smaller bones such as the carpals, phalanges, cuneiform tarsals, and patellae. While a number of subadults are present, proportionately few epiphyses (compared to diaphyses) are included in the remains. Furthermore, single-rooted teeth, such as the incisors and canines, are much less common than their multiple-rooted neighbors. It is likely that during the original disinterment of the burials, these smaller bones were missed and subsequently did not find their way into the common coffin. Thus two episodes of cultural activities affected the assemblage after its initial creation: the excavation and reinterment earlier this century and then the most recent recovery by construction workers and archaeologists. Both episodes, each acting as a sieve to certain bone types, contributed significantly to nonrandom information loss and will substantially affect our ability to reconstruct the living biologies of these individuals.

The impacts of excavation and curation cannot be underestimated and both must be treated as important taphonomic variables. Anyone with experience in the excavation of human remains knows that the skeleton rarely looks as good in the lab as it did just before it was removed from the ground. The simple act of opening the burial exposes the bones to the above-ground environment, where sun-baking and precipitation can create more damage in just a few hours than the skeleton suffered in all of its years beneath the soil. Scratches, nicks, and cuts from trowels frequently occur and can later be mistaken for perimortem trauma. Packaging, transport, and cleaning all may negatively affect the remains. In general, as much cleaning as possible should be accomplished at the recovery scene, to remove damp soils that will only harden and become much more difficult to remove later. Repeated wetting and drying during the transport and cleaning phases inevitably weakens the bone and reduces the amount of analyzable material that will eventually be available to the anthropologist.

The question may arise as to why one would include cultural behaviors, such as burial methods and excavation, as taphonomic variables. Simply put, humans are a major source of modification and alteration that can affect the distribution and preservation of human remains. It is a useful heuristic device that helps the archaeologist, working from the perspective of the skeleton, to perceive the sum total of factors that are likely to influence the survival and morphology of bone over time. However, the unique and complex nature of human modification warrants the inclusion of a third, separate category rather than simply lumping human effects into environmental effects.

## A CASE STUDY IN TAPHONOMIC PROCESSES:
## THE ONEIDA BURIAL SITE

The Oneida Burial Site was excavated in the summer of 1988 through a joint effort by the Public Archaeology Facility at the State University of New York at Binghamton and the New York State Museum at Albany. Human remains were discovered by construction workers on the grounds of the former Rome Developmental Center, a psychiatric institution located two miles outside of the city of Rome in Oneida County, New York. The New York State Department of Correctional Services had acquired the property and its complex of buildings and was in the process of renovating it into a medium-security prison. Razor-wire fences had already been erected around the compound and hundreds of prisoners and guards were in residence when the archaeologists were called in. The construction of new transformer pads and subsurface electrical conduits had disturbed an unmarked burial ground in the central courtyard. Details of the project can be found in Santangelo (1989) and Nawrocki (1989).

Between May and August, 81 burials were excavated and packaged for later analysis at Syracuse University. All were extended, single burials in simple wooden coffins, with little in the way of artifacts or coffin hardware. Fourteen additional burials were located but left unexcavated because they were not in the direct line of proposed construction activities. Human bones emerging from the backdirt piles were a testament to the large number of burials (perhaps more than 100) that had been completely or partially destroyed by the heavy equipment in the days before the archaeologists arrived. I conservatively estimated that an additional 150 burials remain at the site outside of the impact area (Nawrocki, 1989). Santangelo (1989, p. 46) suggests that the cemetery may once have contained as many as 900 interments and covered an area greater than one acre.

### Dating and Demographics

The Oneida Burial Site was most likely associated with the former psychiatric institution. Determining the exact time period of its use, however, proved difficult. No documentation of the cemetery's existence could be located. A county poorhouse and asylum had been established in the vicinity by 1825 and is known to have occupied the spot where the cemetery is located by at least 1860 (Santangelo, 1989, pp. 3–5). Later the state took over the facility and continued to operate the institution until the 1980's, so there were 160 years of continuous occupation of the immediate area. Artifactual data narrowed down the likely time range. The presence of celluloid buttons in most burials indicates a date proceeding 1870, and a mix of both machine cut and wire coffin nails broadly dates the use of the cemetery to the last quarter of the 19th century.

Further clues to the date of the cemetery can be derived from the characteristics of the skeletal sample itself. With the exception of one infant burial (Burial 3) and a few unprovenienced infant bones recovered from the backdirt piles, no subadults are represented in the assemblage (Fleischman, 1989, 1990; Nawrocki, 1989, 1990).

This situation contrasts sharply with the age distribution demonstrated by the Monroe County Poorhouse Cemetery from Rochester, New York, excavated in 1984 by the Rochester Museum and Science Center (Lanphear, 1988, 1990), where 81 of 296 individuals (27%) were less than 20 years old.

The Monroe County cemetery was in use between 1826 and 1863. By 1878, state legislation had "mandated the removal of all children between three and sixteen years of age, disabled or not, from the county almshouses" (Ferguson, 1988, p. 180). The admission statistics from the Oneida County facility reflect this population shift. In 1856, 42 of 222 residents (19%) were under 16 years of age. By 1877, 10% were under 20 years, and in 1884 no residents fell in the 2–16 year category (Ferguson, 1988, p. 106; Santangelo, 1989, p. 6). In 1893 the state purchased the county-run institution and by 1894 the "Rome State Custodial Asylum" was born. At that point the number of children once again began to rise. In 1896, 78 of 99 admissions (79%) were subadults, and the first deaths of children were occurring by the turn of the century. In the nine year span from 1894 to 1902, 5% of the 173 inmate deaths at the institution were of individuals less than 16 years of age (Ferguson, 1988, p. 200; Santangelo, 1989, p. 7).

Thus the lack of subadults in the Oneida skeletal assemblage suggests a date between circa 1880 and 1900—towards the later years of the county operation or the early years of the state operation. Of course, this argument depends on a few assumptions that may or may not be warranted. First, one must assume that subadults were not buried in some other (unexcavated) portion of the cemetery. While segregation of children (particularly infants) at mortuary sites is not unknown, the Monroe County Poorhouse cemetery stands as a nearby example to the contrary. A second assumption is that subadult skeletons, if present, would be as likely to survive and to be recovered as adult skeletons. At Oneida the coffin and graveshaft outlines were well preserved, and even if the bones had not survived, clues as to the presence of at least some subadult burials most likely would have been recognized. Finally, one assumes that the age classes represented in the death sample at least roughly mimic those present in the living resident population. This assumption is more difficult to swallow, especially since death rates in the later subadult range are generally low compared to infants and adults. However, the historical documentation indicates that at least some subadults were dying at Oneida in the early 1900's, and it seems reasonable to assume that they would have been interred in the cemetery along with the adults.

I am not necessarily arguing that one should place great weight on age distributions in determining the dates of historic cemeteries in upstate New York. Instead, this information is offered to underscore the potential complications that cultural practices may inject into the analysis of historic skeletal populations. In the case of Oneida, changing legal and social conventions acted as a fluctuating filter that introduced sampling bias into the death assemblage, which is no longer representative of the late 19th century upstate populations that surrounded the institution. Here we see taphonomic processes of the cultural variety in effect.

This viewpoint can be pursued further. For example, utilizing the results of Fleischman's (1989) analysis of the Oneida assemblage and adding my own observations on many of the skeletons, of 63 for which sex could be determined, 48 are males and 15 are females. This difference is highly significant ($\chi^2 = 17.29$, $df = 1$, $p < 0.001$). A number of workers have noted the tendency for males to outnumber females in skeletal collections and Weiss (1972, p. 240) suggests that some of this bias may result from labeling too many specimens as male. However, when one examines the cultural context of the Oneida assemblage, an additional factor becomes relevant. Ferguson (1988, p. 109) indicates that the county poorhouse typically put male inmates to work on the institutional farm in order to cut maintenance costs and to teach good work habits. In fact, there is evidence to suggest that the poor working class used the almshouses as a "network of hostels for temporary respite as they travelled the country looking for wage labor" (p. 113). It should be no surprise, then, that young adult males were differentially admitted to the institutions as a cheap and willing labor source. In 1902, 415 residents of Rome were male and 135 were female (Ferguson, 1988, p. 201). Of the 1473 deaths at the institution between 1894 and 1919, 69% were males and 31% were females, very close to the ratio in the living residential population (Santangelo, 1989, p. 7). Thus the heavily "biased" skeletal sample at Oneida makes sense in light of late 19th century admissions practices. It raises a cautionary note against blindly seriating a skeletal sample and assuming that half are males and half are females, as Weiss suggests.

A final example of cultural taphonomic variables is the "loss" of the Oneida cemetery in the first place (Nawrocki, 1990, 1991). Engineers, before a large expansion project in the mid-1930s, found human bone in soil borings taken in the immediate vicinity of the burials (Santangelo, 1989, p. 17). Since the cemetery is not marked on any available map or grounds plan of the institution (the oldest of which dates to 1906), it is assumed that its presence had been forgotten by the 1930's or, minimally, it had fallen into disrepair. Yet even after human bone was identified in the soil borings, the institution continued with its expansion plans and likely destroyed hundreds of burials during the construction of new buildings. It is unlikely that this sequence of events—first the "loss" of the cemetery and then its partial destruction—would have occurred if those interred had been members of anything other than the lowest class of individuals (see McGuire, 1989).

### Skeletal Preservation

Examination of maps of the institution dating to the earlier part of the 20th century reveals that the Oneida Cemetery was once placed on a small knoll running east–west and rising some six feet above the surrounding area (Santangelo, 1989, pp 14–17). With the construction activities of the mid-1930s, the knoll was graded and the low areas filled (Nawrocki, 1989). Figure 1 illustrates the resulting effects on the relative depths of the burials. Those near the center of the excavation lay close to the present ground surface, while those at the peripheries were much deeper. This gradual flux was observed over the entire maximum (north–south) length of the excavation (50 m).

During the excavation, we noted that skeletal preservation varied systematically

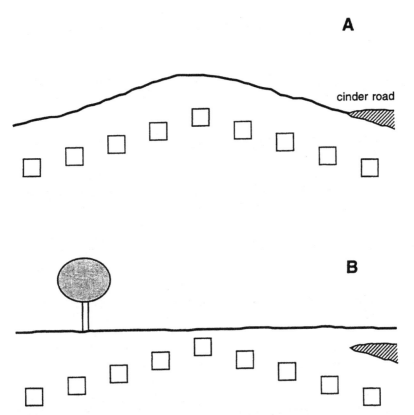

**FIGURE 1.**   Land modification at the Oneida Burial Site. Diagram A shows the site circa 1890–1900, with the burials dispersed along a small knoll. Diagram B demonstrates changes in depth produced by grading activities in the mid-1930s. (Modified from Nawrocki, 1991).

with depth (see Henderson, 1987, p. 52). Those closer to the surface were poorly preserved, being highly fragmented, fragile, and usually incomplete. Areas of the skeleton containing large quantities of spongy bone suffered the most, although even the denser cortices of the long-bone shafts were heavily eroded. In contrast, burials at greater depths were frequently in excellent condition. We recovered fragile ossified thyroid cartilages, small distal phalanges, and thin portions of the facial skeleton in the peripheral areas of the cemetery. It should be noted that this variation in preservation probably did not result from some skeletons having been buried longer than others. The proximity of the interments to one another, as well as the high death rates in the county poorhouses (see Ferguson, 1988, pp. 106–107), suggest that all of the Oneida burials could have originated within a very short period of time, perhaps in only a year or two. Thus, much of the variance in skeletal preservation would have occurred in the 55 years between the grading of the compound and the archaeological recovery.

It is possible to quantify the relationship between depth below surface and skeletal preservation (Pappalardo & Nawrocki, 1991). The first task is to categorize overall skeletal preservation. Some workers have used rather intensive methods to record preservation, including the actual measurement of remaining portions of bone (Walker et al., 1988). The approach used here is simpler and more qualitative. Full-length color photographs were available for 57 of the 81 burials, representing a random subset of the entire assemblage. These photographs were ranked independently by a physical anthropologist (this writer) and an archaeologist from best preserved (1) to worst preserved (57). Since the midsections of the skeletons appeared to withstand the effects of time less well than the extremities (for reasons discussed previously), each analyst constructed two rankings: one based on the preservation of the cranium and long bones, and a second based on the preservation of the ribcage and vertebral column. Thus, each burial received a total of four different rankings. No attempt was made to modify assessments on the basis of root damage or animal activity, and neither analyst had access to depth data at the time of scoring. The use of photos of the burials in situ rather than the measurement or ranking of bones after removal from the ground has the significant advantage of minimizing postexcavation taphonomic effects on the skeleton, producing a more direct assessment of the condition of the bones before archaeological disturbance (see Boddington, 1987, p. 28 for further advantages to using photographs in burial archaeology).

Depth below present ground surface (DEPTH) was measured in centimeters to the floor of the coffin at the head (west) end. For the 57 burials ranked for preservation, depth ranged between 39 and 170 cm (mean = 87 cm, sd = 29.6 cm), including both the shallowest and the deepest burials excavated. All data were analyzed with SYSTAT for the Macintosh (v.5.2.1—Wilkinson, 1992). The first questions to be answered included: 1) How do the rankings of the different areas of the skeleton compare? 2) How well do the rankings of the two analysts compare? 3) How strongly is skeletal preservation associated with depth below surface? Spearman's correlation ($\rho$) is the appropriate measure of association for ranked variables, yielding results that are interpreted in the same fashion as the standard Pearson product–moment correlation ($r$).

For each analyst, the correlation between the rankings of the midskeleton and extremities is high (for this writer, $\rho = +0.85$, $p < 0.001$; for the archaeologist, $\rho = +0.97$, $p < 0.001$; $n = 57$), indicating that both regions reflect the same relative degree of skeletal preservation. The correlations between the analysts' rankings of each skeletal region are also significant (for the midskeleton, $\rho = +0.92$, $p < 0.001$; for the extremities, $\rho = +0.80$, $p < 0.001$), indicating a moderately strong level of agreement between the analysts. On the basis of these results, and for the sake of convenience, all four rankings for each burial were averaged, producing a single summary ranking (PRES).

The Spearman correlation between DEPTH and PRES is significant ($\rho = -0.47$, $p < 0.001$, $n = 57$), confirming our initial observations. The negative value indicates that well-preserved burials (receiving low ranking values) were the most deeply buried. The least squares regression line takes the form

PRES = 45.45—0.19(DEPTH)
($r^2 = 0.125$, $se = 14.96$, $n = 57$; model $F = 7.85$, $p < 0.007$)

Visual inspection of the plot suggested that three of the interments (Burials 53, 55, and 56) were outliers, being less well preserved than their depth would predict. The regression analysis indicates that the leverage of one of these (Burial 53) is indeed relatively high (0.159), as are the Cook's $D$ values for all three (0.15–0.23), showing that each has a strong influence on the regression. These burials came from a tight cluster in the northernmost section of the cemetery and include the most deeply buried skeletons in the assemblage, ranging from 150 to 170 cm below surface. This end of the cemetery was located beneath or adjacent to a thick layer of ash, cinders, and debris dating to the early 20th century, representing a roadbed that once crosscut the central compound of the institution (see Fig. 1). It is possible that leaching chemicals, altered drainage patterns, and compaction differentially accelerated the decomposition process of the skeletons lying beneath the roadbed. After removing them from the analysis, the correlation between DEPTH and PRES rises to −0.574 ($p < 0.001$, $n = 54$). The resulting least-squares regression is

PRES = 56.95—0.34(DEPTH)
($r^2 = 0.279$, $se = 13.84$, $n = 54$; model $F = 20.08$, $p < 0.000$)

Thus, in this sample approximately 28% of the variance in preservation can be accounted for by variation in depth.

These results suggest that depth below surface is an important environmental taphonomic variable influencing the overall preservation of human skeletal remains. A number of specific factors could account for this relationship. First, shallower burials may lay within the seasonal freeze–thaw zone. Groundwater that permeated any cracks within the bone would expand upon freezing, producing fragmentation. Second, animal and plant activity would be more marked at higher levels. Third, soil pH may have varied systematically with depth, producing potentially drastic effects on skeletal preservation (see Gordon & Buikstra, 1981). It is interesting to note that Mant (1987, p. 69) made similar observations concerning soft-tissue decomposition and depth in his exhumations of World War II victims in Germany.

### Individual Variation

Another set of taphonomic variables can be examined using the Oneida data: those involving the individual characteristics of those interred. Data on sex and stature are available for a number of the burials. The mean score for PRES for the nine ranked females is 32.6 ($sd = 11.7$), while that for the 37 ranked males is 24.0 ($sd = 15.2$), suggesting that females are less well preserved than males. This difference, however, is not statistically significant. A Mann–Whitney $U$ Test (generated with the Kruskal–Wallis option of NPAR in SYSTAT) does not reach significance ($U = 108.5, p = 0.11$, $\chi^2 = 2.58, df = 1$). Furthermore, a standard analysis of covariance (ANCOVA) of the form PRES = SEX + DEPTH + ERROR fails to produce a significant $F$-value for SEX ($F = 2.703, p = 0.11, df = 1, n = 46$), although that for DEPTH nearly reaches significance ($F = 3.806, p = 0.058, df = 1$). Both sexes are randomly dispersed with respect to DEPTH (for the ANOVA model DEPTH = SEX + ERROR, $F = 0.004, p = 0.95, df = 1$). Thus, while the sample size is admittedly small, it appears that sex has no strong effect on skeletal preservation, supporting the findings of Walker et al. (1988).

Differences in body size and robusticity, while overlapping basic sex differences, can be analyzed separately. Stature was estimated by myself and Fleischman (1989) from complete long bones using the appropriate regression formulae (Trotter & Gleser, 1952, 1958). Forty individuals with stature estimates were among the 57 ranked for preservation, including 33 males, four females, and three of uncertain sex for which stature was calculated using the male formulae. Mean stature for the 40 individuals is 171.0 cm ($sd = 7.1$ cm). The Spearman correlation between PRES and estimated stature is not significant ($\rho = -0.03, p > 0.80$). The use of maximum femoral length instead of stature does not improve the association with PRES ($\rho = +0.09$, $p > 0.60, n = 28$). The relationships between PRES and other measures of skeletal size were also examined, including the vertical diameter of the femoral head ($\rho = -0.13$, $p > 0.40, n = 42$), vertical diameter of the humeral head ($\rho = -0.17, p > 0.40, n = 23$), and circumference of the tibia at the nutrient foramen ($\rho = -0.03, p > 0.80, n = 25$). These preliminary results suggest that variation in body size, including sexual dimorphism, does not strongly influence overall skeletal preservation.

## CONCLUSIONS

The taphonomic history of an organism can be seen as a complex interplay between the opposing forces of preservation and destruction (Garland, 1989, p. 15). Taphonomists recognize that some processes (such as burial) can help to preserve skeletal material and may result in important information gains (see Gifford, 1981). From the perspective of the analysis of skeletal material from historic cemeteries, however, the ultimate end product of nearly all postmortem processes is generally the loss of biological information. To the extent that skeletal attrition is nonrandom, sampling bias will be introduced into the assemblages studied by anthropologists.

From the preceding discussion it can be seen that sampling bias can occur at one or more of three broad levels of analysis in historic cemeteries (Nawrocki, 1991). First, different areas of individual skeletons may suffer attrition, resulting in systematic overrepresentation of some bones (such as femora) in the burial assemblage and underrepresentation of others (such as carpals). This sort of bias has important ramifications for basic osteological and paleopathological analysis. Techniques used in the determination of race, sex, age at death, and stature from skeletal remains are not equally effective for all types of bones. Disease processes and activity-induced degeneration frequently affects very specific areas of the skeleton, leaving other areas untouched. Thus, differential loss of skeletal elements may hinder our ability to make basic inferences about the lives of the individuals we are studying.

Second, taphonomic processes can lead to differential loss of entire burials. These losses are frequently nonrandom with respect to the biological characteristics or socioeconomic standing of the interred, producing assemblages that are not representative of the population of individuals originally buried in the cemetery. Certain individuals (such as the very young) do not preserve well, and others (such as the poor) may be segregated into areas of the cemetery that are subject to different preservational environments or social attitudes. This sort of sampling bias can greatly influence paleodemographers in their attempt to reconstruct the characteristics of the parent population.

Third, taphonomic processes can lead to the loss of whole cemeteries, making entire subcomponents of a society inaccessible for study. The results, however, can be somewhat counterintuitive. Many if not most of the larger historic period cemeteries excavated in this country in recent decades—such as the Oneida and Monroe County cemeteries—have been associated with poorhouses, institutions, and African-American communities, none of which would necessarily reflect the biology or material culture of middle- or upper-class communities of European origin. In essence, then, it is the well-maintained European cemetery that is lost from study, whereas those of lower socioeconomic status, while perhaps more likely to be completely destroyed, are also more likely to be excavated and studied.

## REFERENCES

Andrews P, Cook J (1985). Natural modifications to bones in a temperate setting. Man 20:675–691.

Behrensmeyer AK, Hill AP (1980). Fossils in the Making: Vertebrate Taphonomy and Paleoecology. Chicago: University of Chicago Press.

Blankman JE (1994). Analysis of a Human Cranium and Mandible Recovered in Indianapolis. Paper presented at the Butler University Undergraduate Research Conference, Indianapolis.

Boddington A (1987). Chaos, disturbance and decay in an Anglo-Saxon cemetery. In A Boddington, Garland AN, Janaway RC (eds.), Death, Decay, and Reconstruction, pp. 27–42. Manchester: Manchester University Press.

Boddington A, Garland AN, Janaway RC (1987a). Death, Decay, and Reconstruction: Approaches to Archaeology and Forensic Science. Manchester: Manchester University Press.

Boddington A, Garland AN, Janaway RC (1987b). Flesh, bones dust and society. In Boddington A, Garland AN, Janaway RC (eds.), Death, Decay, and Reconstruction, pp. 3–9. Manchester: Manchester University Press.

Bonnichsen R, Sorg MH (1989). Bone Modification. Orono, ME: Center for the Study of the First Americans, University of Maine.

Brain CK (1981). The Hunters or the Hunted? An Introduction to African Cave Taphonomy. Chicago: University of Chicago Press.

Brothwell D (1987). Decay and disorder in the York Jewbury skeletons. In Boddington A et al. (eds.), Death, Decay, and Reconstruction, pp. 22–26. Manchester: Manchester University Press.

Catts EP, Haskell NH (1990). Entomology and Death: A Procedural Guide. Clemson, SC: Joyce's Print Shop.

Clark J, Beerbower JR, Kietzke KK (1967). Oligocene sedimentation, stratigraphy and paleoclimatology in the Big Badlands of South Dakota. Fieldiana: Geology Memoir 5:1–158.

Cook DC (1993). Letter to the editor. Archaeology 46(4):10.

Dodson P (1980). Vertebrate burials. Paleobiology 6:6–8.

Ellis GD, Jones JR, Mohow JA (1991). Archaeological Investigations and Recovery of Human Remains from the White River Levee at East Ray Street, Indianapolis, Indiana. Cultural Resources Report, Division of Historic Preservation and Archaeology, Department of Natural Resources.

Evans WED (1963). The Chemistry of Death. Springfield, IL: Charles C. Thomas.

Ferguson P (1988). Abandoned to their Fate: A History of Social Policy and Practice Towards Severely Retarded People in America, 1820 to 1920. Ph.D. Dissertation in Education, Syracuse University.

Fleischman ML (1989). Report on the Skeletal Population of a Paupers' Cemetery, Rome Facility, Rome, New York. Report submitted to the New York State Museum, Albany.

Fleischman ML (1990). Unmarked Paupers' Cemetery at Rome Facility in Rome, New York. Paper presented at the 30th Meeting of the Northeast Anthropological Association, Burlington, VT.

Garland AN (1989). The taphonomy of inhumation burials. In Roberts CA, Lee F, Bintliff J (eds.), Burial Archaeology: Current Research, Methods and Developments, pp. 15–37. BAR British Series 211.

Gifford DP (1981). Taphonomy and paleoecology: A critical review of archaeology's sister disciplines. Advances in Archaeological Method and Theory 4:365–438.

Gordon CC, Buikstra JE (1981). Soil pH, bone preservation, and sampling bias at mortuary sites. American Antiquity 46:566–571.

Hackett CJ (1981). Microscopical focal destruction (tunnels) in exhumed human bones. Med. Sci. Law 21:243–265.

Haglund WD (1991). Applications of Taphonomic Models to Forensic Investigations. Ph.D. Dissertation in Anthropology, University of Washington.

Haglund WD, Reay DT, Swindler DR (1988). Tooth mark artifacts and survival of bones in animal scavenged human remains. J. Forensic Sci. 33:985–997.

Haglund WD, Reay DT, Swindler DR (1989). Canid scavenging/disarticulation sequence of human remains in the Pacific Northwest. J. Forensic Sci. 34:587–606.

Haglund WD, Sorg MH (1993). Taphonomy in the Forensic Context. Session organized for the 45th Meeting of the American Academy of Forensic Sciences, Boston, MA.

Henderson J (1987). Factors determining the state of preservation of human remains. In Boddington A, Garland AN, Janaway RC (eds.), Death, Decay, and Reconstruction, pp. 43–54. Manchester: Manchester University Press.

Janaway RC (1987). The preservation of organic materials in association with metal artifacts deposited in inhumation graves. In Boddington A, Garland AN, Janaway RC (eds.), Death, Decay, and Reconstruction, pp. 127–148. Manchester: Manchester University Press.

Johnson E (1985). Current developments in bone technology. Advances in Archaeological Method and Theory 8:157–235.

Lanphear KM (1988). Health and Mortality in a Nineteenth Century Poorhouse Skeletal Sample. Ph.D. Dissertation in Anthropology, State University of New York at Albany.

Lanphear KM (1990). Frequency and distribution of enamel hypoplasias in a historic skeletal sample. Am. J. Phys. Anthropol. 81:35–43.

Mant AK (1987). Knowledge acquired from post-War exhumations. In Boddington A, Garland AN, Janaway RC (eds.), Death, Decay, and Reconstruction, pp. 65–78. Manchester: Manchester University Press.

Marchiafava V, Bonucci E, Ascenzi A (1974). Fungal osteoclasia: A model of dead bone resorption. Calcified Tissue Research 14:195–210.

Marshall LG (1989). Bone modification and "the laws of burial." In Bonnichsen R, Sorg MH (eds.), Bone Modification, pp. 7–24. Orono, ME: Center for the Study of the First Americans.

Mathews DS (1988). The massacre: The discovery of De Soto in Georgia. In Blakely RL (ed.), The King Site: Continuity and Contact in Sixteenth-Century Georgia, pp. 101–116. Athens: University of Georgia Press.

McGuire RH (1989). The sanctity of the grave: White concepts and American Indian burials. In Layton R (ed.), Conflict in the Archaeology of Living Traditions, pp. 167–184. London: Unwin Hyman.

Micozzi MS (1990). Postmortem Changes in Human and Animal Remains. Springfield, IL: Charles C. Thomas.

Nawrocki SP (1989). Developing Archeological Methodology: The Oneida Burial Project. Report submitted to the New York State Museum, Albany.

Nawrocki SP (1990). Reflections of Social Status in a Late-19th Century Almshouse Cemetery Population Near Rome, New York. Paper presented at the 30th Meeting of the Northeast Anthropological Association, Burlington, VT.

Nawrocki SP (1991). Human Taphonomy and Historic Cemeteries: Factors Influencing the Loss and Subsequent Recovery of Human Remains. Paper presented at the 31st Meeting of the Northeast Anthropological Association, Waterloo, ONT.

Nawrocki SP, Bell EL (1991). Burial Archeology and Human Taphonomy in the Northeast. Session organized for the 31st Meeting of the Northeast Anthropological Association, Waterloo, ONT.

Nawrocki SP, Clark MA (1994). Extreme Dispersal and Damage of Human Skeletal Remains by Farming Equipment. Paper presented at the 46th Meeting of the American Academy of Forensic Sciences, San Antonio, TX.

Nawrocki SP, Pless JE (1993). Transport of Human Remains in Fluvial Environments: A Review. Paper presented at the 45th Meeting of the American Academy of Forensic Sciences, Boston, MA.

Olson EC (1980). Taphonomy: Its history and role in community evolution. In Behrensmeyer AK, Hill AP (eds.), Fossils in the Making: Vertebrate Taphonomy and Paleoecology, pp. 5–19. Chicago: University of Chicago Press.

Pappalardo AM, Nawrocki SP (1991). The Effects of Depth Below Surface, Sex, and Stature on the Preservation of Buried Human Remains. Paper presented at the 31st Meeting of the Northeast Anthropological Association, Waterloo, ONT.

Roberts CA, Lee F, Bintliff J (eds.) (1989). Burial Archaeology: Current Research, Methods and Developments. BAR British Series 211.

Rodriguez WC, Bass WM (1985). Decomposition of buried bodies and methods that may aid in their location. J. Forensic Sci. 30:836–852.

Santangelo, MC (1989). DOCS Oneida Supplement, City of Rome, Oneida County. Report Submitted to the New York State Department of Correctional Services.

Saunders SR (1992). Subadult skeletons and growth related studies. In Saunders SR, Katzenberg MA (eds.), Skeletal Biology of Past Peoples: Research Methods, pp. 1–20. New York: Wiley-Liss.

Shipman P (1981). Life History of a Fossil. Cambridge: Harvard University Press.

Sledzik PS (1994). Hardin, Missouri cemetery disaster. The Connective Tissue 10(1):11.

Smith B (1993). Hardin waging most grisly of flood cleanups. St. Louis Post-Dispatch (August 15).

Trotter M, Gleser GC (1952). Estimation of stature from long bones of American whites and Negroes. Am. J. Phys. Anthropol. 19:213–227.

Trotter M, Gleser GC (1958). A re-evaluation of estimation based on measurements of stature taken during life and of long bones after death. Am. J. Phys. Anthropol. 16:79–123.

Villa P, Mahieu E (1991). Breakage patterns of human long bones. Journal of Human Evolution 21:27–48.

Von Endt DW, Ortner DJ (1984). Experimental effects of bone size and temperature on bone diagenesis. Journal of Archaeological Science 11:247–253.

Waldron T (1987). The relative survival of the human skeleton: Implications for palaeopathology. In Boddington A, Garland AN, Janaway RC (eds.), Death, Decay and Reconstruction: Approaches to Archaeology and Forensic Science, pp. 55–64. Manchester: Manchester University Press.

Walker PL, Johnson JR, Lambert PM (1988). Age and sex biases in the preservation of human skeletal remains. Am. J. Phys. Anthropol. 76:183–188.

Weiss KM (1972). On the systematic bias in skeletal sexing. Am. J. Phys. Anthropol. 37:239–249.

Wells C (1967). Pseudopathology. In Brothwell DR, Sandison AT (eds.), Diseases in Antiquity, pp. 5–19. Springfield, IL: Charles C Thomas.

Wilkinson L (1992). Systat for the Macintosh, Version 5.2. Systat Inc., Evanston, IL.

Willey P, Heilman A (1987). Estimating time since death using plant roots and stems. J. Forensic Sciences 32:1264–1270.

# PART II
# The Assessment of
# Demographic Patterns

# 5 Can Skeletal Samples Accurately Represent the Living Populations They Come From? The St. Thomas' Cemetery Site, Belleville, Ontario

SHELLEY R. SAUNDERS, D. ANN HERRING, and GERALD BOYCE

## INTRODUCTION

Community development often generates archaeological excavation. In the 1980s, St. Thomas' Anglican Church in Belleville, Ontario (Fig. 1) decided to build a parish hall on land adjacent to church property in order to accommodate an expanding congregation. It was known that a 19th-century cemetery existed on the land. A number of old tombstones were still standing on the property even after two major church fires and the effects of time had caused the destruction of much of the evidence of a burying ground. However, the number of intact burials was unknown, as it was believed that many of the interments had been removed to the town's municipal cemetery after St. Thomas' cemetery was closed on April 14, 1874.

Provincial permission to close the cemetery and disinter the remains was received and the church proceeded with the building project. The plans included archaeological excavation of the cemetery and Northeastern Archaeological Associates, an archaeological contract firm, was hired to carry out the disinterments and excavation over the summer of 1989.

Under a previously established court order, the church was given permission for the excavation and study of the skeletal remains over a one-year period before reinterment was required. A detailed series of skeletal analyses, including data collection, X-rays, photography, and tissue sampling, was carried out at the Depart-

*Bodies of Evidence*, Edited by Anne L. Grauer.
ISBN 0-471-04153-X  © 1995 John Wiley & Sons, Inc.

**FIGURE 1.** Map of southern Ontario illustrating the location of Belleville and the parish of St. Thomas' Church.

ment of Anthropology, McMaster University over that one-year period. Ultimately, a large number of researchers from ten different universities in Canada and the United States took part in the skeletal analysis. Work on the skeletal data still continues.

Once the skeletal data collection was completed, another phase of the project began with the systematic assembling of primary source documentary data for St. Thomas' Anglican Church and Belleville. A review of the published literature led us to conclude that the St. Thomas' cemetery site is unique in at least two respects: 1) it represents one of the largest archaeologically excavated historic cemetery samples in North America to date, and 2) the cemetery burials are fully documented—parish records for St. Thomas' as well as other historical documents for the town of Belleville, such as censuses and municipal tax assessment records, are available for the entire period during which the cemetery was used.

Permission was received from the church and the Anglican Church Archives to transcribe St. Thomas' parish registers from 1821 to 1874, the entire period during which the cemetery was used. Separate databases were created for the burial, baptism, and marriage records, the accuracy of the transcriptions was verified, and all transcription errors were corrected. Our intention was to use the burial records (which provided information on virtually everyone buried in the cemetery), as well as information on baptisms and marriages in the parish, to generate historical demographic information that could be compared to the demographic results from the analysis of the skeletal sample. In addition, the parish registers would not only provide an excellent source of historical information on the congregation but would also allow reconstruction of families and a full historical demographic study of the records themselves.

As work progressed, we collected and transcribed decennial government censuses for the Town of Belleville from 1851 to 1881. We will not be reporting on the results of the census analysis in this chapter, but it is worth noting that nominative data on age, sex, place of birth, religion, literacy, occupation, house size and construction, and the extent of agricultural holdings are contained in these rich sources of information on community life in the 19th century.

In this chapter, we focus on the mortality of infants and children as a means of assessing how well skeletal samples can represent the living populations they are drawn from and as a means of evaluating some of the general health characteristics of both St. Thomas' congregation and the greater population of 19th-century Belleville. We focus on infant mortality because it is generally considered to be an important public health index for assessing the sanitary and social conditions that surrounded an infant in life.

## HISTORICAL BACKGROUND

The town of Belleville was first surveyed and named in 1816, at which time it occupied less than 200 acres. Settlement of the town by pioneers was stimulated in the earliest days by the arrival of United Empire Loyalists (UEL's) who maintained allegiance to the British crown and fled the newly independent United States of America. Further waves of settlement occurred after the War of 1812 and into midcentury (Boyce, 1967). These settlers were mainly British subjects from England and Scotland. A large component of Irish immigrants, mostly Roman Catholic, settled in Belleville in the early to mid-19th century.

When the town was established, a detailed census of the existing 45 buildings was completed, along with the names of the owners. However, it wasn't until the 1820s that vital records were maintained with any degree of reliability, coinciding with the establishment of Methodist, Anglican, and Roman Catholic congregations in Belleville. Since civil registration only began in Ontario on July 1, 1869, church records are still considered the most reliable source of information for the early development of Canadian towns.

Belleville's population consisted of a mere 100 people or so at the time of its founding in 1816 but grew to about 700 by the end of the 1820s (Boyce, 1967; Mika & Mika, 1986). The population expanded rapidly to 4,569 by 1851 as the town became a hub for marketing farm and lumber products. By 1874, when St. Thomas' cemetery was closed, Belleville had grown from a small village to a bustling town of some 7,500 people.

St. Thomas' Anglican church was founded on December 26, 1818. Construction of a church building began in 1819 and the first church service was held in June of 1821. St. Thomas' cemetery was the first public burial ground (although a small private cemetery had been established earlier, just outside the original town border). Initially, Methodists, Presbyterians, and members of other denominations were allowed to purchase plots at St. Thomas', but when several other cemeteries eventually were opened by other denominations, this practice declined. Belleville's municipal cemetery was opened in 1874, largely for health reasons and in response to a town council bylaw prohibiting further burials within town limits. Thereafter, burials took place within the municipal cemetery.

## METHODS AND MATERIALS

### Definitions and Words of Caution

One of the problems facing researchers is reaching agreement on common definitions that will allow for accurate comparisons between skeletal and documentary data, as well as between sites (Peterson, 1975; Howell, 1986). In the past, many skeletal researchers have used the term infant to apply to a variety of age spans from 1 to even 5 years; more recently, skeletal biologists appear to be following conventional demographic practice by referring to infants as all individuals who have died between birth and one year of age (Saunders & Spence, 1986; Molleson, 1989; Storey, 1992). The demographic definition of infant mortality, however, refers to all liveborn babies who die before reaching their first birthday. It is rarely possible when excavating burials to distinguish stillbirths (or late fetal deaths) from infants who were born alive but died shortly after birth.

Demographers also conventionally divide infant deaths into two categories: 1) neonatal deaths, which occur from birth to 27 days; 2) postneonatal deaths, which occur from 28 to 364 days. Neonatal mortality is considered to be a reflection of the endogenous state of the infant (genetic and congenital abnormalities, maternal health and nutrition, and circumstances surrounding birth), whereas postneonatal mortality is judged a better indicator of aspects of the infant's environment (nutrition, infectious disease, and living conditions) (Bourgeois-Pichat, 1951a,b).

While skeletal remains and records provide information on health and disease in infants and, by inference, in the community as a whole, each type of data also presents a different facet of the problem of such reconstruction. Recorded causes of death in burial records approximate health conditions around the time of the infant's death. Analysis of cause of death data is useful for reconstructing changes in morbidity and mortality over time, identifying epidemics, detecting seasonal patterns in mortality, inferring breast feeding practices, and assessing the presence of acute infections and noninfectious conditions in a community (Knodel & Kintner, 1977; Meindl, 1977; Meindl & Swedlund, 1977; Dyhouse, 1978; Hansen, 1979; Knodel, 1983; Trapp et al., 1983; Cheney, 1984; Thompson, 1984; Sawchuk et al., 1985; Swedlund, 1990; Lee, 1991; Sawchuk, 1993). No matter what the source, however, cause of death information must be used with extreme caution. A physician's decision to assign a particular cause of death is influenced by his or her knowledge of a patient, diagnostic ability, approach to disease causation, and understanding of pathological processes, and is a reflection of prevailing philosophies, taxonomies, and perceptions of disease (Sartwell & Last, 1980, p. 20). As it is unusual for clergymen to have medical training, ascriptions of cause of death in parish records are even more unreliable than those contained in civil and medical records.

In the present study, the demographic definition of infant mortality was used for the documentary data. In the case of the skeletal sample, all babies buried beside their mothers or in separate graves were deemed liveborn and those estimated by dental development to be up to but not including one year were included in the infant category.

Skeletal remains, in contrast to parish records, recapitulate the lifetime of nutritional and disease experiences of an individual. The skeletons of infants and children can provide evidence of chronic physiological stress, such as defects in tooth enamel (Goodman & Rose, 1990), anemias (Stuart-Macadam, 1992), altered bone metabolism, dietary composition, and intragroup dietary differences (Tuross et al., 1990; Katzenberg et al., 1993). Growth and development patterns, which are critical components for evaluating the quality of a child's health, have been assessed by comparing the relative sizes of subadult long bones to modern standards and to other skeletal samples (Jantz & Owsley, 1984; Cook, 1984; Mensforth, 1985; Lovejoy et al., 1990; Hoppa, 1992; Saunders, 1992; Saunders et al., 1993a).

Recently, it has been argued that it is not possible to detect associations between aggregate-level measures of skeletal stress (morbidity) or mortality as studied by paleodemographers and paleopathologists and the risks of illness and death experienced by individual members of past populations (Wood et al., 1992). These authors attribute the difficulty to two main problems. The first problem concerns selective mortality or the fact that we are working with a sample of dead individuals, not all of the individuals who were at risk for disease at particular ages. The second refers to hidden or undetectable variability of the risks of developing disease or of dying. It is asserted that the skeletal evidence pertaining to transitions in subsistence patterns, such as the adoption of agriculture, is equally consistent with either an improvement in health or a deterioration in health over time.

However, others have responded that because most skeletal indicators of health are represented by lesions that reflect survival for some time after the morbidity event, they are not directly tied to mortality (Goodman, 1993; Saunders & Hoppa, 1993) and therefore should not necessarily be affected by selective mortality. In addition, it is important to examine a variety of indicators of health and nutrition in order to resolve any paradoxical interpretations. Finally, appropriate hypothesis building in skeletal studies of past populations requires that we take cultural and social factors into account (Goodman, 1993). Such ideal opportunities are offered by historic-cemetery studies, such as the St. Thomas' project, where interpretations from skeletal material can be compared, evaluated, and amplified by those from historical documents and writings.

### St. Thomas' Parish Records

The parish registers of St. Thomas' Anglican Church were kept by the church's ministers beginning with the first baptismal service on July 24, 1821 and continuing up to the present day. Data include name(s), age(s), date of the event (whether burial, baptism, or marriage), name of the registrar, death date of a burial, cause of death, and occasional notes on family relationships. All of the records up to and including 1899 were transcribed to a database management program and checked twice by different individuals for transcription errors.

A total of 1,564 interments were recorded for the cemetery during its 53-year period of use. Not all of these 1,564 interments could be included in statistical calculations because of the incompleteness of recorded information. Notations in the burial records indicate, however, that an additional 17 individuals were buried in other locations. This illustrates the recorders' attention to detail, but it was never-theless necessary to apply a series of historical demographic tests to the parish registers to evaluate their quality (Drake, 1974). The tests involved determining: 1) the adequacy of sample size (a minimum of 100 registry entries per year); 2) whether there were obvious and serious gaps in the registers and evidence of underregistra-tion; 3) whether persons buried in other churchyards were so indicated in the records; and 4) whether recorded sexes and ages were accurate or estimates.

Analysis of the quality of St. Thomas' registers (Rogers, 1991; DeVito, n.d.) showed that in rare, isolated cases individuals had been buried without being recorded in the burial records. There are no significant gaps in the registers; however, the total number of vital events (sum of all baptisms, marriages, and burials) is somewhat reduced between 1831 and 1835, although the number of burials was unaffected (Fig. 2). Another dip in the baptisms was noted in 1863, the result of the establishment of Christ Church, a second Anglican Church in Belleville. This discovery, and the knowledge that members of Christ Church's congregation were buried in St. Thomas' cemetery, led us to collect the Christ Church parish records and include them in our historical demographic analysis. As mentioned earlier, parishioners buried elsewhere were so noted in the register. Individuals of unknown sex represent a nonsignificant proportion of the total sample (less than 2%) and those of unrecorded age appear to be randomly distributed throughout the age range. These findings led us to conclude that the register data could be confidently treated as a reliable source for comparison to skeletally derived sex and age profiles.

The burial register indicated that 701 infants and children died under the age of 15. The exact ages of 637 (91%) could be determined from the burial entries, but 64 individuals had nonspecific ages listed, such as "infant" or "child." By cross-checking the latter against the baptismal registers, it was possible to identify the exact ages of

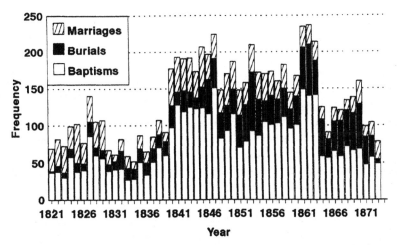

**FIGURE 2.** Total vital events (baptisms, marriages, and burials) per year at St. Thomas' Church, 1821–1874.

36 of these, increasing the registry sample of identifiable subadults to 673, or 96% of the recorded children. This is a good example of how record-linkage techniques improve the quality of parish record data.

### Skeletal Data

During the summer of 1989, a total of 579 grave shafts were excavated from an area of 1.75 acres, representing approximately one-third of the original grounds of St. Thomas' cemetery (Saunders et al., 1993b). The well-drained, sandy soil promoted such excellent bone preservation that more than 60% of adult burials were of good to almost perfect preservation (Jimenez, 1991). Good preservation was taken to mean only slight damage to the proximal or distal ends of long bones or to the vertebral processes. Fully 87% of all adult skeletons were sufficiently complete to evaluate trauma and infection on *all* bones (Saunders et al, 1994).

A total of 604 individuals were identified from the 579 grave shafts, demonstrating that some burials contained more than one individual, often a mother and child or infant. Of the 604 individuals, approximately 577 were complete enough for detailed examination. It was determined that 282 individuals were immature or under the age of 15 years (subadults), while the remainder were older adolescents or adults. A total of 149 infants were identified among the 282 subadults.

Estimation of age-at-death of the adults in the skeletal sample included the observation of a number of morphological features as well as the histological analysis of bone thin sections. Changes to the pubic symphysis and the auricular surface of the hip bone, metamorphosis of the sternal rib ends, and dental wear and degenerative changes have been recorded. A test of these methods using a small subsample of personally identified adults ($n = 55$) has shown that the summary age of a series of morphological indicators provides the closest approximation to chronological age (Saunders et al., 1991). However, these results still suffer from the perennial problem of underaging of older adults (Jackes, 1992). We are currently attempting to test and apply a variety of age-distribution models to the adult age data (Paine, 1989; Konigsberg and Frankenberg, 1992).

The determination of the sex of adults was based almost entirely on intact morphological features of the bony pelvis (Rogers, 1991), and a comparison and statistical test of the sex ratios of the skeletal and overall interrment sample (based on parish registers) showed no significant differences. Tests of the accuracy of morphologically determined sex were highly reliable (Rogers & Saunders, 1994).

Of the 282 subadults, 266 were given a dental age based on the tooth formation standards for three deciduous and 12 permanent mandibular teeth of Moorrees et al. (1963a,b). An earlier study had shown that these were the most reliable standards and the least likely to produce any bias in overall mean dental age estimates (Saunders et al., 1993a). It was necessary to assign ages to the remaining 16 individuals in the subadult sample from long-bone diaphyseal lengths derived from the total sample.

Despite the fact that there are published regression equations for determining the sex of subadult skeletons from tooth dimensions (DeVito & Saunders, 1990), we did not attempt to determine the sex of the subadult skeletal remains. It is possible that tooth measurements will show evidence of mortality selection in archaeological skeletal samples, producing abnormally high ratios of females (Saunders, 1992).

A variety of skeletal indicators have been used to evaluate health-stress levels or morbidity rates in past populations. These include enumerated cases of mortality in various age categories, adult stature, subadult bone size, enamel hypoplasia of the teeth, bone infection and trauma, skeletal markers of anemia, arthritis, and dental caries (Buikstra & Cook, 1980). While all of these indicators were assessed for the St. Thomas' skeletal sample, the present study is restricted to the assessment of subadult mortality profiles and measures of subadult bone growth. Mortality profiles were constructed from dental age estimates considered to be most accurate as described above. Diaphyseal lengths for all long bones as well as the ilium and scapula were recorded to the nearest whole millimeter by one investigator.

Skeletal-growth profiles (SGPs) were created by plotting distributions of diaphyseal lengths against estimates of chronological age based on tooth formation. The growth profiles were constructed for comparison with the modern standards of Maresh (1970) and other archaeological samples. These included a protohistoric Arikara sample from South Dakota (Merchant & Ubelaker, 1977) and subadult skeletons from a British 10th-century Anglo–Saxon cemetery, the Raunds Site (Hoppa, 1992). Means and 95% confidence intervals for each age sample were also calculated. Tests of discordancy to detect true outliers in the St. Thomas' sample were run on $z$-scores calculated from the mean and standard deviation of each appropriate sample. The SGPs were constructed using the left-side bones, with replacement by the right when necessary, so that single individuals were represented only once in a given SGP.

## RESULTS AND DISCUSSION

The following section considers the possible evidence for bias in the skeletal sample due to differential preservation and compares the proportions of subadult age categories in the skeletal and records sample. Following this, an examination of historical documents provides some explanation for differential mortality and interment of infants over the course of the cemetery's use. We also divide infant mortality into neonatal and postneonatal categories in order to delineate the role played by sanitary-social, and other environmental conditions in infant mortality and survival. The Bourgeois-Pichat (1951a,b) method for inferring factors affecting infant death, particularly the role of breastfeeding and weaning, is applied to the records and skeletal samples. Finally, we examine infant and child bone growth and size as indicators of general causes of death in the Belleville sample.

### Bone Preservation

There is a widespread belief that infants' and childrens' bones, because they are small and fragile, do not preserve as well as adult bones, and that this poor preservation results in subadult underrepresentation and skeletal samples that are not representative of living populations (Johnston & Zimmer, 1989; Storey, 1992). At least, an apparent lack of subadult individuals, particularly infants, can severely hinder paleodemographic analysis of skeletal samples (Jackes, 1992; Storey, 1992). On the other hand, while subadult bone is known from experimental studies to be less dense and to have higher organic and less mineral content than adult bone (Currey & Butler, 1975; Specker et al., 1987; Gordon & Buikstra, 1981), the lack of subadults in many archaeological collections is more likely due to differential burial practices and inexperienced or biased excavation (Saunders, 1992).

The St. Thomas' skeletal sample showed evidence of relatively good preservation of subadult bones. The estimated proportions of total subadults to adults in the skeletal sample matched closely with the known proportions calculated from the burials listed in the parish registers (Saunders, 1992) (see Table 1). In addition, a significant and unusually high proportion (98%) of the subadults showed preservation of either dental or skeletal age indicators, when compared to the adult skeletons.

### Infants in Skeletal and Documents Samples

On the other hand, when we looked at the proportions of infants to other ages in the documents versus those observed in the skeletal sample, differences were found. A likelihood ratio chi square test of the proportions of individuals under one year of age and all other age groups (combined) in the two samples showed that significantly fewer infants were listed in the burial records while significantly more were found in the skeletal sample (Table 2) (Herring et al., 1994). This is a somewhat surprising result in view of the expectation from the literature that infant skeletons should be underpreserved in archaeological samples.

Of course, it is possible that some infants, especially the very young, were interred

**TABLE 1. St. Thomas' Cemetery Site Comparison of Subadults to Adults.**

|  | Skeletons | | Records | |
|---|---|---|---|---|
|  | N | % | N | % |
| Subadults | 282 (1.06)[a] | 50.5 | 710 (−0.64) | 46 |
| Adults | 277 (−1.00) | 49.5 | 825 (.60) | 54 |
| Total | 559 | | 1535 | |

Note: Likelihood ratio chi square = 2.89, $p$ = .089 (not significant).
[a]Values in brackets are likelihood ratio chi square residuals. A value greater than 1.64 indicates a cell is significant at the .05 level.

with their mothers without being recorded in the burial registers. In fact, the archaeological excavation of the cemetery revealed that there were more than a dozen recorded instances of infants found in the same grave or buried above an adult female. Alternatively, some infant burials may not have been recorded simply because infant death was common and not accorded the attention given to older individuals. However, these explanations are difficult to reconcile with the good quality of the burial registers and the very complete data provided for the infants listed in them. Indeed, examination of the recorded names and ages in the burial records detected ten cases

**TABLE 2. St. Thomas' Cemetery Study Comparison of Infants to All Other Ages.**

|  | Skeletons | | Records[a] | |
|---|---|---|---|---|
|  | N | % | N | % |
| Infants | 149 (2.25)[b] | 26.7 | 293 (−1.40) | 20.4 |
| Others | 410 (−1.20) | 73.3 | 1141 (.75) | 79.6 |
| Total | 559 | | 1434 | |

Note: Likelihood ratio chi square = 8.79, $p$ = .003.
[a]Individuals whose exact ages were not recorded in the records were excluded from these calculations.
[b]Values in brackets are likelihood ratio chi square residuals. A value greater than 1.64 indicates a cell is significant at the .05 level.

of deaths of women and young babies or infants with the same surname. We cannot determine, however, whether these individuals were actually buried together. One possible explanation for the discrepancy might be the surreptitious practice of burying infants unrecorded and under cover of darkness to avoid payment for a plot, but it is not possible to detect evidence of such a practice from the conditions of the excavated burials.

We interpret the overrepresentation of infants in the skeletal sample to be a product of temporal bias in the archaeological excavation of the site. According to the parish registers, the proportions of infant burials by decade increases over the period of cemetery use. Specifically, infant burials were significantly underrepresented from 1820-1839 (Herring et al., 1994). It is suspected that the excavated area contained a disproportionately large part of the cemetery used from the 1840s onwards.

Historical evidence offers some ideas for the relative dearth of infants in the earlier decades of St. Thomas' cemetery use. In the 1820s and 1830s, church membership was largely rural (Fig. 3). The lack of doctors in Belleville, the high fees charged by those in practice at the time, coupled with the travel distance from home to town, probably lessened the inclination to seek treatment in town for a sick child or a church burial for a dead one. It is well known, moreover, that infants were often interred in family plots on the farm during the pioneer period. Later, when the expanse and population of the town had grown, most members of the parish lived in town and were likely to bury dead infants at the church.

The *Belleville Intelligencer* also provides accounts of the discovery of infants who died under suspicious circumstances.

INQUEST.—An inquest was held yesterday evening before Coroner John P. Macdonnell on the body of an infant found on the bay shore, near Bleecker's grove. The body

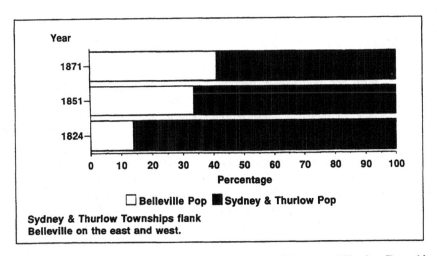

**FIGURE 3.** The population of Belleville as a percentage of Sidney and Thurlow Townships, 1824–1871.

was considerably decomposed, but the medical witnesses thought the child had been born alive. The jury said in their verdict that the "child was either still-born or could but have lived a few moments, and that it was placed in the position found by some person or persons unknown to this jury." (*Belleville Daily Intelligencer*, August 21, 1867).

CHILD FOUND IN THE WOODS.—An infant girl, about four weeks old, was found in the woods west of Stirling, lying on the ground near some bushes, entirely deserted. Mr. Wm. Shaw very humanely took it to his house, where it has been well taken care of. Immediate search was made for the mother who so inhumanely deserted her infant babe, and fortunately for the character of Stirling she was discovered. She turns out to be a *lady* from Belleville, who has taken this course to rid herself of her child, and as the authorities of Stirling have been so active in the matter, it is hoped she will receive a punishment suitable to such a crime. (*Belleville Intelligencer*, August 3 1866).

At this point, we are unable to ascertain whether infants who died under such circumstances were buried in the hallowed ground of church cemeteries or were laid to rest elsewhere. Historical accounts reveal that overlaying, a euphemism for infanticide (Hansen, 1979), was not unknown in 19th century Upper Canada (Siegel, 1984). Sex differences in the risk of infant death can be important indicators of preferential treatment, vulnerability to disease, and attitudes toward infants and children (Damme, 1978; Hansen, 1979; Siegel, 1984). There is no way, however, to directly assess whether infanticide or preferential treatment/neglect of one sex occurred among St. Thomas' parishioners. It is extremely difficult to determine the sex of an infant from skeletal evidence alone because the secondary sex characteristics in bone develop much later when the child undergoes sexual maturation during puberty. Estimates of infant mortality by sex from the parish registers nevertheless suggest that neither sex was receiving preferential burial treatment or, by inference, substantial advantages in life that would have enhanced survival to one year of age (Herring et al., 1994).

## Breakdown of Infant Mortality

There is a broad but mistaken assumption that mortality rates among infants will be highest at birth and will slowly decline thereafter, leading us to expect mostly newborn deaths in any mortality sample. However, postneonatal mortality has exceeded neonatal mortality in industrialized countries up until the 1930s (Forfar & Arneil, 1978). This situation still pertains in developing countries and therefore could be extrapolated to prehistoric and early historic societies. As explained earlier, postneonatal mortality is largely rooted in environmental factors such as poor sanitation and poor nutrition, whereas neonatal mortality is largely due to the physiological and organic weaknesses of infants and by the problems suffered by their mothers during pregnancy. But when stillbirth mortality is added to neonatal mortality (perinatal mortality), the rates almost always exceed those of postneonatal mortality. Theoretically, with good age estimation techniques and an unbiased sample of infant skeletons, it should be possible to separate these age categories of infant death and to determine their relative frequency. However, if excavators recover relatively larger proportions of neonatal deaths compared to the rest of infants, then there is some justification for arguing that this is further evidence of biased mortuary practices (Saunders & Spence, 1986).

We therefore excluded a very small number of individuals whose age estimates showed that they were preterm, and then compared the proportions of postneonates to neonates in St. Thomas' burial records and skeletons. The proportions proved to be virtually identical: 74% of the infant skeletons and 73% of the recorded infant burials were aged as postneonates (Fig. 4). This not only reveals the important role played by sanitary, social, and other environmental conditions in infant mortality at St. Thomas' (Herring et al., 1994), but also demonstrates that the infant category as a whole, and not just the neonatal group, was overrepresented in the sample.

### Sanitary and Social Conditions

Previous investigation of the 292 infant deaths listed in the burial register has shown that environmental factors influenced the patterning of infant death (Herring et al., 1994). The summer months proved to be a relatively dangerous time for St. Thomas' babies, with 39% of all infant burials clustering significantly between June and August. Diarrhoeal diseases were deadly for infants during times of drought and in the heat of summer in many historical populations (Boatler, 1983; Cheney, 1984; Sawchuk, 1993; Sawchuk et al., 1985). The often poor quality of weaning foods, such as gruels, coupled with the tendency to dilute them with contaminated water, made ba-

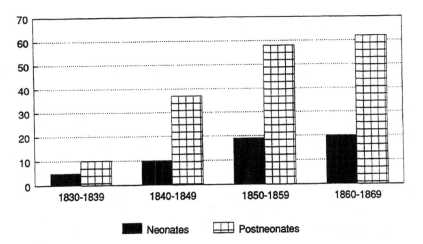

**FIGURE 4.** Neonatal versus postneonatal infant mortality by decade, St. Thomas' Anglican Church burial register.

bies particularly susceptible to gastrointestinal disease and to the weanling diarrhea complex (Sawchuk, 1993; Sawchuk et al., 1985; Thompson, 1984; Hardy, 1984; Wohl, 1983). We also know that by the mid-19th century the quality of Belleville's water supply was of concern to citizens (Moodie, 1853) and authorities alike (Bell, 1876).

We have observed, nevertheless, that overall infant mortality was moderate at St. Thomas' during the period and seems to have ranged no higher than 81–130 deaths per 1000 livebirths, even when the population of the town was expanding rapidly between 1850 and 1874 (Herring et al., 1993). It is well known that breast-fed babies are more likely to survive the first year of life than those who are artificially fed, when sanitary and social conditions are poor. This positive association between breast feeding and infant health is further buttressed by the observation that infant mortality tends to increase in the months following weaning, often in conjunction with a rise in the weanling diarrhea complex. Is it possible that breast feeding was buffering St. Thomas' infants from the environmental hazards in the town?

The classic biometric method for inferring endogenous and exogenous causes of infant death, developed by Bourgeois-Pichat in the late 1940s and early 1950s, can be used to make inferences about breast feeding and weaning practices (Bourgeois-Pichat, 1951a,b). Bourgeois-Pichat demonstrated that there is a linear relationship between accumulated infant mortality after the first month and age in days, when age is transformed logarithmically via the formula log $(n + 1)^3$, where $n$ is age in days since birth. The linear relationship between age and cumulative mortality breaks down under certain conditions. When infants are fed artificially, the mortality slope is steeper in the first half of the year than in the second. This excess cumulative mortality in early infancy is attributed to the absence of passive immunity and nutritional benefits conferred by breast milk, coupled with early exposure to the unsanitary conditions surrounding artificial feeding. It is also associated with high rates of infant mortality. For breast-fed infants, cumulative mortality rises gradually in the first half of the year, then rises more sharply in the later months. By the sixth month, the immunoprotective and nutritional advantages of breast milk have diminished and so the excess cumulative mortality seen thereafter reflects the effects of the infant's exposure to environmental insult. Especially important are the nutritive quality of supplemental foods, hygienic conditions surrounding artificial feeding, and the overall health of the baby's environment. In historical populations where sanitary conditions were poor, breast-fed infants tended to have lower rates of death than artificially fed ones (Knodel & Kintner, 1977, pp. 393–397).

We plotted the cumulative infant mortality rates for the cohort of 292 infants whose burials were recorded in St. Thomas' register between 1821 and 1874, in days, and converted them to a logarithmic scale as described earlier. The number of infants at risk of dying in the parish was derived from the baptismal registers for St. Thomas' and Christ Church Anglican Churches, yielding a total of 4,267 infant christenings during the study period.

The results clearly indicate a breast-feeding population (Fig. 5). The slope of the line cants upward from 5–12 months of age, indicating excess mortality in the latter

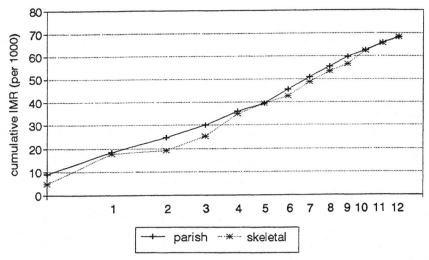

**FIGURE 5.** Biometric distribution of cumulative infant mortality, St. Thomas' burial register, 1821–1874.

part of the first year of life, relative to the early months. Furthermore, comparison of the ratio of the slope of cumulative mortality from 6–12 months to the slope from 1–6 months, gives a value of 1.3, placing the St. Thomas' infants firmly within Knodel and Kintner's (1977, p. 398) breast-feeding category. The same analysis was conducted on the skeletal sample. An age distribution of infant deaths (cast by month) was constructed according to the Bourgeois-Pichat method using the dental age estimates (Saunders et al., 1993a). In order to define the population of infants at risk of dying, we made the assumption that the proportion of excavated infant skeletons to infants listed in the burial register (51%) was the same as for listed baptisms (or 51% of 4,267 infants baptized). This allowed the calculation of cumulative infant mortality rates. They were transformed to a logarithmic scale.

As Fig. 5 shows, the skeletal results are similar to those from the parish-record analysis. There is excess cumulative mortality in the 6–12 month period, relative to 1–6 months, typical of breast-fed babies. The ratio of slopes, which is 1.6, also supports the inference that infants were breast fed.

We infer from these results that a substantial segment of Anglican mothers were breast feeding their babies until about 5 months of age, when they began to introduce supplemental foods to their babies' diets. Of course, this is just an approximation. We have no way of determining the actual proportion of breast-fed infants or of knowing the extent of variation in maternal weaning practices.

This is an important point, because the term "weaning" has several meanings. Strictly speaking, it refers to the process by which an infant is encouraged to eat foods other than breast milk. The concept of weaning also incorporates the complete cessation of breast feeding at a specific time, referred to as the "weaning age." As

Fildes (1986) and others (Dettwyler, 1987) note, there is no universal rule regarding when solid foods begin to be introduced or when breast feeding is terminated; neither is there a universal pattern in the style of weaning: it may be abrupt, gradual and protracted, or syncopated. It varies cross-culturally and through time, and may even vary from child to child in a single family, depending on the desires and circumstances of the mother and the demands of the child.

For the purposes of this study, we consider weaning age to be the process by which the infant is regularly receiving supplemental foods, with or without additional breast milk. Our data suggest that this process began around 5–7 months among Anglican women in mid-19th century Belleville. Since breast-fed infants are at a significant advantage relative to artificially fed babies, and since it appears that St. Thomas' mothers breast fed their babies, by and large, when the nutritional and immunoprotective properties of breast milk are at their peak, this probably helped to buffer their infants from causes of death associated with poor hygiene and nutrition, contaminated water, and infectious disease. This, in turn, may have helped to dampen infant mortality and keep it at moderate levels.

## Skeletal Growth Profiles

Other indications of the relationship between the environment and death were revealed through the analysis of cross sectional growth profiles in St. Thomas' subadult skeletal sample (Saunders et al., 1993b). The evidence suggests that the skeletal sample follows a pattern of growth not unlike that of modern children, up to at least 12 years of age, with perhaps the exception of under-2-year olds who are slightly smaller than the modern standards (Fig. 6). Comparisons with two other archaeological samples, a protohistoric Arikara sample from South Dakota and subadult skeletons from the Raunds Site, a 10th-century AD Anglo-Saxon cemetery, suggest that these two older samples suffered a reduced level of general health, likely associated with malnutrition and infection, as shown by their relatively reduced or stunted skeletal size.

These observations support the conclusion that most St. Thomas' children who died did so from acute conditions or accidents and not chronic disease-related factors that would tend to compromise skeletal growth. The slightly lower growth rates in the St. Thomas' children under 2 years of age may otherwise be the result of intrinsic stresses associated with poor maternal health during pregnancy. This is supported by the many growth and nutritional studies that have identified the first 3 years of life as a particularly crucial period. It was not until the turn of the century that there would be drastic changes in Western urban centers, with higher incomes and better living standards, which improved the nutrition, hygiene, and sanitary environment of mothers and their infants.

Certainly, there is evidence of an overrepresentation of 6–7 year old deaths in the skeletal sample, possibly due to drowning deaths (Saunders et al., 1993b). This cause of death was relatively common for this age group since the town often experienced severe spring run-offs and flooding to which adventuresome children were attracted, sometimes fatally.

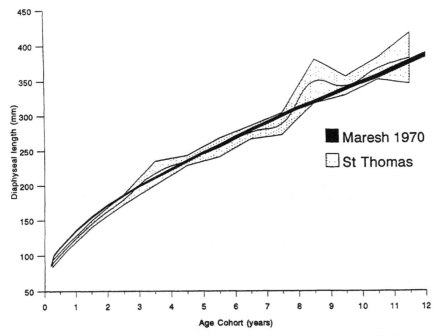

**FIGURE 6.** Skeletal growth profile for the femur, modern standards versus St. Thomas' Anglican Church subadult sample.

## CONCLUSIONS

Although documentary records and skeletal remains provide radically different types of information on human populations, our study of St. Thomas' Anglican cemetery has afforded fascinating insights into the complementarity of the two kinds of data. Both indicate the important role played by environmental factors in infant and childhood death in 19th-century Belleville. The predominance of postneonatal mortality among infants and the seasonal clustering of infant deaths in the summer months, when higher risks of the weanling diarrhea complex were present, point to less than ideal sanitary–social conditions in the town. Entries in St. Thomas' and Christ Church burial registers indicate that children were exposed to serious acute infections, such as cholera, smallpox, measles, meningitis, scarlet fever, typhoid fever, and whooping cough throughout the study period. However, the practice of breast feeding during the first 5 months of life probably helped to shield many infants from these conditions and to maintain infant mortality rates at relatively moderate levels. Patterns of skeletal growth support the hypothesis that the most serious environmental problems faced by infants and children took the form of acute infections, rather than chronic undernutrition or chronic infectious diseases.

While there are clearly problems with attempting detailed demographic analyses of St. Thomas' parish through use of the skeletal sample or parish registers (Saunders et al, 1994) the skeletal sample is judged sufficiently representative to provide significant information about these people's lives. Even though infant deaths may be overrepresented in the skeletal sample, the concordance between broad demographic categories of age and sex, coupled with the converging lines of documentary and skeletal evidence toward the importance of acute infectious disease, still provide meaningful insight into health and disease in 19th-century Belleville.

## ACKNOWLEDGMENTS

We are grateful to St. Thomas' Anglican Church and to the Anglican Church of Canada for permission to work with Belleville's parish records. Thanks also go to Carol DeVito, Tina Moffat, Tracy Farmer, Rob Hoppa, and Kathryn Denning for assistance in preparing the data and historic documents for our study period. This research was supported by SSHRC Grant #410-92-1493.

## REFERENCES

Bell JT (1876). Epidemic Diseases and Their Prevention in Relation to the Water Supply of the Town of Belleville. Belleville, Ontario: Intelligencer Office.

Belleville Daily Intelligencer (1866). August 3.

Belleville Daily Intelligencer (1867). August 21.

Boatler JF (1983). Patterns of infant mortality in the Polish community of Chappell Hill, Texas, 1895–1944. Hum Biol 55(1):9–18.

Bourgeois-Pichat J (1951a). La Mésure de la Mortalité Infantile. I. Principes et Méthodes. Population 6:223–248.

Bourgeois-Pichat J (1951b). La Mésure de la Mortalité Infantile. II. Les Causes de Décès. Population 6:459–480.

Boyce G (1967). Historic Hastings. Belleville, Ontario: Belleville Hastings County Council.

Buikstra JE, Cook DC (1980). Paleopathology: An American account. Ann Rev Anthropol 9:433–470.

Cheney RA (1984). Seasonal aspects of infant and childhood mortality: Philadelphia, 1865–1920. Inter J Interdis Hist XIV(3):561–585.

Cook DC (1984). Subsistence and health in the Lower Illinois Valley: Osteological evidence. In Cohen MN, Armelagos GJ (eds.), Paleopathology at the Origins of Agriculture, pp. 237–271. Orlando, FL: Academic Press.

Currey JD, Butler G (1975). The mechanical properties of bone tissue in children. J Bone and Jt Surg 57A:810–814.

Damme C (1978). Infanticide: the worth of an infant under law. Med Hist 22:1–24.

Dettwyler KA (1987). Breastfeeding and weaning in Mali: Cultural context and hard data. Soc Sci and Med 24(8):633–44.

DeVito C (nd). Drake's analysis: St. Thomas' Anglican Church, 1821–1874.

DeVito C, Saunders SR (1990). A discriminant function analysis of deciduous teeth to determine sex. J For Sci 35(4):845–858.

Drake M (1974). Historical Demography: Problems and Prospects. Milton Keynes, UK: The Open University Press.

Dyhouse C (1978). Working-class mothers and infant mortality in England, 1895–1914. Journal of Social History 12(2):248–252.

Fildes VA (1986). Breasts, Bottles and Babies: A History of Infant Feeding. Edinburgh: Edinburgh University Press.

Forfar JO, Arneil GC (1978). Textbook of Pediatrics. Edinburgh: Churchill Livingstone.

Goodman AH (1993). On the interpretation of health from skeletal remains. Curr Anthropol 34:281–288.

Goodman AH, Rose JC (1990). Assessment of systemic physiological perturbations from dental enamel hypoplasias and associated histological structures. Yrbk Phys Anthropol 33:59–110.

Gordon CC, Buikstra JE (1981). Soil pH, bone preservation and sampling bias at mortuary sites. Am Antiq 48:566–571.

Hansen E de GR (1979). "Overlaying" in 19th-century England. Infant mortality or infanticide? Hum Ecol 7(4):333–351.

Hardy A (1984). Water and the search for public health in London in the eighteenth and nineteenth centuries. Med Hist 28:250–282.

Herring DA, Saunders SR, Boyce G (1994). Bones and burial registers: Infant mortality in a 19th century cemetery from Upper Canada. Coun for Northeast Hist Arch J 20:54–70.

Herring DA, Moffat T, Saunders SR, Sawchuk LA (1993). Weaning babies in 19th Century Belleville. Paper presented at the Annual Meeting of the Canadian Association for Physical Anthropology, St. John's, Newfoundland, Canada.

Hoppa RD (1992). Evaluating human skeletal growth: An Anglo-Saxon example. Inter J Osteoarch 2(4):275–288.

Howell N (1986). Demographic anthropology. Annual Reviews of Anthropology 15:219–306.

Jackes M (1992). Paleodemography: problems and techniques. In Saunders SR, Katzenberg MA (eds.), The Skeletal Biology of Past Peoples: Advances in Research Methods, pp. 189–224. New York: Wiley-Liss.

Jantz RL, Owsley DW (1984). Long bone growth variation among Arikara skeletal populations. Am J Phys Anthropol 63:13–20.

Jimenez SB (1991). Analysis of Patterns of Injury and Disease in an Historic Skeletal Sample from Belleville, Ontario. Master's Thesis, McMaster University, Hamilton, Ontario.

Johnston FE, Zimmer LO (1989). Assessment of growth and age in the immature skeleton. In İşcan MY, Kennedy KAR (eds.), Reconstruction of Life from the Skeleton, pp. 11–22. New York: Liss.

Katzenberg MA, Saunders SR, Fitzgerald WR (1993). Age differences in stable carbon and nitrogen isotope ratios in a population of prehistoric maize horticulturalists. Am J Phys Anthropol 90:267–281.

Knodel J (1983). Seasonal variation in infant mortality: An approach with applications. Annales de demographie historique 208–230.

Knodel J, Kintner H (1977). The impact of breast feeding patterns on the biometric analysis of infant mortality. Demography 14(4):391–409.

Konigsberg LW, Frankenberg SR (1992). Estimation of age structure in anthropological demography. Amer J Phys Anthropol 89(2):235–256.

Lee CH (1991). Regional inequalities in infant mortality in Britain, 1861–1971: Patterns and hypotheses. Population Studies 45:55–65.

Lovejoy CO, Russell KF, Harrison ML (1990). Long bone growth velocity in the Libben Population. Am J Hum Biol 2:533–542.

Maresh MM (1970). Measurements from roentgenograms. In McCammon RW (ed.), Human Growth and Development, pp. 157–199. Springfield, IL:Charles C. Thomas.

Meindl RS (1977). Environmental and Demographic Correlates of Mortality in 19th Century Franklin County, Massachusetts. Ph.D. Diss., Department of Anthropology, University of Massachusetts, Amherst.

Meindl RS, Swedlund AC (1977). Secular trends in mortality in the Connecticut Valley, 1700–1850. Hum Biol 49:389–414.

Mensforth RP (1985). Relative tibia long bone growth in the Libben and Bt-5 prehistoric skeletal populations. Am J Phys Anthropol 68:247–262.

Merchant VL, Ubelaker DH (1977). Skeletal growth of the protohistoric Arikara. Am J Phys Anthropol 46(1):61–72.

Mika N, Mika H (1986). Belleville, the Seat of Hastings County. Belleville: Mika Publishing Co.

Molleson T (1989). Social implications of mortality patterns of juveniles from Poundbury Camp, Romano-British cemetery. Anthropol Anz 47:27–38.

Moodie S (1853). Life in the Clearings versus the Bush. 1989 reprint copy, New Canadian Library. Toronto: McClelland and Stewart.

Moorrees CFA, Fanning EA, Hunt EE (1963a). Age variation of formation stages for ten permanent teeth. J Dent Res 42:1490–1502.

Moorrees CFA, Fanning EA, Hunt EE (1963b). Formation and resorption of three deciduous teeth in children. Am J Phys Anthropol 21:205–213.

Paine RR (1989). Model life table fitting by maximum likelihood estimation: A procedure to reconstruct paleodemographic characteristics from skeletal age distributions. Amer J Phys Anthropol 79:51–61.

Petersen W (1975). A demographer's view of prehistoric demography. Curr Anthropol 16:227–245.

Rogers TL (1991). Sex Determination and Age Estimation: Skeletal Evidence from St. Thomas' Cemetery Belleville, Ontario. Master's Thesis, McMaster University, Hamilton, Ontario.

Rogers TL, Saunders SR (1994). Accuracy of sex determination using morphological traits of the human pelvis. J For Sci 39:1047–1056.

Sartwell PE, Last JM (1980). Epidemiology. In Last JM (ed.), Maxcy-Rosenau Public Health and Preventive Medicine, 11th edition, pp. 9–85. New York: Appleton-Century-Crofts.

Saunders SR (1992). Subadult skeletons and growth related studies. In Saunders SR, Katzenberg MA (eds.), The Skeletal Biology of Past Peoples: Advances in Research Methods, pp. 1–20. New York: Wiley-Liss.

Saunders SR, Spence MW (1986). Dental and skeletal age determinations of Ontario Iroquois infant burials. Ontario Archaeology 46:45–54.

Saunders SR, Fitzgerald C, Dudar C, Rogers TL (1991). A test of several methods of skeletal age estimation using a documented archaeological sample. J Can Soc For Sci 25(2):97–118.

Saunders SR, DeVito C, Herring DA, Southern R, Hoppa R (1993a). Accuracy tests of tooth formation age estimations from human skeletal remains. Amer J Phys Anthrop 92(2):173–188.

Saunders S, Hoppa R, Southern R (1993b). Diaphyseal growth in a nineteenth century skeletal sample of subadults from St. Thomas' Church, Belleville, Ontario. Intl J Osteoarch 3:1–139.

Saunders SR, Hoppa R (1993). Linear growth, malnutrition, morbidity and mortality: Biological mortality bias in nonadult skeletal samples. Yrbk Phys Anthropol 36:127–151.

Saunders SR, Herring DA, Sawchuk LA, Boyce G (1994). The nineteenth-century cemetery at St. Thomas' Anglican Church, Belleville: skeletal remains, parish records and censuses. In Saunders SR, Herring DA (eds.), Grave Reflections: Portraying the Past through Cemetery Studies, pp. 93–117. Toronto: Canadian Scholars Press.

Sawchuk LA (1993). Societal and ecological determinants of urban health: A case study of pre-reproductive mortality in 19th century Gibraltar. Soc Sci and Med 76(7):875–892.

Sawchuk LA, Herring DA, Waks L (1985). Evidence of a Jewish advantage: A study of infant mortality in Gibraltar, 1840 to 1959. Am Anthropol 87(3):616–625.

Siegel LS (1984). Child health and development in English Canada, 1790–1850. In Roland CR (ed.), Health, Disease and Medicine. Essays in Canadian, pp. 360–380. Hamilton, Ontario: The Hannah Institute for the History of Medicine.

Specker BL, Brazerol W, Tsang RC, Levin R, Searcy J, Steichen J (1987). Bone mineral content in children 1 to 6 years of age. Am J Dis Child 141:343–344.

Storey R (1992). Life and Death in the Ancient City of Teotihuacan. Tuscaloosa: The University of Alabama Press.

Stuart-Macadam P (1992). Porotic hyperostosis: A new perspective. Am J Phys Anthropol 87(1):39–48.

Swedlund AC (1990). Infant mortality in Massachusetts and the United States in the nineteenth century. In Goodman AC, Armelagos GJ (eds.), Diseases in Populations in Transition, pp. 161–182. New York: Bergin & Garvey.

Thompson B (1984). Infant mortality in nineteenth-century Bradford. In Woods R, Woodward J (eds.), Urban Disease and Mortality in Nineteenth-Century England, pp. 120–147. New York: St. Martin's.

Trapp PG, Mielke JH, Jorde LB, Eriksson AW (1983). Infant mortality patterns in Aland, Finland. Hum Biol 55(1):131–149.

Tuross N, Fogel ML, Owsley DW (1990). Tracing human lactation with stable nitrogen isotopes. 2: Studies with subfossil human skeletal tissue. Paper presented to the 88th Annual Meeting of the American Anthropological Association, Washington, DC.

Wohl AS (1983). Endangered Lives: Public Health in Victorian Britain. London: J.M. Dent & Sons Ltd.

Wood JW, Milner GR, Harpending HC, Weiss KM (1992). The osteological paradox: problems of inferring prehistoric health from skeletal samples. Curr Anthropol 33:343–370.

# 6 A Piece of Chicago's Past: Exploring Childhood Mortality in the Dunning Poorhouse Cemetery

ANNE L. GRAUER and ELIZABETH M. McNAMARA

## INTRODUCTION

Paleodemographic evaluation of skeletal populations is frequently used as a means of detecting the presence of stressors in past populations (see, e.g., Lallo, 1973; Green et al., 1974; Kennedy, 1984; Swedlund & Armelagos, 1976; Palkovich, 1980; Grauer, 1989, 1991; Larsen & Milner, 1994, to name a few). Its use in the reconstruction of the past, however, is not without controversy. Researchers such as Angel (1969), Bocquet-Appel and Masset (1982, 1985), and Howell (1982) have criticized paleo-demographic analysis for its use of absolute age at death calculations from skeletal material, the inability of the results to accurately reflect mortality patterns of the archaeological population being examined (the mortality curve mimics the reference population employed to age the skeletal material), the necessity to assume stable population dynamics, and the lack of living populations with similar demographic structure as those created from skeletal populations [see Roth (1992) for a more detailed review of the controversies].

Many, if not all, of these issues have been addressed by paleodemographers and paleopathologists as a means of strengthening the discipline (see Jackes, 1992). For instance, the use of multiple techniques for aging and sexing skeletal material, as well as a refinement of these techniques, has allowed researchers to successfully achieve a greater degree of accuracy in ascertaining developmental age at death. Greene et al. (1986), using Weiss' (1973) model life tables, refuted the notion that demographic

*Bodies of Evidence*, Edited by Anne L. Grauer.
ISBN 0-471-04153-X © 1995 John Wiley & Sons, Inc.

results from archaeological populations mimicked the pattern of the reference population by showing that their skeletal sample from Kulubnarti was not a replica of the reference population used to age the adult skeletal material. Similarly, the criticism aimed at the necessity to assume population stability (a concern that has been voiced again recently by Wood et al., 1992) has also been addressed. Moore et al. (1975), Johansson & Horowitz (1986), Horowitz et al. (1988), and Goodman (1993) have urged researchers to continually be sensitive to the effects of population instability, whether due to fluctuating fertility rates, patterns of migration, or cultural or behavioral patterns. However, calculating an archaeological population's mortality rate first, under the assumption that the population is stable, allows the researcher to explore through the use of comparison and computer simulation the potential for instability within that specific population (Roth, 1992).

In light of the potential and controversy surrounding the use of paleodemography, a study was undertaken specifically to explore subadult mortality patterns in the Dunning Cemetery population. The goal of our study was to gain insight into the origin of this skeletal population. Was, for instance, the Dunning Cemetery population a reflection of the living population of the city of Chicago during that time? And similarly, was the mortality pattern of the skeletal population comparable to other poorhouse cemetery populations (i.e., the Monroe County Poorhouse cemetery population)? It was hoped that through means of comparison the promise and problems of the calculated patterns of mortality would be evident, thereby providing insight into life in 19th-century Chicago.

## THE SAMPLE

In the summer of 1990 excavations took place on the west side of Chicago to save remnants of the earliest Dunning Cemetery. The excavated portion of the cemetery is believed to have been associated with the Cook County poor farm, established in 1851, the almshouse, completed in 1854, and the insane asylum built in 1868 (Keene, 1989, 1991). Historical sources suggest that the cemetery at this location was used by the poorhouse from approximately 1851 until 1869, when permission was requested from the city to remove the bodies and rebury them in a location immediately to the west. It appears, however, that not all remains were relocated, for archaeologists successfully exhumed 120 individuals.

Although records are sparse, there is some information concerning the conditions of the institution. In 1870, a report filed by the Board of State Commissioners of Public Charities of the State of Illinois criticized the facilities as miserably planned, badly managed, and grossly overcrowded. A later report, provided in 1876 by the acting warden of the Cook County Insane Asylum and Poor House, contained detailed information concerning the demography and description of the facility. The relative dearth of historical records, especially pertaining to the earliest facilities at Dunning (due perhaps to the Chicago Fire of 1871), has highlighted the value of skeletal analysis as a means of reconstructing the past.

# METHODS AND TECHNIQUES

## Skeletal Analysis

Skeletal age at death was assessed using the Paleopathology Association Skeletal Database Committee Recommendations (Buikstra et al.). These include, for subadult specimens, an examination of dental developmental stages (see Moorrees et al., 1963a,b; Smith, 1991), dental eruption rates (Ubelaker, 1989), epiphyseal formation and fusion (Bass, 1987; Krogman and Iscan, 1986), and long-bone length (Ubelaker, 1989). Age at death determination for adult material was made using dental attrition rates (Brothwell, 1989; Lovejoy, 1985; Smith, 1984, 1991), the pubic symphysis (Suchy et al., 1986; Krogman and Iscan, 1986), the auricular surface of the ilium (Lovejoy, 1985; Bedford et al., 1989), and degree of cranial suture closure (Meindl and Lovejoy, 1985).

Age-estimate techniques were applied and recorded independently of one another for each skeleton and averaged for a final age determination. A minimum of three individuals working independently (or three separate groups of individuals) evaluated the skeletal material using as many techniques as possible per skeleton. The final age estimate for each skeleton was determined by averaging the conclusion reached by each individual or group.

## Demographic Analysis

Several historical sources provided demographic information on Cook County, which includes the city of Chicago. For this study we used three census reports: the 1860 U.S. Federal Census (Kennedy, 1864); the 1870 U.S. Federal Census (Walker, 1872); and the 1870 Chicago, Illinois Census Index (Steuart, 1990). The latter census, a local enumeration, was undertaken to rectify what Chicago officials believed was an underrepresentation of the population by the 1870 U.S. Federal Census.

The 1860 U.S. Federal Census provided specific population statistics for Cook County, Illinois. This included a detailed demographic profile of the county by age, sex, and race. The 1870 U.S. Federal Census provided less detailed information. Here, the statistics supplied for Cook County focused upon males, particularly adult males. In this census, statistics compiled from individuals living in Cook County were grouped into large age categories. These categories included the number of individuals aged 5–18 (total of males and females), 18–45 (males only), and over 21 (males only). Details, however, concerning the age, sex, and race composition of the population of the state of Illinois were provided. Combining these two sets of information allowed us to calculate the possible age profile of Cook County. This was accomplished by first comparing the percentage of males and females recorded for Cook County between the ages of 5–18 with those for the state of Illinois. The overall percentage of males and females recorded in the two populations was also compared. Finding these percentages to be similar, we continued by taking the percentage of individuals for a specific age category in the state of Illinois and multiplying it by the total population recorded for Cook County.

We recognize that two important assumptions are being made here. First, we have assumed that if the percentage of males and females in the county and state were similar, then the age profile within each sex would also be similar. Second, we have assumed that the population of individuals under the age of five share similar profiles, even though information on individuals under the age of five is not provided for Cook County. Since our goal in this study is to explore the potential for using historic demographic data in skeletal analyses, and not to make a determination of the precise age profile of the residents at the Dunning Poorhouse in the 19th century, we concluded that these calculations could provide us with a heuristic tool.

Demographic information was also obtained from the mortality report for the city of Chicago, 1867, as recorded in the Annual Report of the Health Officer to the Board of Police, Fire, and Health Commissioners of the City of Chicago. Lastly, the Acting Warden's Annual Report of the Cook County Insane Asylum and Poor House, 1876, provided information concerning the facilities shortly after the excavated portion of the cemetery was no longer used.

## RESULTS

A total of 120 skeletons were examined from the Dunning Cemetery. Of these, 106 were assigned an age at death, while 14 could not be assigned to an age category. The demographic profile (see Table 1) indicates that 34.9% of the population died under the age of 15, 29.2% died between the ages of 15 and 25, and 35.9% died over the age of 25.

The subadult mortality rate in the Dunning population shows a clear pattern of decreasing mortality by age. Age interval 0–.9, for instance, displays the highest mortality rate (35.1%) of all age categories below 15 years of age, while the lowest rate of mortality occurs at 10–14.9 years (8.1%).

**TABLE 1. The Demographic Profile for the Dunning Cemetery Skeletal Population**

| Age | n | % |
| --- | --- | --- |
| 0–.9 | 13 | 12.2 |
| 1–2.9 | 10 | 9.4 |
| 3–4.9 | 7 | 6.6 |
| 5–9.9 | 4 | 3.7 |
| 10–14.9 | 3 | 2.8 |
| 15–19.9 | 15 | 14.1 |
| 20–24.9 | 16 | 15.0 |
| 25–34.9 | 17 | 16.0 |
| 35–44.9 | 12 | 11.3 |
| 45–54.9 | 7 | 6.6 |
| 55+ | 2 | 1.8 |

**TABLE 2. Mortality for the City of Chicago as Reported in the Annual Report of the Health Officer in 1867.**

| Age | Total number of deaths reported |
|---|---|
| Under 5 | 2,918 |
| 5–10 | 360 |
| 10–20 | 269 |
| 20–30 | 643 |
| 30–40 | 654 |
| 40–50 | 431 |
| 50–60 | 230 |
| 60–70 | 185 |
| 70–80 | 101 |
| 80–90 | 27 |
| 90–100 | 3 |
| over 100 | 3 |
| unknown | 113 |
| Total | 5,937 |

The mortality report for the city of Chicago for the year 1867, appearing in the Annual Report to the Health Officer, indicates that 2,918 children below the age of 5 (out of 5,937 total deaths reported in the city) died from various causes (Table 2). The total number of deaths recorded for subadults aged between 5 and 10 years was 360, and the total number of deaths of individuals aged between 10–20 years was 269. It appears, therefore, that 49.1% of all deaths recorded in 1867 in the city of Chicago were of children below the age of 5.

The results of our examination of the 1860 and 1870 U.S. Federal Census data and the Chicago, IL 1870 Census Index appear in Table 3. Here it can be seen that the

**TABLE 3. Census Information Concerning Subadults from 1860 U.S. Federal Census, the 1870 U.S. Federal Census, and the Chicago, IL 1870 Census Index**

| Age at Death | 1860 U.S. Federal Census | | 1870 U.S. Federal Census | | Chicago, IL 1870 Census Index | |
|---|---|---|---|---|---|---|
| | n | % | n | % | n | % |
| 0–.9 | 5,797 | 4.0 | 10,930 | 3.1 | 86 | .029 |
| 1–4.9 | 21,251 | 14.7 | 42,917 | 12.3 | 341 | .114 |
| 5–9.9 | 16,601 | 11.5 | 46,776 | 13.4 | 879 | .294 |
| 10–14.9 | 12,331 | 8.4 | 44,386 | 12.7 | 1,702 | .569 |
| % of subadults in the total population | 38.6% | | 41.4% | | 1.0% | |

**TABLE 4. Mortality Patterns of Subadults from Dunning Cemetery and the Monroe County Poorhouse Cemetery**

| Age at Death | Dunning Poorhouse Skeletal Sample ($n = 37$) | | Monroe County Poorhouse Skeletal Sample ($n = 58$) | |
|---|---|---|---|---|
| | $n$ | $\%$ | $n$ | $\%$ |
| 0–.9 | 13 | 35.1 | 20 | 34.5 |
| 1–2.9 | 10 | 27.0 | 9 | 15.5 |
| 3–4.9 | 7 | 18.9 | 17 | 29.3 |
| 5–9.9 | 4 | 10.8 | 8 | 13.8 |
| 10–14.9 | 3 | 8.1 | 4 | 6.9 |

percentage of subadults recorded for each age interval and the percentage of subadults as a proportion of the total population is similar for the years 1860 and 1870, according to the U.S. Federal Censuses. The demographic profile of subadults constructed from the Chicago, IL 1870 Census Index (Steuart, 1990), however, indicates that a total of 3008 subadults (aged between 0–15 years) were reported by census officials for the city, out of a total population of 298,977, representing 1.0% of the total living population.

The demographic pattern of subadult mortality in the Dunning population is compared to that reported for the Monroe County Poorhouse in Table 4 (adapted from Lanphear, 1988). Information adapted from Lanphear indicates that subadult mortality rates for the Monroe County Poorhouse Cemetery peak at 0—.9 years of age (34.5%) and 3—4.9 years of age (29.3%), and decrease in the following age categories.

Kolmogorov–Smirnov Two Sample Tests were applied in order to examine the cumulative differences between the census reports and between the Dunning population and the Monroe County Poorhouse (Tables 5 and 6). Statistically significant results were noted in all comparisons except those made between the two archaeological populations.

## DISCUSSION

The Dunning Cemetery skeletal analysis suggests that subadult underenumeration was not a substantial bias in this archaeological population. Weiss (1973) asserts that the general pattern of human subadult mortality in anthropological populations is one of very high infant mortality, which decreases between the ages of 1–5, and further declines until ages 10–15. This pattern is clearly reflected in the subadult mortality rate for the Dunning population.

**TABLE 5. Results of Kolmogorov–Smirnov Cumulative Difference Tests for Census Data and the Dunning Poorhouse Skeletal Material.**

| | Kolmogorov–Smirnov Cumulative Differences | | | |
|---|---|---|---|---|
| Age at Death | 1860 Federal vs. 1870 Federal | 1870 Federal vs. 1870 Local | Dunning Cemetery vs. 1860 Federal | Dunning Cemetery vs. 1870 Federal |
| 0–.9 | .0286* | .0468* | .247 | .2756* |
| 1–2.9 | — | .1421* | — | .3968* |
| 1–4.9 | .1117* | — | .328* | — |
| 3–4.9 | — | .2294* | — | .4397* |
| 5–9.9 | .0861 | .2597* | .139 | .2251* |
| 10–14.9 | 0 | 0 | 0 | 0 |
| | $D_{.01} = .0081$ | $D_{.01} = .030$ | $D_{.01} = .268$ | $D_{.01} = .268$ |

*Statistically significant.

An evaluation of the 1867 Mortality Report for the City of Chicago, included in the Annual Report of the Health Officer (1867), suggests that the early subadult mortality pattern noted in the Dunning skeletal sample was perhaps not unusual for the city as a whole. The actual numbers of deaths recorded, however, may be inflated, since the Health Officer was quick to note the debilitating presence of cholera and smallpox in the city: "The past year has been an eventful one concerning the health of this city, the cholera making its appearance during the summer adding largely to the mortality report, the small pox visiting us during the winter months, but in a very mild form, the percentage of deaths being very light" (Annual Report of the Health

**TABLE 6. Kolmogorov–Smirnov Test of Cumulative Difference for the Dunning Poorhouse Skeletal Subadult Population and the Monroe Poorhouse Skeletal Subadult Population***

| | Dunning Poorhouse Subadult Skeletal Sample | | Monroe Co. Poorhouse Subadult Skeletal Sample | | |
|---|---|---|---|---|---|
| Age at Death | f | % | f | % | D |
| 0–.9 | 13 | .351 | 20 | .345 | .006 |
| 1–2.9 | 10 | .622 | 9 | .5 | .122 |
| 3–4.9 | 7 | .811 | 17 | .793 | .018 |
| 5–9.9 | 4 | .919 | 8 | .931 | .012 |
| 10–14.9 | 3 | 1.0 | 4 | 1.0 | 0 |
| | | | $D_{.01} = .343$ | | |

*Adapted from Lanphear, 1988.

Officer, 1867, p. 3). Numbers of deaths in the city as a whole might therefore be inflated. An argument may be made, however, that the condition does not single out young children, so that the percentage of children dying is a reasonable representation of death patterns in this urban environment with or without pestilence.

The examination of the 1860 and 1870 Federal Census data, along with the Chicago, IL 1870 Census Index, was used to provide insight into the living population in the city during the years that the earliest Dunning Cemetery was in use. Comparisons made between the 1860 and the 1870 U.S. Federal Censuses suggest that the population in Cook County was experiencing tremendous growth, resulting in a tenfold increase in population size from roughly 30,000 known inhabitants in 1850, to approximately 300,000 by 1870 (Szucs, 1990).

While the proportion of subadults to adults in the population and the proportion of subadults in each age category appears to remain similar in the 1860 and 1870 U.S. Federal censuses, the Kolmogorov–Smirnov Two Sample Test indicates that the differences are great enough to treat the two populations as distinctly different. This result must be accepted with extreme caution. Since the subadult age intervals with the greatest cumulative differences are the youngest, and it is precisely these age categories that we reconstructed for the city of Chicago and Cook County from the 1870 U.S. Census data for the state of Illinois, it is wholly possible that this statistical difference is an artifact of our assumption that the demographic pattern for the state of Illinois mirrored that of Cook County.

Our comparison between the two censuses taken in 1870 was equally problematic. The startling differences noted in both the proportion of subadults to the adult population and the percentage of individuals recorded in each subadult age interval led us to explore the nature and purpose of these reports. Investigation revealed that both the 1870 U.S. Federal Census and the Chicago, IL 1870 Census were undertaken with the intent to determine the number of political representatives to which the city and state were entitled. Counting adult inhabitants may have been of more concern than enumerating their offspring. This appears to be true especially for the local reenumeration undertaken in 1870 for Chicago. The Chicago, IL 1870 Census Index reports that only 1% of the total population was below the age of 15. The mortality records for the city, however, compiled with the assistance of physicians in 1872, indicate that 5,901 children under the age of 5 died in that year (Andreas, 1886). This figure is extraordinarily high considering that only 3008 subadults are reported to have been living in the city two years earlier. Therefore, while the 1860 and 1870 U.S. Federal censuses might arguably have favored the recording of adults in the population, the Chicago, IL 1870 Census most certainly fell victim to this bias.

In spite of these obstacles, an examination of the U.S. Federal Census data for both 1860 and 1870 may serve to highlight some general population trends. First, regardless of the possible underenumeration of subadults in the living population (seen in its extreme in the Chicago Census Index), the reports suggest that a minimum of 38.6% and 41.4% of the population for Cook County were under the age of 15 in 1860 and 1870, respectively. This proportion of subadults in the population is similar to that constructed for the Dunning Cemetery population (34.9%). Second, the recognizable demographic trend for subadults in the census data is one of increasing numbers of individuals as subadult age increases. This pattern is converse to that recorded in the 1867 Mortality Report and the pattern constructed for the Dunning skeletal sample. This finding is not unexpected, since census data relies upon tallies of the living population and mortality reports (recorded and skeletally derived) focus upon patterns of death. Obviously, if a population maintains a constant or increasing fertility rate, then one can expect the numbers of infants and subadults to show up in either the tallies of the living or the dead at any particular time.

Do these findings suggest, therefore, that the Dunning skeletal sample is an adequate reflection of the population living in Chicago between 1860 and 1870? If the similar proportion of subadults to adults in the living and cemetery populations are used as a measure of similarity, then the answer might cautiously be yes. The preliminary assumption adopted in paleodemographic analysis is that of population stability; that is, an archaeological population is first treated as static and viewed as a cohort. If this is a true condition of the skeletal population, then in this instance we would expect that the proportions of individuals detected in the archaeological sample faithfully reflect the proportions of individuals in the once-living population. While the overall proportion of individuals in the populations (the Dunning Cemetery and the 1860 and 1870 U.S. Federal censuses) appear to be similar, the differences are statistically significant.

Adopting the notion, however, that there are similarities between the demographic patterns of the Dunning Cemetery population and the contemporary living population in the city of Chicago does not inconclusively lead us to believe that the Dunning population can be treated as a cohort. In other words, regardless of the similarities, it is unlikely that the Dunning Cemetery population, and the population of Chicago, for that matter, were stable. Migration into the city appears to be the premier mechanism of population growth. Perhaps, in spite of a bias in the census data toward the enumeration of adults, there was the real feature of continued migration of adults into the region and a high mortality rate for infants born locally.

The Dunning Cemetery population undoubtedly felt the repercussions of regional demographic change, if not mirrored them. The tenfold increase in population size for Cook County and the city of Chicago between the years 1850 and 1870 had a definitive impact on the city's and county's charitable institutions. The reported problem of overcrowding prompted Cook County to agree to build a substantially larger facility in 1869–1870 that would separately house residents of the poorhouse (also known as the poor farm) and the insane. It is precisely this expansion that allowed us to determine a terminal date of 1869 for the early cemetery site.

Records for this later facility, published for the years 1875–1876, provided by the Acting Warden of the Cook County Insane Asylum and Poor House, suggest that 1,240 individuals were admitted to the poorhouse that year out of a total of 1,872 residents. This gigantic proportion of new residents was not highlighted by the Warden as unusual. As such, these later records may serve as a warning about using the earlier cemetery data as a cohort, or assuming that the sample of subadults from the Dunning Cemetery represents a static population.

Although data from the Monroe County Poorhouse skeletal population does not follow the Dunning pattern of subadult mortality faithfully, there appears to be no statistically significant difference between these two archaeological populations. It may cautiously be proposed that the similarities between these two poorhouse skeletal populations stem from the unique but similar nature of the facilities. Inhabitants of our nation's poorhouse were obviously not simply adults, and indirectly reflect a dynamic and burgeoning urban population.

## CONCLUSION

The goal of this study was to assess the mortality pattern of the Dunning Cemetery population through comparison with federal and local census data from Chicago, Chicago mortality records, and the results of the skeletal analysis of the Monroe County Poorhouse. The results indicate that the Dunning skeletal population appears similar to that reported in the Monroe County Cemetery. The Dunning Cemetery population, however, differs significantly from reported demographic data for the city of Chicago and Cook County in 1870. It has been asserted that this data cannot be used as an accurate reflection of life and death patterns of the city, and that comparisons made between the census report and the constructed demographic profile of the Dunning Cemetery population are problematic.

What, then, have we learned about the subadult mortality pattern in the Dunning Cemetery population? It appears most probable at this time that the proportion of subadult skeletons in the cemetery population is not an adequate reflection of the proportion of children living at the facility at any one time. While we have found no record to date of the number of subadults admitted into or born into the facility during its earliest years, information highlighting the crowded conditions, the need for expansion, the extraordinary increase in population size in the city and county due to migration, along with poorhouse records indicating the high number of new residents sent to the facility each year, suggests that the population in Chicago, not to mention the poorhouse, was remarkably dynamic. Since reports elucidate the number of individuals sent to the poorhouse during a given year, the poorhouse population can be seen as a migrant one. It is possible, therefore, that the number of subadults would be proportionately lower than that of adults if the living population in the facility could be examined. Additionally, evidence suggests that infant and juvenile mortality rates for the city and county during 1860–1870 were high. Hence, an argument can be made that children entering the poorhouse were more likely to die, and thus begin to contribute to a greater proportion of the skeletal material in the cemetery.

## ACKNOWLEDGMENTS

We would like to thank several individuals and institutions for their assistance, support, and encouragement during this project. In particular, we are indebted to Debra Brown, Christine Engle, Diane Houdek, Theresa Jolly, Rakhi Khanna, Cinthia Leman, Alexia Sabor, Sital Shah, Julie Smentek, Paula Tomczak, and Patrick Waldron for their countless hours of participation and assistance in the laboratory and library. Our appreciation is also extended to Dr. Kenneth Johnson for putting up with our constant intrusions to ask questions concerning demographic patterns. We gratefully acknowledge the support and encouragement provided by Loyola University of Chicago. We extend our appreciation to the volunteers at the National Archives—Great Lakes Region for their patience and experience. We owe thanks to Leland Development Corporation, National Terminals Corporation, and the state of Illinois for support of the excavations and preliminary analysis of the skeletal material. The continuing research into historic poorhouse cemeteries and the synthesis of students into the scientific process is funded by National Science Foundation Grant No. SBR-9350256.

# REFERENCES

Acting Warden's Annual Report of the Cook County Insane Asylum and Poor House (1876).

Andreas AT (1886). History of Chicago. Chicago: AT Andreas.

Angel JL (1969). The bases of paleodemography. Am J Phys Anthropol 30:427–437.

Annual Report of the Health Officer to the Board of Police, Fire and Health Commissioners of the City of Chicago, 1866–67. (1867). Chicago: "Illinois Staats-zeitung" Steambook and job printing establishment.

Bass W (1987). Human Osteology. Columbia: Missouri Archaeological Society.

Bedford ME, Russell KF, Lovejoy CO (1989). The utility of the auricular surface aging technique (abstract). Am J Phys Anthropol 78:190–191.

Bocquet-Appel JP, Masset C (1982). Farewell to paleodemography. Journal of Human Evolution 11:321–333.

Bocquet-Appel JP, Masset C (1985). Matter of moment. Journal of Human Evolution 14:107–111.

Brothwell DR (1989). The relationship of tooth wear to aging. In Iscan MY (ed.), Age Markers in the Human Skeleton, pp. 303–316. Springfield, IL: Charles C Thomas.

Buikstra J, Ubelaker D, Jaas J (nd). Standards for Data Collection from Human Skeletal Remains. Proceedings of a seminar at the Field Museum of Natural History.

Goodman AH (1993). On the interpretation of health from skeletal remains. Current Anthropology 34(3):281–288.

Grauer AL (1989). Health, Disease and Status in Medieval York. Ph.D. Dissertation, University of Massachusetts, Amherst.

Grauer AL (1991). Patterns of life and death: The palaeodemography of Medieval York. In Bush H, Zvelebil M (eds.), Health in Past Societies. British Archaeological Reports International Series 567. Oxford: Tempvs Reparatvm.

Green S, Green S, Armelagos GJ (1974). Settlement and mortality of the Christian Site (1050 A.D.–1300 A.D.) of Meinarti (Sudan). Journal of Human Evolution 3:297–316.

Greene DL, Van Gerven DP, Armelagos GJ (1986). Life and death in ancient population: bones of contention in paleodemography. Human Evolution 1(3):193–207.

Horowitz S, Armelagos GJ, Wachter K (1988). On generating  birthrates from skeletal populations. Am J Phys Anthropol 76:189–196.

Howell N (1982). Village composition implied by a paleodemographic life table: the Libben Site. Am J Phys Anthropol 59:263–270.

Jackes M (1992). Paleodemography: Problems and techniques. In Saunders SR, Katzenberg MA (eds.), Skeletal Biology of Past Peoples: Research Methods, pp. 189–224. New York: Wiley-Liss.

Johansson RS, Horowitz S (1986). Estimating mortality in skeletal population: Influence of growth rate on the interpretation of levels and trends during the transition to agriculture. Am J Phys Anthropol 71:233–250.

Keene D (1989). Final Report-Archaeological Investigations: Dunning Cemetery Site. Loyola University of Chicago: Archaeological Research Lab.

Keene (1991). Dunning Site–Archaeological Investigation: Report Number 3. Loyola University of Chicago: Archaeological Research Lab.

Kennedy CG (1864). Population of the United States in 1860; Compiled from the Original Census Returns of the Eighth Census. Washington: Government Printing Office.

Kennedy KA (1984). Growth, nutrition and pathology in changing paleodemographic settings in South Asia. In Cohen M, Armelagos GJ (eds.), Paleopathology at the Origins of Agriculture, pp. 169–192. New York: Academic Press.

Krogman WM, Iscan MY (1986). The Human Skeleton in Forensic Medicine, 2nd ed. Springfield, IL: Charles C Thomas.

Lallo JW (1973). The Skeletal Biology of Three Prehistoric American Indian Societies from Dickson Mounds. Ph.D. Dissertation, University of Massachusetts, Amhearst.

Lanphear H (1988). Health and Mortality in a Nineteenth-Century Poorhouse Skeletal Sample. Ph.D. Dissertation, State University of New York, Albany.

Larsen CS, Milner GA (1994). In the Wake of Contact: Biological Responses to Conquest. New York: Wiley-Liss.

Lovejoy CO (1985). Dental wear in the Libben population: its functional pattern and role in the age determination of adult skeletal age at death. Am J Phys Anthropol 68:47–56.

Meindl RS, Lovejoy CO (1985). Ectocranial suture closure: A revised method for the determination of skeletal age at death based on the lateral-anterior sutures. Am J Phys Anthropol 68:57–66.

Moore JA, Swedlund AC, Armelagos GJ (1975). The use of life tables in paleodemography. In Swedlund AC (ed.), Population Studies in Archaeology and Biological Anthropology: A Symposium. Society of American Archaeology: Memoir No. 30, pp. 57–70.

Moorrees CE, Fanning E, Hunt E (1963a). Age variation and formation stages for ten permanent teeth. Journal of Dental Research 42(6):1490–1502.

Moorrees CE, Fanning E, Hunt E (1963b). Formation and resorption of three deciduous teeth in children. Am J Phys Anthropol 21:205–213.

Palkovich AM (1980). Pueblo Population and Society: Arroyo Hondo Skeletal and Mortuary Remains. Arroyo Hondo Archaeological Series, Vol. 3.

Roth EA (1992). Applications of demographic models to paleodemography. In Saunders SR, Katzenberg MA (eds.), Skeletal Biology of Past Peoples: Research Methods, pp. 178–188. New York: Wiley-Liss.

Smith BH (1984). Patterns of molar wear in hunter-gatherers and agriculturalists. Am J Phys Anthropol 63(1):39–56.

Smith BH (1991). Standards of human tooth formation and dental age assessment. In Kelley

MA, Larsen CS (eds.), Advances in Dental Anthropology, pp. 143–168. New York: Wiley-Liss.

Steuart B (1990). Chicago, IL (Including Cook Co.) 1870 Census Index. Bountiful, UT: Precision Indexing.

Suchy JM, Wiseley DV, Katz D (1986). Evaluation of the Todd and Mckern–Stewart methods for aging the male os-pubis. In Reichs KJ (ed.), Forensic Osteology: Advances in the Identification of Human Remains, pp. 33–67. Springfield, IL: CC Thomas.

Swedlund A, Armelagos GJ (1976). Demographic Anthropology. Dubuque, Iowa: Wm. C. Brown.

Szucs L (1990). Foreword. In Steuart BW (ed.), Chicago, IL (Including Cook Co.) 1870 Census Index. Bountiful, UT: Precision Indexing.

Ubelaker D (1989). Human Skeletal Remains. Chicago: Aldine.

Walker FA (1872). Ninth Census—Volume I. The Statistics of the Population of the United States, Embracing the Tables of Race, Nationality, Sex, Selected Ages, and Occupations. Washington: Government Printing Office.

Weiss KM (1973). Demographic models for Anthropology. American Antiquity 38(2):Part 2, Memoir 27.

Wood JW, Milner GR, Harpending HC, Weiss KM (1992). The osteological paradox: Problems of inferring prehistoric health from skeletal samples. Current Anthropol 33:4, 343–370.

# 7 Bones in the Basement: Bioarchaeology of Historic Remains in Nonmortuary Contexts

JUDITH M. HARRINGTON and ROBERT L. BLAKELY

## INTRODUCTION

Archaeologists seek to understand a past society through reading the material remains left by its members (Johnsen & Olsen, 1992). Material remains may consist of cultural items manufactured and used by the social group, or of natural items used in a cultural manner. One example of the latter is the human body, a natural object that carries many powerful symbols (Shanks & Tilley, 1982) and which, after death, becomes a cultural product commonly used in various ways in mortuary contexts. When the material remains include human bodies, mummies, skeletons, or bones, opportunities to understand the past are increased, since investigative methods can be expanded to include bioarchaeological data as well as data generated from artifacts and other strictly cultural items.

Peebles (1977, p. 124) observed that "A human burial contains more anthropological information per cubic meter of deposit than any other type of archaeological feature." However, precisely because human remains harbor so much symbolism, they pose investigative problems usually not encountered in analyses of nonhuman artifacts. These problems can be compounded further when the remains—once symbols in a mortuary context—are subsequently extracted from that context and deposited a second time in an altogether different context.

The unusual historical context of the material excavated from the Medical College of Georgia in Augusta required the development of a research design that relied as heavily upon theory as it did upon methodology. Two theoretical approaches toward understanding the past became critical to our project. The first was the approach known as "processual archaeology." This approach emphasizes the objectivity of

*Bodies of Evidence*, Edited by Anne L. Grauer.
ISBN 0-471-04153-X  © 1995 John Wiley & Sons, Inc.

archaeological inquiry and the scientific process of acquiring knowledge. It also seeks to explain human behavior in relation to social systems comprised of functionally interdependent parts of a whole (Trigger, 1989). A society is broken down into subparts, each of which is interrelated with every other part and to the whole. A change in any part of society inevitably affects all other parts. Thus, material culture can be viewed not only as a reflection of human behavior, but becomes an integral part of it (Rathje, 1977).

This approach has its critics, though. Among them is Ian Hodder (1982), who believes that the link between meaning and material culture is tenuous at best and illusory at worst. Material culture not only reflects what people do, as the adherents of processualism claim, but it also distorts, inverts, and misrepresents what they do and how they structure themselves. It may reflect what they would like to do, or how they believe they should be structured (Shanks & Tilley, 1982).

According to postprocessualists such as Hodder (1986), processualists make assumptions about the material remains they study that are culture- and/or theory-specific. Instead of an "independent," "objective" observer of cultural process, the archaeologist is a product of his or her own belief system and a particular cultural/theoretical orientation, and imposes that upon the society under study. Since archaeologists are themselves participants in the reconstruction of a past society, they cannot be working from a neutral base of observation (Gibbon, 1989).

Ideally, archaeologists should make assumptions based only upon the past context of the material remains. Like other anthropologists, the archaeologist should attempt to put himself or herself into the position of the society being studied, or the viewpoint of the inhabitants, in order to understand the context of the site. To the extent that traces (chunks?) of the present intrude into this context, the reality of the past is obscured; so too will be the intentions of the people who left the remains (Johnsen & Olsen, 1992).

An understanding of another archaeological paradigm known as discard theory has also proved useful to our analysis of the Medical College of Georgia skeletal remains. Several models and formulae have been used to interpret human discard behavior (see Schiffer, 1987, pp. 50–58). Archaeologically, garbage is no simple matter. Human discard, or trash, normally consists of items that are lost, abandoned, disposed, or cached—cultural deposition resulting from human discard behavior (Schiffer, 1987). Schiffer (1987, p. 58) distinguishes between primary discard—an artifact that is discarded at its location of use—and secondary discard—an artifact that is discarded elsewhere. During regular maintenance or cleaning of an activity area, primary-discard items are gathered up to be discarded secondarily. If there are several different activity areas at a site, then refuse from those areas is frequently combined and carried off to be dumped at a secondary location. A modern example of this comes from the city or town. Each office in a building may have a wastebasket, which is regularly emptied into a larger receptacle, which in turn is emptied into yet a larger receptacle. Eventually, all the refuse from the building is picked up by sanitation workers, who combine it with the refuse from other buildings—houses, offices, stores, hospitals, and so on—en route to a vast midden. This is an example of what Schiffer (1987, p. 66) calls a "waste stream."

According to Schiffer (1987, p. 66), each site has a unique structure of waste streams that can be analyzed to further provide information about the activities at the site. We believe that the waste stream model, along with other archaeological paradigms and osteological analyses, can be used to help interpret activities at the Medical College of Georgia.

In order to interpret the historical context of the remains in the basement at the Medical College of Georgia, we made several assumptions about the explanatory power of individual bones and the representativeness of the sample from which they were extracted. These assumptions, in their generic form, are common to many bioarchaeological analyses within processual archaeology. Since most of the skeletal material recovered consisted of individual bones, we assumed first that meaningful data about individuals (e.g., gender, age category at death, "race")—within an acceptable margin of error—can be obtained from single bones (see Krogman & Iscan, 1986; Iscan & Kennedy, 1989). We also assumed that these data, taken collectively, can provide meaningful information about the demographic composition of the skeletal sample (see, for example, Miller-Shaivitz & Iscan, 1991).

The recovery operations of the salvage excavation and construction crew resulted in the retrieval of most of the skeletal material in the basement—some 10,000 bones. And the archaeological sampling design, we believe, produced a representative sample of the material in the basement (Blakely, 1992; Harrington & Blakely, 1993). Moreover, although a few of the dissected cadavers may have been reinterred elsewhere (Allen, 1976, p. 193), there is no reason to suspect that they comprised an unrepresentative portion of the sample. Underenumeration of young individuals is a common problem in archaeological samples due to the friableness of immature bones, but that was not the case at the Medical College of Georgia because of the excellent state of preservation of the skeletal material.

The intent of this project is to take an interdisciplinary approach towards the understanding of the past. Our goal is to gain insight into the lives of individuals whose bodies were found in the basement of the Medical College of Georgia as well as to shed light upon 19th-century social and medical practices that were responsible for creating this unusual human and material assemblage.

## THE MEDICAL COLLEGE OF GEORGIA PROJECT

In 1989, construction workers renovating the old Medical College of Georgia building unearthed human skeletal remains and artifacts in the dirt floor of the basement. After determining that the remains were not recent, the Georgia Bureau of Investigation contacted Dr. Robert Blakely about the feasibility of conducting salvage archaeology at the site. At the request of college officials, construction was halted for a week to permit archaeological recovery of a portion of the material in the basement floor.

The masonry Greek Revival-style building was built in 1837, and served as the Medical College of Georgia's only teaching facility until 1912 (Spalding, 1987). During the Civil War, the building was used for the treatment of injured and ill

Confederate soldiers (Moores, 1984). Throughout most of the 19th century, however, the building served as classroom and laboratory in which medical students dissected human cadavers as part of their training. Because dissection was illegal in Georgia until 1887 (Allen, 1976), the practice was carried out surreptitiously. Cadavers occasionally were purchased from Baltimore, New York City, and Savannah, but most seem to have been obtained locally (Allen, 1976). A slave and later employee at the college, known locally as "the resurrection man," would slip out under cover of darkness to remove fresh corpses from their graves in nearby cemeteries and deposit them at the college (Allen, 1976). He apparently disposed of most of the dissected material in the basement of the building.

The excavation of the basement uncovered hundreds of skeletonized body parts. The bones are well-preserved, some with soft tissue still present. Most of the remains, it appears, had been tossed on the earthen floor, covered with a layer of dirt, then capped with quicklime to reduce the stench. Thus, as body parts accumulated, the floor slowly rose with the accretion of remains. A latrine containing some dissected material was found in a corner of the building. A large, wooden vat, recognized by the metal bottom and stays, held dozens of articulated and disarticulated bones. Historic records mention the use of a vat in which cadavers and body parts were preserved in whiskey (Allen, 1976). Skeletal material was found in all areas of the basement except a front room where a stairway had once ascended to the first floor. Perhaps the smell of decomposing flesh wafting up the stairwell was the motivation for keeping this area clear.

Following the emergency excavation, the construction crew sifted through screens the "rubble" removed from the basement during the course of construction. Although the provenience is far less precise, the material recovered by the screening more than doubled the number of bones and artifacts available for study.

Hundreds of material artifacts were recovered in the course of excavation. These included ceramic jugs, scalpels, syringes, thermometers, coins, buttons of glass, metal, wood, fabric (including coffin lining), belt buckles, leather shoes, remnants of a small furnace, charcoal, and glass bottles used for both medicinal and domestic purposes. Some bottles contain residues of their original contents; one holds liquid preserving human organ tissue. Also found were numerous animal bones, among them a partial deer skeleton, a cockspur from a fighting cock, and ubiquitous rat bones. Traces of peanut shells were scattered everywhere. Most of the artifacts date to the 19th century and, together with the skeletons, hold important clues to the activities undertaken in the basement, to 19th-century medical practices, and to the health and nutrition of that segment of the population represented by the remains. (See, for example, Dillingham, 1994.)

## METHODOLOGY

### Inventory of Commingled and Disarticulated Bones

One of the most challenging aspects of the Medical College of Georgia skeletal project was how to generate demographic data from the skeletal sample. An excavation of complete skeletons would have provided reasonably reliable information on age at death, sex, and "race" within the population. The Medical College of Georgia skeletal material, however, consisted of dissected body parts rather than fully articulated skeletons. Regardless, because of the excellent state of preservation and the fact that body parts from the same individual were often deposited near one another, modest success was achieved toward reassembling partial individuals. A software package entitled "Skeletal Material Analysis Program (SkelMAP)" developed by Burleson and Trevathan (1991), which contains a "commingling" menu, helped us to assign long bones to a few individuals. But the fact remains that it has not been possible to reassemble the vast majority of the bones.

The unit of analysis, therefore, was the individual bone rather than the skeleton. Data were gathered and analyzed by bone type. Unlike traditional cemetery settings, where the researcher knows at the outset of data collection the provenience, condition, and number of discrete burials, in ossuary settings the researcher must prepare an inventory of bones—individual and articulated—in order to know how to proceed with data collection and analysis. Moreover, for the sake of efficiency, the inventory must anticipate contingencies likely to be encountered in the course of enumeration, such as individual bones thought at first to be from separate individuals, but later determined to be part of an articulation from one person.

An inventory instrument was developed (see Harrington, 1991) whereby each human bone and tooth recovered at the site was given a number, and observations recorded, including provenience, bone name, articulations with other bones, side (when applicable), percentage of whole bone present, condition, postmortem treatment (e.g., dissection, animal gnawing, etc.), robusticity, size, gender (when possible), age category (when possible), "race" (determined, when possible, by discriminant function formulae), anomalies, pathologies (including location, severity, and extent of bone remodeling), and comments. The variables were computerized, and analyses were performed using SPSS for Windows.

## Osteological Data

Osteological data used in the demographic assessment were gathered from all intact or nearly intact crania, pelves, femora, and tibiae. Reasonably reliable criteria for determining "race," gender, and age category at death have been developed for these individual bones or regions of the skeleton (St. Hoyme & Iscan, 1989).

We decided to rely upon data gathered from the tibiae to demographically reconstruct the population for two reasons. First, the sample size, while small ($n = 22$), was over 200% larger than that of any other skeletal element in this collection. Moreover, the accuracy of determination of "race" from the tibia for males (which make up about 77% of the sample of tibiae) is higher than it is for any other bone or region of the skeleton (Krogman & Iscan, 1986, p. 290). Second, evaluating the population by other anatomical features resulted in striking discrepancies. For example, of the three intact adult crania, none was African American. An examination of seven intact adult pelves found three African Americans. Two African Americans were assigned using seven intact adult femora, and 17 African Americans were classified using the

22 intact adult tibiae. Other discrepancies were apparent in sample sizes and gender ratios.

Possible explanations for these disparities include: 1) differential preservation of skeletal elements in the earthen floor; 2) differential archaeological recovery of skeletal elements; 3) selective disposal of cadaver parts by anatomy professors, medical students, and grave robbers; 4) small sample sizes; and 5) unreliability of "race" and gender assignments by discriminant function formulae. Differential preservation and recovery of skeletal elements was judged to be an unlikely explanation. It is conceivable, however, that anatomists, students, and grave robbers selectively withheld certain cadaver parts from disposal. Most likely to have been retained are crania and those bones with "curious" or illustrative pathological lesions. There is little doubt that the small sample sizes and the inherent problems associated with "race" determination using discriminant function formulae are factors.

Our discussion of osteological methods is therefore limited to those employed for collecting data from the tibia. Age at death was determined for whole and fragmentary tibiae, which totalled 48 individuals. The complete fusion of the distal epiphysis (Bass, 1987) was used to divide the sample roughly into adults and subadults. Care was taken to include only one tibia from those individuals for which both tibiae were present. Pairing was based principally on length, shape, rugosity, color, and preservation. Gender was assigned to whole tibiae of adult specimens using discriminant function formulae developed by Iscan and Miller-Shaivitz (1984). Gender was not assigned to subadults because of the incomplete development of juvenile bones. Accuracy of gender determination reportedly varies from 77.5% to 87.5% (Iscan & Miller-Shaivitz, 1984, p. 55).

Discriminant function formulae were applied to adult tibiae to assign "race." There is, in this, a "catch-22": The discriminant functions require that either "race" or gender be known in order to ascertain the other. To circumvent this problem, we first arbitrarily called all individuals African American, and determined gender using the appropriate formulae. We then arbitrarily called all individuals European American, and again determined gender using the appropriate formulae. Any bone assigned male by one formula and female by the other was eliminated from further consideration. "Race" then was assigned to the remaining 22 individuals, using discriminant function formulae provided by Krogman and Iscan (1986). The accuracy of "race" determination from the tibia is reported to range from 70.5% for females to 82.9% for males (Krogman & Iscan, 1986, pp. 290–291).

## Historical Information

The search for documents to enhance the bioarchaeological research is ongoing. There is a large body of literature, including anecdotal notes and serious scholarship, on the practice of grave robbing in the United States and Europe (see, for example, Adams, 1972; Bailey, 1896; Ball, 1989; Breeden, 1975; Cole, 1964; Gallagher, 1967; Kaufman & Hanawalt, 1971). The material is depressingly full of accounts of dissection of and medical experimentation on the destitute and disempowered—particularly African Americans and other people of color in the United States (Fry, 1975; Haller, 1972; Humphrey, 1973; Richardson, 1987; Savitt, 1978, 1982; Wilf, 1988).

We have been less successful in locating census data from Augusta and surrounding Richmond County with which to compare demographic data obtained from the skeletal remains, and we question the reliability of the census counts we have found. In the nineteenth century, enumerators of Federal censuses often had little education and were not always committed to the task (Moran, 1986). Mistakes have been noted in gathering, tabulating, and transcribing raw data. Nevertheless, according to Marcellus Barksdale, Professor of African American History at Morehouse College in Atlanta, there is reason to believe that the decennial censuses in the 19th-century South were reasonably accurate, especially for African Americans. Before emancipation, accurate enumeration of slaves was an economic concern of considerable importance. After the Civil War, ideas of social Darwinism that swept through the South argued for accurate censuses of blacks and whites alike (Marcellus Barksdale, personal communication 1993).

To compare data on "race," we used the Federal decennial censuses of Augusta from 1840 to 1880, corresponding roughly to that time from the founding of the Medical College of Georgia to the time when dissection was made legal in Georgia. Despite the fact that this was a period of unprecedented social, economic, and political change in the South, enumerations of blacks and whites in Augusta do not fluctuate dramatically (Cashin, 1980, p. 309). Therefore, figures for the five decennial censuses were averaged. Data on gender were available only for Richmond County and only for 1850 (De Bow, 1854).

Skeletal age at death was compared with mortality data rather than with census counts of the living. Since cemetery records and death certificates for 19th-century Augusta appear to be incomplete and unreliable, particularly for the poor, the itinerant, and people of color (Allen, 1976), we relied on mortality figures for the middle section of Georgia, a region encompassing 27 counties, including Richmond County (De Bow, 1855). Mortality is not recorded according to "race."

## RESULTS AND DISCUSSION

The distribution by "race" and gender of tibiae in the Medical College of Georgia sample based on discriminant function values derived from Iscan and Miller-Shaivitz (1984) and Krogman and Iscan (1986) can be seen in Fig. 1. The final sample size of 22 tibiae included 13 black males, four black females, four white males, and one white female. All differences mentioned below are statistically significant at the .05 level of confidence or beyond. The results indicate that there is a preponderance of black men, followed by black women, white men, and white women in the skeletal sample. A comparison of the "racial" breakdown of the skeletal sample with census counts of Augusta from 1840 to 1880 indicates that, while African Americans made up between 37% and 49% of Augusta's population, they comprised 77% of the skeletal sample.

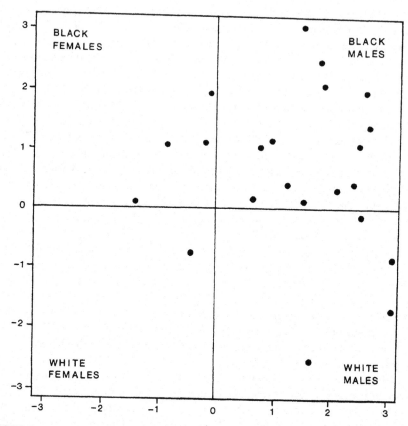

**FIGURE 1.** Distribution by "race" and gender of tibiae from the Medical College of Georgia (*n* = 22). Coordinates based on discriminant function values derived from Iscan and Miller-Shaivitz (1984) and Krogman and Iscan (1986).

An assessment of gender reveals that approximately 77% of the tibiae are male, compared with slightly less than half of the population of Richmond County in 1850. Because most of the remains seem to be African American, a comparison was made by gender between African Americans in the skeletal sample and in Richmond County in 1850. Women comprised over half of the African American population in Richmond County, but less than one in four tibiae in the skeletal sample.

Mortality in middle Georgia for the year ending July 1, 1850, shows that about 64% of the deaths were among subadults, whereas only 10% of those in the skeletal sample were subadults. Although the mortality data in 1850 are not recorded by "race," Allen (1976, p. 195) reports that immediately following the Civil War, the mortality rate among African Americans in Augusta was more than twice that for whites, a figure that could account for part of the overrepresentation of African Americans in the skeletal sample.

The results of the skeletal analysis indicate that this assemblage is derived from a somewhat different archaeological context than that from which most human remains are recovered. In most funerary contexts, mortuary ritual is viewed as reification of social structure—a copy, more or less direct, of social personae and the larger social organization of which the deceased were part (Binford, 1972; Brown, 1971, 1981; O'Shea, 1984; Saxe, 1970; Tainter, 1978). Schiffer (1987, p. 85), following Binford (1972), observes that people who were treated differently in life also were treated differently in death. Mortuary theory in archaeology seeks to understand and "decode" the rituals and symbolism associated with the disposal of the human body after death (Schiffer, 1987; Shanks & Tilley, 1982).

Our conviction is that the Medical College of Georgia skeletal remains fall into the category of natural objects used culturally. The human corpses were first treated culturally when, immediately after death, primary inhumation took place in a cemetery. Shortly after this, the bodies were exhumed and transported to the Medical College of Georgia to be used as teaching aids. When their usefulness to the professors and students was over, the remnants of the corpses were combined with other waste streams from other parts of the institution.

We assume, in adopting the waste stream model, that the dissected cadaver parts were regarded as trash by the anatomy professors, medical students, and workers/grave robbers at the college. And, although the remains may still have possessed powerful symbolism, it is unlikely that their deposition in the basement was accompanied by the mortuary ceremonialism that surrounded their initial interment.

The discarded body parts, therefore, were no longer in a mortuary context; they had become garbage to those in charge of their disposal. The fact that they were considered garbage means that they retained a certain social personae. That is, in death, just as in life, the people victimized by anatomists and grave robbers were considered useful commodities that could be cavalierly discarded when their usefulness was over. The fact that they were treated as contraband also means that they retained a powerful symbolism in the eyes of the public and, at least in a legal sense, in the eyes of the personnel at the Medical College of Georgia.

The archaeological context shows clearly that the anatomy professors, medical students, and other workers at the college regarded the dissected cadavers in nearly the same way as the "other rubbish" recovered in the basement. We suppose that the treatment of human remains at the college may have been somewhat different before and after 1887, when dissection became legal in Georgia. Before 1887, the basement offered a convenient and discrete solution to the problem of the disposal of illicit material. Because we are attempting to reconstruct the behaviors and intentions of the anatomy professors and grave robbers, we believe that discard theory provides the primary approach and mortuary theory the secondary approach for the analysis of the Medical College of Georgia remains.

Other archaeological contexts in which one or more conditions matched those encountered in the Medical College of Georgia research were also examined. Owsley (1993) reports a similar finding in New Orleans, Louisiana. There investigators recovered 19th-century cadavers interred in the Charity Hospital Cemetery. According to Owsley (1993, p. 154), "In addition to demographic data, the analysis revealed many sawed and cut bones resulting from autopsy, anatomical dissection, medical experimentation, and medical intervention (e.g., amputation)." A difference—and it is a fundamental one—is that the New Orleans remains constitute largely intact skeletons, whereas the Medical College of Georgia remains constitute largely disarticulated and commingled bones. The latter necessarily limits the amount and types of information available from skeletal biology, whereas the former can yield more reliable demographic and paleopathological data. Both can provide useful and unique information on the behaviors, attitudes, and knowledge of institutional personnel in Augusta, Georgia, and New Orleans.

All secondary burial contexts share certain characteristics with the Medical College of Georgia site and can suggest methodological protocols that can be useful in our research. A number of pre-Columbian and post-Columbian Native Americans disposed of the dead by defleshing or burning the corpse or by allowing it to decay, and then periodically gathering the bones or other remains into bundles before burying them in pits or mass graves known as ossuaries. In the eastern United States, the 17th-century Huron, 18th-century Choctaw, and 18th-century Nanticoke, among others, disposed of the dead in ossuaries (Ubelaker, 1974). Ossuary archaeological contexts—particularly disarticulated and/or commingled remains—pose methodological problems similar to those encountered in the Medical College of Georgia research. Despite the fact that both ossuaries and the Medical College of Georgia contain secondary burials, they are quite different as mortuary sites. Secondary interment in ossuaries was almost always accompanied by ritual (O'Shea, 1984; Ubelaker, 1974), whereas at the Medical College of Georgia any funerary rituals long preceded the disposal of the cadavers in the basement.

These data suggest that, as a result of either accessibility, selectivity, or both, anatomy professors and grave robbers at the Medical College of Georgia obtained disproportionate numbers of African Americans, males, and adults as cadavers for dissection. These findings were not unexpected, given the prevailing social attitudes and economic realities of the day.

The most striking feature of the dissecting-room sample is the preponderance of African Americans. It is possible that the percentage of African Americans could be even higher than we have estimated. Not only is the determination of "race" from skeletal biology problematic, so is the definition and application of the concept of "race" throughout American history. To white Southerners in the 1800s, African Americans were a socially, genealogically, and quasipolitically defined group based on certain phenotypic criteria, usually skin color (Shanklin, 1994). But African Americans have historically exhibited differing degrees of European American and Native American admixture upon what is principally an African substratum of phenotypes. It is not inconceivable, therefore, that bones classified as "white" by discriminant function formulae were actually considered "black" in the 19th-century American South.

There are many reasons why most of the corpses taken for dissection were African Americans. Throughout the 1800s, trafficking in black cadavers was common both south and north of the Mason-Dixon Line (Wilf, 1988). Humphrey (1973) reports that slave owners sometimes sold or donated the bodies of deceased slaves to medical schools. Free blacks, who made up about 10% of the antebellum black population in southern cities (Savitt, 1978), also would have been a source of cadavers, as would the scores of itinerant blacks who came through the cities in the years following the Civil War. Fry (1975) contends that threats of dissection and grave robbing in the Reconstruction and Jim Crow South served as an extralegal mechanism of social control of African Americans by whites. If her thesis is correct, then dissection and grave robbing were analogous to lynching and other terrorist activities carried out by the Ku Klux Klan and other groups of white supremacists.

It comes as no surprise that African Americans, devalued in life, also were devalued in death. Grave robbers knew that the graves of the poor—often people of color—were the most vulnerable (Jackson, 1993; Wilf, 1988). Throughout America, dissection of blacks was undertaken more often than dissection of whites. The *Transylvania Journal of Medicine and the Associate Sciences* (1828–1839) and *Transylvania Medical Journal* (1849–1851) of Kentucky reported that 80% of all postmortem examinations were performed on blacks—this in a state where the population was overwhelmingly white (Savitt, 1982, p. 338). At Johns Hopkins University in Baltimore between 1898 and 1904—a time when dissection was legal—two-thirds of the cadavers were African American (Humphrey, 1973, p. 824).

Grave robbers in the South regularly shipped the bodies of southern blacks to northern medical schools (Humphrey, 1973). Southern medical schools even boasted that their cities' large African American populations offered ample supplies of anatomical material. The Medical College of South Carolina advertised in a circular in 1831 that it obtained "subjects . . . for every purpose" from the African American rather than the white population of Charleston so as to carry out "proper dissections . . . without offending any individuals . . . " (Savitt, 1982, p. 339). Dissection and medical experimentation were humiliations imposed upon the disempowered (Humphrey, 1973; Savitt, 1982).

## CONCLUSIONS

We have just begun to explore the clandestine world of grave robbing and dissection in the 19th-century South in general and at the Medical College of Georgia in particular. Where does the research project go from here? More data on skeletal biology need to be amassed in order to reconstruct the nutrition and health environments of the populations that comprise the skeletal sample. We need to locate additional historic documents on discriminatory grave robbing and medical beliefs and practices in the South throughout the 1800s. Jackson (1993, p. 26) recommends that we examine the records of segregated hospitals in Augusta and the letters of abolitionists.

An exercise in "experimental anatomy" will entail dissecting a modern cadaver using 19th-century techniques and equipment. Composite "skeletal maps" derived from the Medical College of Georgia bones, showing locations, angles, and depths of cuts, will serve as a blueprint for the experimental dissection. Nineteenth-century medical tools on loan to us will be used to perform the dissection. By comparing dissection cut marks on the bones of blacks and whites and men and women in the archaeological sample, we may be able to discover differences in dissection by "race" and gender, which may illuminate social attitudes prevalent among practitioners at the Medical College of Georgia. The "experimental anatomy" also will provide insights into dissection methods of the 19th century, which are poorly known from the medical literature.

Analyses of the artifacts recovered in the basement will potentially assist in the reconstruction of waste streams, thereby shedding light on the types and locations of both routine and periodic activities undertaken in the basement and on the floors of the building above. Because human bones were most likely considered trash by those who deposited them, they can be treated as artifacts as well. Clearly, "discard behaviors" must be discerned before "use behaviors" can be inferred (Rathje & McCarthy, 1977).

Ethnographic interviews will be gathered from residents in Augusta who knew people with recollections of, or rumors about, covert activities at the Medical College of Georgia before 1912. Informants will be questioned about their knowledge of resistance to any such activities by people traditionally viewed as passive victims of a macabre business in an oppressive society. We hope to offer tools by which the people can continue on their own to explore their past and to become partners with them in the dissemination of their heritage.

Interviews, however, are problematic. As Page (1986, p. 279) notes, "The narrator [informant] . . . is a human being who is likely to have prejudices and quirks which filter his memories and give a somewhat distorted perspective to his account." The ethnographic interview, however, as part of postprocessual archaeology, gives history back to people (Hastorf & Hodder, 1991). The narrative interview may counterbalance the tendency of social scientists to fit data to theory (Hodder, 1991). Accessing the past in this way allows for the telling of stories as well as the testing of formal hypotheses. It opens the past to public debate (Hodder, 1991).

All human societies process their dead. It might be through primary inhumation, cremation, or secondary burial (Schiffer, 1987, p. 83). It becomes obvious, then, that the human body—both before and after death—carries with it many symbols, and is considered important enough not to be discarded thoughtlessly. We agree. The skeletal remains from the Medical College of Georgia eventually will be cremated and, in a public ceremony, interred in Mt. Olive Cemetery in Augusta.

## ACKNOWLEDGMENTS

This research was supported, in part, by grant RK-20029-93 from the National Endowment for the Humanities and by grant 93-021 from the Georgia State University Research Enhancement Program.

# REFERENCES

Adams N (1972). Dead and Buried: The Horrible History of Body Snatching. Aberdeen: Impulse.

Allen L (1976). Grandison Harris, Sr.: Slave, resurrectionist and judge. Bulletin of the Georgia Academy of Science 34:192–199.

Bailey JB (1896). The Diary of a Resurrectionist, 1811–1812. London: Sonnenschein.

Ball JM (1989). The Body Snatchers: Doctors, Grave Robbers, and the Law. New York: Dorset (originally published in 1928).

Bass WM (1987). Human Osteology: A Laboratory and Field Manual. Special Publication No. 2. Columbia: Missouri Archaeological Society.

Binford LR (1972). An Archaeological Perspective. New York: Seminar Press.

Blakely RL (1992). Covert Medical Practices in Nineteenth–Century Georgia. Grant proposal submitted to the National Endowment for the Humanities on file at Georgia State University.

Breeden JO (1975). Body snatchers and anatomy professors: Medical education in nineteenth-century Virginia. Virginia Magazine of History and Biography 83:321–345.

Brown JA (1971). Introduction. In Brown JA (ed.), Approaches to the Social Dimensions of Mortuary Practices. Memoirs of the Society for American Archaeology 25:1–5.

Brown JA (1981). The search for rank in prehistoric burials. In Chapman R, Kinnes I, Randsborg K (eds.), The Archaeology of Death, pp. 25–38. New York: Cambridge University Press.

Burleson CH, Trevathan WR (1991). Computer-aided analysis of human skeletal material. Practicing Anthropology 13(2):30–31.

Cashin EJ (1980). The Story of Augusta. Augusta, GA: Richmond County Board of Education.

Cole H (1964). Things for the Surgeon: A History of the Resurrection Men. London: Heinemann.

De Bow JDB (1854). Statistical View of the United States: Compendium of the Seventh Census. Washington, DC: US Senate.

De Bow JDB (1855). U.S. Census Office. Mortality Statistics of the Seventh Census of the United States, 1850. Washington, DC: ADP Nicholson.

Dillingham P (1994). Diet in the Urban Environment: A Trace Element Analysis of a Nineteenth-Century Cadaver Sample from the Cluskey Building, Medical College of Georgia, Augusta. MA thesis, Department of Anthropology, University of Tennessee, Knoxville.

Fry GM (1975). Night Riders in Black Folk History. Knoxville: University of Tennessee Press.

Gallagher T (1967). The body snatchers. Am Heritage 18(4):64–73.

Gibbon G (1989). Explanation in Archaeology. New York: Basil Blackwell, Inc.

Haller JS (1972). The Negro and the southern physician: A study of medical and racial attitudes, 1800–1860. Medical History 16:238–253.

Harrington JM (1991). A New Inventory Method for Commingled or Ossuary Remains. Paper presented at the annual meeting of the American Association of Physical Anthropologists, Milwaukee.

Harrington JM, Blakely RL (1993). Rich Man, Poor Man, Beggar Man, Thief: The Selectivity Exercised by Grave Robbers at the Medical College of Georgia. Paper presented at the annual meeting of the American Association of Physical Anthropologists, Toronto.

Hastorf C, Hodder I (1991). Archaeology and the other. In White KD (ed.), Archaeology and Indigenous Peoples: Ethical Issues and Questions. Anthropology UCLA, Vol 18, No 1, pp. 1–11. Los Angeles: UCLA Anthropology Graduate Student Association.

Hodder I (1982). Theoretical archaeology: A reactionary view. In Hodder I (ed.), Symbolic and Structural Archaeology, pp. 1–16. Cambridge: Cambridge University Press.

Hodder I (1986). Reading the Past: Current Approaches to Interpretation in Archaeology. Cambridge: Cambridge University Press.

Hodder I (1991). Interpretive archaeology and its role. Am Antiquity 56(1):7–18.

Humphrey DC (1973). Dissection and discrimination: The social origins of cadavers in America, 1760–1915. Bulletin of the New York Academy of Medicine 49:819–827.

Iscan MY, Kennedy KAR (eds.) (1989). Reconstruction of Life from the Skeleton. New York: Liss.

Iscan MY, Miller-Shaivitz P (1984). Determination of sex from the tibia. Am J Phys Anthropol 64:53–57.

Jackson H (1993). The Politics of Dissection: The Social Origins of the Bones Found at the Medical College of Georgia. Manuscript on file at Georgia State University.

Johnsen H, Olsen B (1992). Hermeneutics and archaeology: On the philosophy of contextual archaeology. Am Antiquity 57(3):419–436.

Kaufman M, Hanawalt LL (1971). Body snatching in the Midwest. Michigan History 55:22–40.

Krogman WM, Iscan MY (1986). The Human Skeleton in Forensic Medicine (2nd ed). Springfield, IL: Charles C Thomas.

Miller-Shaivitz P, Iscan MY (1991). The prehistoric people of Fort Center: physical and health characteristics. In Powell ML, Bridges PS, Mires AMW (eds.), What Mean These Bones? Studies in Southeastern Bioarchaeology, pp. 131–147. Tuscaloosa: University of Alabama Press.

Moores RR (1984). The Medical College of Georgia's venerable old lady. Ancestoring 9:16–28.

Moran MH (1986). Using census materials in ethnohistoric reconstruction: An example from South Carolina. In Wiedman D (ed.), Ethnohistory: A Researcher's Guide. Studies in Third World Societies No. 35, pp. 61–76. Williamsburg, VA: Department of Anthropology, College of William and Mary.

O'Shea JM (1984). Mortuary Variability: An Archaeological Investigation. Orlando, FL: Academic Press.

Owsley DW (1993). New perspectives on 19th century surgical practice through bioarchaeological research (abstract). Am J Phys Anthropol Suppl 16:154.

Page JB (1986). The use of reminiscences and oral tradition in the study of ethnohistory. In Wiedman D (ed.), Ethnohistory: A Researcher's Guide. Studies in Third World Societies No 35, pp. 275–296. Williamsburg, VA: Department of Anthropology, College of William and Mary.

Peebles CS (1977). Biocultural adaptation in prehistoric America: An archeologist's perspective. In Blakely RL (ed.), Biocultural Adaptation in Prehistoric America. Southern Anthropological Society Proceedings, No. 11, pp. 115–130. Athens: University of Georgia Press.

Rathje W (1977). In praise of archaeology: le projet du garbage. In Ferguson L (ed.), Historical

Archaeology and the Importance of Material Things. Special Publication Series. Society for Historical Archaeology 2:36–42.

Rathje W, McCarthy M (1977). Regularity and variability in contemporary garbage. In South S (ed.), Research Strategies in Historical Archaeology, pp. 261–286. New York: Academic Press.

Richardson R (1987). Death, Dissection and the Destitute. London: Routledge and Kegan Paul.

St. Hoyme LE, Iscan MY (1989). Determination of sex and race: Accuracy and assumptions. In Iscan MY, Kennedy KAR (eds.), Reconstruction of Life from the Skeleton, pp. 53–93. New York: Liss.

Savitt TL (1978). Medicine and Slavery: The Diseases and Health Care of Blacks in Antebellum Virginia. Urbana: University of Illinois Press.

Savitt TL (1982). The use of blacks for medical experimentation and demonstration in the Old South. J of Southern History 48:331–348.

Saxe A (1970). Social Dimensions of Mortuary Practices. PhD dissertation, University of Michigan. Ann Arbor: University Microfilms.

Schiffer MB (1987). Formation Processes of the Archaeological Record. Albuquerque: University of New Mexico Press.

Shanklin E (1994). Anthropology and Race. Belmont, CA: Wadsworth.

Shanks M, Tilley C (1982). Ideology, symbolic power and ritual communication: A reinterpretation of Neolithic mortuary practices. In Hodder I (ed.), Symbolic and Structural Archaeology, pp. 129–154. Cambridge: Cambridge University Press.

Spalding P (1987). The History of the Medical College of Georgia. Athens: University of Georgia Press.

Tainter JA (1978). Mortuary practices and the study of prehistoric social systems. In Schiffer MB (ed.), Advances in Archaeological Method and Theory, Vol 1, pp. 105–141. New York: Academic Press.

Trigger BG (1989). A History of Archaeological Thought. Cambridge: Cambridge University Press.

Ubelaker DH (1974). Reconstruction of Demographic Profiles from Ossuary Skeletal Samples. Smithsonian Contributions to Anthropology, No 18. Washington, DC: Smithsonian Institution Press.

Wilf SR (1988). Anatomy and punishment in late eighteenth-century New York. J Social History 22:507–530.

# 8 An Assessment of Health and Mortality of Nineteenth Century Rochester, New York Using Historic Records and The Highland Park Skeletal Collection

ROSANNE L. HIGGINS and JOYCE E. SIRIANNI

## INTRODUCTION

The study of historic human populations through the analysis of associated skeletal material and written records is emerging as an important area of physical anthropology. Evidence of the growing interest in this type of research was seen at the 1993 meeting of the American Association of Physical Anthropologists, where a symposium was held concerning the representativeness of historic-cemetery collections. In addition to demographic profiles (Saunders et al., 1993; Sirianni, 1993; Sirianni-Higgins, in press) researchers addressed a variety of issues such as the practice of surgery in the 19th century (Owsley, 1993) and health status in the 18th and 19th centuries (Bowman et al., 1993; Sirianni, 1993; Sirianni-Higgins, in press). Cox (1993) cautioned that anthropological osteologists must also be trained historians and be careful not to misinterpret or accept unequivocally information contained in historic documents. Bowman et al. (1993) warned that different documents can often give conflicting information. Despite the potential sources for error, written records still add to the depth of skeletal analysis.

In 1984 the Monroe County Parks Department in Rochester, New York uncovered human skeletal remains while constructing a public facility at Highland Park. Approximately 300 skeletons were excavated by the Rochester Museum and Science Center. It is assumed that this cemetery was associated with a nearby almshouse, an

*Bodies of Evidence*, Edited by Anne L. Grauer.
ISBN 0-471-04153-X  © 1995 John Wiley & Sons, Inc.

**FIGURE 1.** Monroe County Poorhouse, established 1826.

insane asylum, a work house, and later, a penitentiary (Fig. 1). These facilities were in use from 1826 until the end of the Civil War. When the almshouse was no longer in use, the poor were buried in a pauper section of the Mt. Hope Cemetery.

From 1832 to 1860, interment records were kept by the city sextant for all the residents of Rochester, whether or not they were buried at Mt. Hope. After 1860, only deaths of those who were interred at Mt. Hope were recorded. These records are a valuable source of information because they contain many death records from residents of the Monroe County Poorhouse and associated facilities. Previously, the only known death records of poorhouse residents, the Town of Brighton Vital Records, spanned a time period of four years (1847–1850). The analysis of the Mt. Hope death records and the Town of Brighton Vital Records allows us to investigate to what extent the Highland Park Skeletal Collection is representative of The Monroe County Poorhouse residents, it also allows us to assess the health status of poorhouse inmates relative to the general population of Rochester during the 19th century.

The purpose of this research is to compare the estimated demographic profile and health status of subadults and adult females of the skeletal sample with the Brighton town records, and further, to compare the disease-specific mortality of this group to the women and children of the city of Rochester, using the data from the Mt. Hope Cemetery.

## MATERIALS AND METHODS

### The Skeletal Sample

The sample consists of 65 subadult and 77 female skeletons (Table 1). The basic demographic estimates for the adults were calculated using multiple means of assessment and have been reported by Dannenhoffer (1990). We reexamined the material

**TABLE 1. Sample Sizes of Three Populations Used in the Analysis of 19th Century Health and Mortality**

|  | Subadults | Adult Females | Total |
|---|---|---|---|
| Highland Park Skeletal Collection | 65 | 77 | 142 |
| Town of Brighton Vital Records | 82 | 68 | 150 |
| Mt. Hope Cemetery Interment Records | 1,744 | 1,071 | 2,815 |

to affirm the original assessments. Age profiles were then constructed for the subadult (Sirianni, 1993; Sirianni & Jennings, 1990) and adult material. Individuals were recorded as adult in both the skeletal and documentary evidence if their age at death was assessed to be over 15 years. Adult age-group intervals spanned 10-year periods, except for the youngest adult age category (i.e., 15–19 years old, 20–29 years old, 30–39 years old, up to 90–99 years old). The skeletal age at death was capped at 69 years old.

Assessments of health reported for subadults (Sirianni & Jennings, 1990) and adults (Lanphear, 1988) were compared with the samples derived from both sets of historic records. The focus of this study was to determine the dental-health status of females and subadults in the skeletal collection. Hence, the number of caries per tooth, premortem tooth loss, the number of abscesses per alveolar socket, and the frequencies of dental calculus and enamel hypoplasia were recorded for each tooth type as a measure of health in this study. All recorded lesions were macroscopically visible.

### Historic Records

*Mt. Hope Cemetery Interment Records.*    The Mt. Hope interment records contain vital information for over 14,000 residents of Rochester. From this, a sample of 2,815 cemetery records of women and children was drawn using a random-numbers table to select pages (Table 1). For each individual, the name, age, sex, cause of death, place of residence, and place of interment was recorded. The records listing vital information for poorhouse residents were extracted and included in the sample of poorhouse residents from the Brighton town records. Thus, the Mt. Hope sample represents residents of the greater Rochester population, and the Brighton town records represents all known information concerning poorhouse residents.

*Town of Brighton Vital Records.*    The addition of poorhouse death data from the Mount Hope records to the Town of Brighton Vital Records results in a total of 150 death records for women and children at the poorhouse (Table 1). The name, age, sex, cause of death, and occupation (if listed) were recorded for each individual.

*Causes of Death.*    Many of the listed causes of death in the historical records were ambiguous at best, such as "drinking cold water" or "mortification." These causes of death were included in the category of "other" because, though individually they accounted for very few deaths, they were sufficient in number to be counted as a group. Other diseases such as "inflamed bowel," diarrhea, dysentery, and "summer complaint" all refer to gastrointestinal disorders, which were most likely difficult to distinguish. These types of diseases were grouped into a general category of gastro-intestinal diseases. Respiratory diseases refer to illnesses such as "inflamed lungs," bronchitis, and "lung disease." However, diseases such as cholera and tuberculosis, which occurred in sufficient numbers to be counted and more reliably diagnosed, were presented as individual categories.

## RESULTS

### Demographic Profile: Subadults

The profiles for estimated ages at death in the skeletal collection and in Brighton town records are similar (Fig. 2). In both, neonatal and infant deaths account for the largest

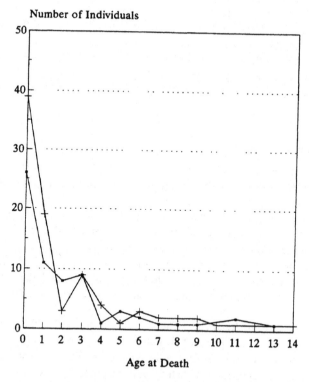

**FIGURE 2.** Age distribution of infants and children at the poorhouse: a comparison of skeletal remains and the Brighton town records.

proportion of deaths among the subadults. Approximately 40% of the immature skeletons and 45% of the children in the town records associated with the poorhouse were under one year of age. A pattern of high subadult mortality before the age of four was noted for all three of the samples (Fig. 3).

### Health Status: Subadults

The Mt. Hope interment records indicate that 21% of the subadults in Rochester were stillborn. However, only 2.6% are historically recorded in the Brighton town records for the poorhouse. This low percentage appears consistent with the number of neonates calculated in the skeletal remains. When considering the causes of infant and childhood deaths (Table 2), stillbirths were extracted from the total number of subadult deaths before the percentages were calculated. A comparison between the causes of death in various age categories for subadults from the poorhouse (Brighton town records) and the greater Rochester area (Mt. Hope records) can be seen in Table 2. Gastrointestinal diseases accounted for the largest percentage of deaths in all age categories of the Mt. Hope children, and also accounted for a great number of deaths among poorhouse children. Consumption was the leading cause of death among infants at the poorhouse, followed by gastrointestinal diseases and respiratory diseases. Consumption also accounted for considerably more deaths among infants and children of all ages at the poorhouse than among infants and children from the Mt. Hope sample. Childhood diseases, particularly measles, were the leading cause of death among children between the ages of one and four at the poorhouse. Convulsive disorders continued to decline with increased age among the Mt. Hope subadults,

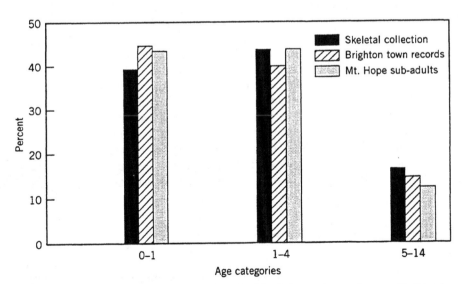

**FIGURE 3.** Comparison of age at death for subadults living at the poorhouse with those in the Mt. Hope interment records.

**TABLE 2. Leading Causes of Death in Subadults: A Comparison of the Brighton Town Clerk's Records (BTC) and the Mt. Hope Cemetery Records (MTH)**

| | Age categories (years) | | | | | |
| | Birth–1 | | 1–4 | | 5–14 | |
| Cause of death | BTC (%) | MTH (%) | BTC (%) | MTH (%) | BTC (%) | MTH (%) |
|---|---|---|---|---|---|---|
| Gastrointestinal | 18.4 | 30.3 | 23.5 | 30.7 | 15.4 | 24.4 |
| Consumption | 29.0 | 4.7 | 14.7 | 7.5 | 38.5 | 17.3 |
| Other respiratory | 18.4 | 5.6 | 5.9 | 7.3 | 7.7 | 6.1 |
| Convulsions/fits | 5.3 | 8.6 | 0.0 | 2.5 | 0.0 | 1.5 |
| Childhood diseases | 7.9 | 5.2 | 29.4 | 16.1 | 0.0 | 9.6 |
| Worms | 0.0 | 0.0 | 8.8 | 1.3 | 0.0 | 0.5 |
| Typhus | 0.0 | 0.0 | 5.9 | 0.0 | 15.4 | 0.0 |
| Teething | 0.0 | 2.2 | 0.0 | 3.8 | 0.0 | 0.0 |
| Accidents | 0.0 | 0.3 | 0.0 | 3.7 | 0.0 | 7.6 |
| Miscellaneous | 2.6 | 34.2 | 11.8 | 23.2 | 15.4 | 28.9 |
| Unknown | 18.4 | 8.9 | 0.0 | 3.9 | 7.7 | 4.1 |

whereas they are not recorded beyond infancy among poorhouse subadults. There were no recorded deaths due to typhus fever among children from the Mt. Hope sample, however deaths from typhus fever recorded at the poorhouse nearly tripled with increased age. Interestingly, there were no accidental deaths or deaths attributed to teething recorded at the poorhouse.

*Dental Health.* In both the deciduous and permanent dentitions of the subadult skeletons, the maxillary incisors exhibit a higher frequency of carious lesions than the mandibular incisors (Table 3). Furthermore, canines and premolars have fewer caries than the morphologically more complicated molars. An example of these carious lesions can be found in Fig. 4. Out of 22 individuals with enamel hypoplasia, 13 have deciduous dentitions. In the individuals with deciduous dentitions, the hypoplastic lesions appear on the anterior teeth either as a row of pits encircling an incisor crown (Fig. 5a) or as an enamel defect on the labial surface of a canine (Fig. 5b). Both defects appear to predispose the teeth to carious lesions. The location of the groove and bands of enamel hypoplasia on the permanent teeth indicate that, for the most part, stressful events occurred early in childhood.

## Demographic Profile: Adult Women

A comparison between the age at death of females from the historic records and the skeletal collection can be found in Fig. 6. The resulting profiles are visually similar, with the greatest number of women dying between the ages of 20–29 years old. Not

TABLE 3. The Percentage of Carious Teeth in Subadults from the Highland Park Skeletal Collection

| Tooth type | Teeth (n) | Caries (n) | Percentage |
|---|---|---|---|
| Deciduous maxillary | | | |
| Incisors | 62 | 26 | 41.9 |
| Canines | 36 | 0 | 0 |
| Molars | 102 | 10 | 9.8 |
| Deciduous mandibular | | | |
| Incisors | 89 | 2 | 2.2 |
| Canines | 44 | 3 | 6.8 |
| Molars | 112 | 22 | 19.6 |
| Total | 445 | 63 | 14.2 |
| Permanent maxillary | | | |
| Incisors | 50 | 8 | 16.0 |
| Canines | 23 | 0 | 0 |
| Premolars | 48 | 0 | 0 |
| Molars | 58 | 28 | 48.3 |
| Permanent Mandibular | | | |
| Incisors | 59 | 4 | 6.8 |
| Canines | 25 | 0 | 0 |
| Premolars | 48 | 3 | 6.3 |
| Molars | 62 | 26 | 35.1 |
| Total | 373 | 69 | 18.5 |

surprisingly, the highest percentage of recorded and skeletally determined deaths occurred between the ages of 20–49 years old. The greatest apparent difference between recorded information on deaths in the poorhouse (as derived from the Brighton town records) and the skeletal assessment occurs in the age categories 30–39 and 60–69. This feature, however, may be a limitation of the skeletal aging techniques used. Since some of the poorly preserved or particularly ambiguous skeletons were assigned to either a "young adult" or "old adult" age category, and then included in either the 30–39 or 60–69 age interval, these intervals might have inflated numbers. The absence of individuals in the oldest age intervals (70–99 years old) is also an artifact of the skeletal aging techniques which cap maximum age at death of the skeletal material at 69 years old.

## Health Status: Adult Women

A comparison between the leading causes of death among women from the poorhouse and women buried in the Mt. Hope cemetery can be seen in Table 4. Consumption was the leading cause of death in both groups of women, accounting for over one-third of all deaths. Typhus fever, the second leading cause of death among

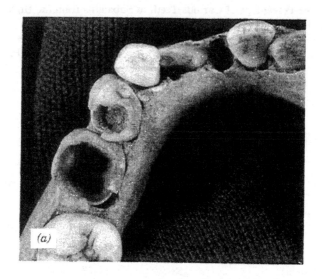

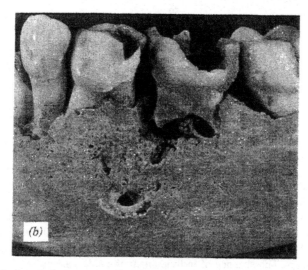

**FIGURE 4.** Carious lesions on mandibular deciduous molars: a) occlusal view: b) buccal view.

poorhouse women, accounted for only 1% of the deaths among the Rochester women, as recorded in the Mt. Hope sample. Cholera accounted for a higher percentage of deaths at the poorhouse, while other gastrointestinal diseases took a similar toll on both groups. The occurrence of respiratory diseases and child-bed fever, while minor in both samples, were almost negligible at the poorhouse.

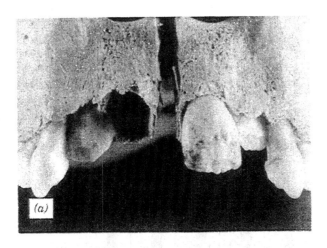

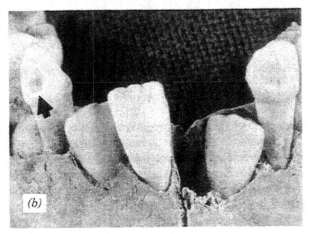

**FIGURE 5.** a) Enamel hypoplasia on the labial surface of a permanent maxillary central incisor; b) enamel defect on the labial surface of a deciduous mandibular canine.

*Dental Health.* The total percentage of teeth with carious lesions among adult females is 37.4% (Table 5), with the highest percentages of these lesions located on both the maxillary and mandibular molars. Calculus was found on 29.0% of the teeth, with the highest percentages being located on the mandibular incisors, canines, and premolars. The total percentage of enamel hypoplasias observed in the mandibular dentition (5.4%) was more than twice that observed in the maxillary dentition (2.2%). This can be attributed to the high percentage of enamel hypoplasias recorded for mandibular canines (13.7%). The overall percentage of teeth displaying enamel hypoplasia in this skeletal sample, however, is rather low (4.0%).

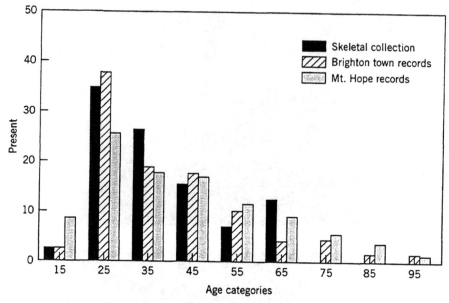

**FIGURE 6.** Age at death: poorhouse and nonpoorhouse women.

The total percentages of premortem tooth loss (Table 6) are similar for both the maxillary and the mandibular dentitions among adult females in the Highland Park Collection. The total percentage of premortem tooth loss in the population appeared relatively high (23.2%). While a similar pattern was observed regarding abscesses in the maxillary and mandibular dentition, the overall frequency of this condition per tooth was small. Periodontal disease appears to be more commonly found in the mandibular dentition and occurs in 10.9% of the teeth.

**TABLE 4. Major Causes of Death for Poorhouse Women and Women from the Greater Rochester Area**

| Causes of death | Poorhouse women (%) | Rochester women (%) |
|---|---|---|
| Consumption | 26.5 | 38.0 |
| Gastrointestinal diseases | 7.4 | 7.7 |
| Cholera | 11.8 | 6.4 |
| Respiratory diseases | 1.5 | 4.8 |
| Child-Bed fever | 1.5 | 4.4 |
| Typhus fever | 19.1 | 1.0 |

**TABLE 5. Percentage of Caries, Dental Calculus, and Enamel Hypoplasia in Adult Females of the Highland Park Collection**

| Teeth | n | Caries (%) | Calculus (%) | Hypoplasia (%) |
|---|---|---|---|---|
| Maxillary | | | | |
| Incisors | 165 | 29.7 | 11.5 | 3.0 |
| Canines | 946 | 17.2 | 11.7 | 2.1 |
| Premolars | 153 | 40.5 | 21.6 | 2.0 |
| Molars | 214 | 61.7 | 34.1 | 1.9 |
| Subtotal | 626 | 41.4 | 21.7 | 2.2 |
| Mandibular | | | | |
| Incisors | 219 | 12.3 | 45.2 | 6.4 |
| Canines | 117 | 20.5 | 37.6 | 13.7 |
| Premolars | 222 | 30.3 | 33.3 | 3.6 |
| Molars | 223 | 66.8 | 24.7 | 1.8 |
| Subtotal | 781 | 34.2 | 34.8 | 5.4 |
| Total | 1407 | 37.4 | 29.0 | 4.0 |

**TABLE 6. Percentage of Premortem Tooth Loss, Abscesses and Periodontal Disease per Tooth Socket among Adult Females of the Highland Park Collection**

| Teeth | Premortem loss | Abscesses | Periodontal disease |
|---|---|---|---|
| Maxillary | | | |
| Incisors | 14.5 | 2.6 | 3.8 |
| Canines | 10.1 | 0.8 | 2.5 |
| Premolars | 38.2 | 3.7 | 3.7 |
| Molars | 23.1 | 6.4 | 14.2 |
| Subtotal | 22.8 | 3.9 | 7.2 |
| Mandibular | | | |
| Incisors | 10.6 | 1.4 | 20.8 |
| Canines | 11.7 | 2.8 | 13.8 |
| Premolars | 17.4 | 4.2 | 12.5 |
| Molars | 41.0 | 5.3 | 10.0 |
| Subtotal | 23.6 | 3.7 | 13.8 |
| Total | 23.2 | 3.8 | 10.9 |

## DISCUSSION

### Representativeness

The data presented here suggest that the demographic pattern recorded in the Town of Brighton Vital Records are reflected in the Highland Park skeletal collection. Infant mortality was high in both samples, accounting for over 40% of all subadult deaths. Also, mortality among subadults in both the town records and the skeletal collection declined drastically after the first year, and continued to decline with increased age. When the adult females in these two samples are compared, the demographic profile is, again, similar. The highest percentage of deaths occurs for both groups between the ages of 20 and 49. However, as previously discussed, the high percentage of skeletal specimens in both the 30–39 and 60–69 year age categories may be the result of the techniques chosen to age the skeletal material. It should also be noted that the low percentage of female deaths in the skeletal collection and recorded in the Brighton town records of late childhood and early adulthood age (ages 5–19) may be because many orphaned children were removed from the poorhouse and placed in orphanages, (McKelvey, 1947). Consequently, the mortality statistics for these ages may reflect the fact that few children and young adults in these age groups lived at the poorhouse.

The patterns of dental health in the skeletal specimens may provide clues concerning the types and amount of stress that poorhouse residents endured. The presence of hypoplastic lesions, especially in both the adult and the subadult specimens, may be interpreted as signs of the presence of prenatal, infant, and childhood stress. The high percentage of carious lesions per tooth and premortem tooth loss recorded among the adult female specimens also suggests a bleak picture of the health status at the poorhouse. These indicators of stress, however, are not equal in their interpretive value. For instance, while the presence of enamel hypoplasia in the population can serve to suggest that stressors were present in that population, the lesions only highlight experiences of childhood stress. Adults in the Highland Park skeletal population displaying enamel hypoplasias, for instance, are providing us with a clue that their childhood was perhaps a difficult one. We cannot assume, however, that these adults grew up in the poorhouse and therefore we cannot assume from this specific data that life in the poorhouse for children was stressful. The presence of enamel hypoplasia on deciduous dentition, nevertheless, can provide us with insight into the conditions of adult women. Since deciduous dentition forms *in utero*, developmental interruptions to the enamel of deciduous teeth suggest that fetal and maternal health were compromised. Similarly, the presence of enamel hypoplasias in the deciduous dentitions of subadults may suggest that not only were prenatal conditions poor, childhood experiences were also stressful, leading ultimately to death before maturity for subadults living in the poorhouse.

The high percentages of caries and premortem tooth loss in the Highland Park skeletal collection is not particularly surprising. A population relying on public and private charity for survival is unlikely to have access to dental care. If the diet of the poorhouse relied heavily upon carbohydrates, often recognized as an inexpensive food source, the percentage of caries in the population could be expected to be high. With high rates of caries, one may expect high percentages of premortem tooth loss, due either to extraction or eventual decay of the entire tooth.

## The Poorhouse and the City of Rochester

A comparison of disease-specific mortality using the two sets of historic records suggests that the causes of mortality at the Monroe County Poorhouse did not differ considerably from those recorded for the greater Rochester area. Among the children, the only considerable difference in mortality was the higher percentage of deaths from consumption observed at the poorhouse. The mortality rate for children under the age of five in Rochester during the 19th century was astounding. In 1860, nearly half of the deaths, excluding stillbirths, were of children under the age of five (Rosenberg-Naparsteck, 1983). The high percentage of deaths attributed to gastrointestinal diseases recorded for both groups is consistent with other studies (McKelvey, 1956; Rosenberg-Naparsteck, 1983). Although cholera accounted for a small percentage of deaths in both sets of death records, many sources confirm that, in fact, cholera infantum was a major cause of death for infants and children (McKelvey, 1956; Rosenberg-Naparsteck, 1983; Lanphear, 1988; Preston & Haines, 1991). Rosenberg-Naparsteck (1983) reported that in 1870 cholera infantum killed 150 infants from July through September. She discussed a host of other gastrointestinal diseases referred to as "summer complaint," which also accounted for the deaths of many infants and children in Rochester during the 19th century. These diseases were noted for their high frequency during the summer months when bacterial growth in the water and sewage was rampant. She also reported that contaminated milk was a major source of the diseases that killed infants and children. Not only did milk sour while sitting on delivery wagons, it was often diluted with disease-infested water or taken from tuberculous cows. Interestingly, she suggested that milk-related deaths appeared to be lower at the poorhouse, perhaps because mothers breast fed or milk was fresh due to the presence of milking cows on the premises. This may suggest that the high percentage of deaths due to gastrointestinal illnesses at the poorhouse can be attributed to squalid living conditions. Typhus fever, which was recorded as a cause of death among children in the Brighton town records and not in the Mt. Hope records, is carried by lice (via rats) and is associated with unsanitary living conditions.

The low percentage of death due to childhood diseases noted in the Mt. Hope records and the Brighton town records is interesting. Very few deaths are recorded as being due to whooping cough, scarlet fever, and other childhood diseases. Although measles accounted for many of the recorded deaths of children between the ages of 1–4 in the poorhouse, and croup accounted for the deaths of more infants than children, many other known childhood conditions were not mentioned. In both sets of historical records gastrointestinal illnesses were among the leading causes of death, if not the leading cause of death for children from birth through age 14. This suggests that these diseases were killing children before they might have contracted the childhood diseases.

The age at death profiles historically recorded for Rochester and the poorhouse suggest that more poorhouse women were dying before age 40, and more women buried at Mt. Hope were surviving to old age. However, the differences are slight and the majority of all women in Rochester appear to have been dying young. Death records from a local Catholic church in 1826, known as St. Luke's Church, substantiate this result. These records indicate that twice as many deaths occurred between the ages of 20 to 40 among parishioners than among all deaths over age 40 (McKelvey, 1956).

Our results, indicating that consumption, gastrointestinal diseases, and cholera were the leading causes of death for both groups of women, suggest that factors shared by these women made them equally susceptible to the spread of disease. The city's well water was often contaminated by run-off from outhouses and cow sheds, and the construction of a sewer did not even begin until 1876. Even when the sewers were in use, inadequate design and poor construction resulted in improper drainage and contamination (McKelvey, 1956; Rosenberg-Naparsteck, 1983). For these reasons, city dwellers were just as vulnerable to the spread of cholera and other gastrointestinal diseases as were the residents of the poorhouse.

It is not surprising that consumption (now referred to as pulmonary tuberculosis) was observed as the leading cause of death for both groups of women. This disease, which is spread by bacteria expelled by the lungs into the air, may have accounted for so many deaths at the poorhouse due to the overcrowded and poorly ventilated conditions. Interestingly, many of the tenement buildings in the city of Rochester were also described as being poorly ventilated and overcrowded (McKelvey, 1956). The inhabitants of such buildings were every bit as likely to contract consumption as were the residents of the poorhouse.

Tuberculosis continued to plague Rochester up to the turn of the century when health officials began taking steps to stop the spread of what became known as the "white plague." These steps included the separation of consumptives from other patients at hospitals and provisions for adequate ventilation. By 1919, the occurrence of tuberculosis had greatly diminished and was continuing to decline (McKelvey, 1956).

A careful examination of the other causes of death for these two groups did reveal some differences in disease-specific mortality. The second leading cause of death for poorhouse women was typhus fever which accounted for only 1% of the deaths in the Mt. Hope sample. Also, child-bed fever accounted for less than 2% of deaths among poorhouse women, and more than twice that among women listed in the Mt. Hope records. Both midwives and physicians practiced the delivery of infants in Rochester and the unsanitary practices of both were noted to have been responsible for the spread of child-bed fever (Rosenberg-Naparsteck, 1983). The Brighton town records list the births of 70 infants at the poorhouse between the years 1847–1850. However, the procedures of childbirth at the poorhouse are unknown. While the difference in sample sizes between the poorhouse women and town of Rochester might account for some of the differences of percentages of disease, there may also be some difference in childbirth procedures at the Monroe County Poorhouse that accounts for such a small occurrence of child-bed fever.

## CONCLUSION

This research supports other studies (Lanphear, 1988; Sirianni & Jennings, 1990) that reported a good match between the skeletal evidence and the associated historic records from the town of Brighton, New York. The dental analysis reported in this study also substantiates the conclusion that the women and children from the Monroe County Poorhouse experienced poor health and nutritional stress. Furthermore, this analysis builds on previous studies that have utilized the Highland Park collection and the Town of Brighton Vital Records (Rosenberg-Naparsteck, 1983; Lanphear, 1988; Sirianni & Jennings, 1990) through the comparison of disease-specific mortality between poorhouse inmates and the residents of the city of Rochester. The evidence presented here suggests that the causes of mortality experienced by poorhouse inmates did not differ considerably from those who lived in Rochester and the surrounding area. This further indicates that there were factors shared by poorhouse inmates and other city residents, such as overcrowded living conditions and a contaminated water supply, which resulted in equal susceptibility to certain life-threatening diseases.

## ACKNOWLEDGMENTS

For their help in this ongoing project, we wish to thank the following: Ruth Rosenberg-Naparsteck, Robert J. Gustafson, Jack McKinney, The Friends of Mt. Hope, Mary Lou Tyndall, Carol O'Kell, Tim O'Connel, Rochester County Clerk's Office, The Rochester Museum & Science Center, Lorraine Saunders, Maureen McMahon, Bob Higgins, and Jean Grela. This research was supported in part by a Biomedical Research Support Grant obtained by Dr. A.T. Steegmann, Jr.

## REFERENCES

Bowman JE, MacLaughlin SM, Scheuer JL (1993). A study of the documentary and skeletal evidence relating to 18th and 19th century crypt burials in the city of London: The St. Brides Project. Am J Phys Anthropol Suppl 16:60.

Cox MJ (1993). A dangerous assumption: Anyone can be an historian! The lessons from Christ Church, Spitalfields, London. Am J Phys Anthropol Suppl 16:75.

Dannenhoffer, RP (1990). A look at the demographic makeup of the Highland Park Cemetery collection. Am J Phys Anthropol 81:213.

Lanphear KM (1988). Health and Mortality in a Nineteenth Century Poorhouse Skeletal Sample. PhD Dissertation SUNY Albany.

McKelvey B (1947). Historic origins of Rochester's social welfare agencies. Rochester History 9:21–36.

McKelvey B (1956). The history of public health in Rochester, New York. Rochester History 18:21–28.

Owsley DW (1993). New perspectives on 19th century surgical practice through bioarchaeological research. Am J Phys Anthropol Suppl 16:154.

Preston SH, Haines MR (1991). Fatal Years: Child Mortality in Late Nineteenth Century America. Princeton: Princeton University Press.

Rosenberg-Naparsteck R (1983). Life and death in nineteenth century Rochester. Rochester History 1055:2–23.

Saunders SR, Herring DA, Sawchuck LA, Boyce G (1993). The nineteenth century cemetery at St. Thomas' Anglican church, Belleville: Skeletons, parish records and the censuses. Am J Phys Anthropol Suppl 16:173.

Sirianni JE, Jennings E (1990). Demography and disease of the immature skeletons from the Highland Park Cemetery. Am J Phys Anthropol 81:296.

Sirianni JE (1993). A comparison of the death records from the Monroe County Poorhouse with skeletal evidence from the associated Highland Park Cemetery. Am J Phys Anthropol Suppl 16:181.

Sirianni JE, Higgins RL (in press). Representativeness: A comparison of the Highland Park Skeletal Collection with the Town of Brighton vital records and the Mt. Hope internment records.

# PART III
# Reconstructing Patterns
# of Health and Disease

# 9 Cross Homestead: Life and Death on the Midwestern Frontier

CLARK SPENCER LARSEN, JOSEPH CRAIG, LESLIE E. SERING,
MARGARET J. SCHOENINGER, KATHERINE F. RUSSELL,
DALE L. HUTCHINSON, and MATTHEW A. WILLIAMSON

## INTRODUCTION

The opening of the American Midwest to settlement by Euroamericans in the early
19th century saw an influx of thousands of immigrants within a few decades. The
settlement of the rich prairie farmland of central Illinois in the 1820s was virtually
complete by midcentury. To the region immediately surrounding Springfield came
families and individuals representing diverse economic backgrounds. Despite the
variation in degree of wealth, all newcomers shared remarkably similar circumstances
once arriving in the region, including physically demanding labor, strenuous travel
over long distances to obtain services and goods not available in the immediate
region, exposure to hazardous conditions such as food shortages following drought
and other natural disasters, disease, periodic undernutrition, and general lack of health
care (Faragher, 1986). In this chapter, we document evidence of health status and
lifestyle of tenant farmers—the Cross family and their close relatives—based on the
study of human remains recovered from the homestead cemetery. Although the
sample is small by comparison with others discussed in this volume, it provides
insight into a variety of issues regarding health and well-being on the Midwestern
frontier. Moreover, it contributes to a growing body of research that is beginning to
shed light on the problems and potential for synthesizing historical documentation
with osteological analysis.

## BIOARCHAEOLOGY IN THE HISTORICAL SETTING

Starting with Shapiro's (1930) modest study of crania from New York City, and later
built upon by Angel's (1976) ambitious investigation of Euroamerican and African

*Bodies of Evidence*, Edited by Anne L. Grauer.
ISBN 0-471-04153-X   © 1995 John Wiley & Sons, Inc.

American skeletal remains from the 17th through the 19th centuries, there has been a marked increase in reports on post-Colonial era burials, especially in the last two decades (see Owsley, 1990). In recent years, for example, a spate of reports have appeared documenting Euroamerican remains from various settings, such as towns and cities (Pfeiffer et al., 1989; Elia & Wesolowsky, 1991), plantations (Thomas et al., 1977; Little et al., 1992), farms (Wood et al., 1986; Saunders & Lazenby, 1992), and military or other conflict situations (Finnegan, 1976; Cybulski, 1988; Pfeiffer & Williamson, 1991). Although many of the samples are limited in size, the accumulation of a biological database has promoted the study of relationships between the physical and cultural environments and the recent history of the human condition (Owsley, 1990) as well as the testing of misunderstandings regarding human health and physical constitution in the historic past in North America (Angel, 1976).

The discovery of human remains from the Cross cemetery affords us an opportunity to examine these characteristics from an early to middle 19th century setting that has only rarely been explored by archaeologists and biological anthropologists in the American Midwest. These remains allow us to characterize key aspects of the human biology of one of the first pioneer families in central Illinois. The cemetery dates from the period of the late 1820s to 1849, marking the first and last burials, respectively. Thus, the series is representative of the Cross family and close relatives over a fairly restricted period of time. Lastly, the series is significant in that it adds to a growing body of bioarchaeological data available for the United States and Canada dealing specifically with historic-era, Euroamerican burials.

## ARCHAEOLOGICAL AND HISTORICAL CONTEXT

During the fall of 1991, workers preparing to move a 19th century farmhouse from an area slated for a housing development on the outskirts of Springfield, Illinois, encountered the fragments of three stone grave markers. These markers revealed that one male, Alvin Cross, and two of his daughters, Lavina Cross Williams and Mary Ann Cross Mitchel, were interred in a small, family cemetery between 1846 and 1849. The markers were contained in wooden frames that probably postdated the original placement of the grave markers. Geophysical investigations and mechanical stripping of the cemetery demonstrated that the markers had been displaced and were not associated with specific graves. Initial field testing also revealed that instead of three graves there were outlines representing grave shafts for 29 interments.

The Cross cemetery is unregistered and falls under the protection of the Illinois Skeletal Remains Protection Act (Illinois Revised Statutes 1989, Chapter 127, paragraph 2660, et seq.), which provides for preservation of unregistered human graves on public and private land within the State of Illinois. Because the property was slated for development, a plan of archaeological investigation was submitted to the Illinois Historic Preservation Agency.

Archaeological excavations revealed that the 29 grave shafts were present within a 300 m² area (Fig. 1). Following mechanical removal of most of the grave-shaft fill, exposure of skeletal remains followed standard archaeological procedures of docu-

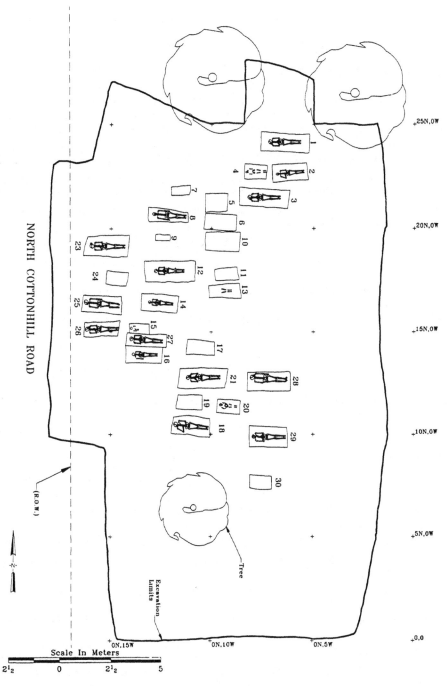

**FIGURE 1.** Map showing locations of interments in the Cross family cemetery (adapted from Craig & Larsen, 1993).

mentation and removal of skeletal remains. Eleven adults and 18 juveniles were found. Twelve juveniles were represented by complete or partial skeletons. The remaining six juvenile graves contained no human remains owing to lack of bone preservation, but the diminutive size of the grave shafts strongly suggested the presence of children. All adult grave pits contained human remains.

Archaeological excavations on the site revealed that the original grave shafts had been dug following a two-step procedure. First, a primary burial shaft comprising a long, rectangular pit was excavated, and second, at the base of the shaft, a secondary shaft or crypt (hole fitted to the shape of the coffin) was excavated. Following the preparation of the primary and secondary shafts, the coffin—with the head end to the west—was lowered by ropes, and the shaft was backfilled. All graves were probably marked with wood, none of which survived to the late 20th century. The three stone markers may have been placed at the time of burial. However, the grave marker for Alvin Cross is not listed in probate documents, and suggests that his widow (Margaret Cross) purchased the markers some years after burial.

Without exception, coffin remains in the Cross cemetery were very simple, consisting of nails, nail fragments, wood fragments, and several coffin screws. No other hardware (e.g., handles, nameplates, hinges) appeared to have adorned the coffins. Based on the shape of the crypt outline, all coffins were break-side or pinched-toe styles. Three individuals—all less than six years of age—were not interred in coffins. Presence of copper pins as well as copper staining on a number of crania indicate that the deceased were probably placed in shrouds. Only three individuals showed evidence of clothing, including nearly 200 seed beads in the shoulder and head region of an infant (probably sewn on a burial garment) and trouser and shirt buttons on two adults.

The paucity of coffin furniture and presence of few headstones indicates the limited economic means of the Cross family and others buried in the cemetery. Unfortunately, the virtual lack of diagnostic artifacts precludes us from precisely dating the use of the cemetery. Archival and historical documents as well as the 1849 date on a grave marker (for Alvin Cross) indicate that the terminal date is 1849. By the early 1850s, the property passed into the hands of a family that appears to have placed their dead in a nearby Catholic cemetery. The initial use of the cemetery probably dates to 1829 or shortly thereafter, when Alvin Cross and his family moved to Sangamon County (Power, 1876). Identifiable nails from grave crypts are early style machine-headed cut nails, which have a terminal production date during the late 1830s (Nelson, 1968), confirming the use of the cemetery in the third decade of the 19th century.

## LIFE ON THE ILLINOIS PRAIRIE

Interpretations of human health and lifeways of Illinois pioneers have been largely based on available archival documents and historical narratives. These records provide a rich and important source of contextual information for interpreting the human remains from the Cross cemetery. Much of the discussion below is drawn from John Mack Faragher's (1986) history of the settlement of Sugar Creek, a 19th century farm community located several miles from the Cross Homestead.

Survival in the Illinois frontier during the early 19th century was a struggle with the harshness of the climate, accidental trauma, disease, and other negative circumstances. Throughout the 1830s, the period of some of the heaviest settlement in Sangamon County, weather wreaked havoc on life-sustaining agricultural pursuits of early pioneers. The decade opened with the "Winter of the Deep Snow," in which three feet of snow fell beginning in December of 1830. The loss of life due to starvation and exposure was high during this time. Other severe storms were documented, and accounts of tornadoes, paralyzing cold, oppressive heat, hail, wind, and rain resulting in the deaths of settlers and destruction of essential fields of wheat and corn are plentiful. Many descendants of pioneers interviewed by Power (1876) relayed stories of trampling by farm animals, prairie fires, drowning, disease, and deprivation.

Although the aforementioned hardships were unrelenting threats to life and well-being, most deaths in frontier Illinois appeared to have been caused by a host of childhood diseases, or pneumonia, tuberculosis, and intestinal disorders. Outbreaks of "brain fever" (typhoid) were common in the late summer and fall when flies—the carrier of the typhoid bacilli—thrived in pools of raw sewage and offal common to every pioneer farm. Preston Breckenridge, newly arrived in Sangamon County in 1834, recalled that a period of hot weather following an especially wet summer produced numerous pools of stagnant water and decaying vegetation, which permeated the air with a foul odor. He remarked further that "chills and bilious diseases prevailed to such an extent that in many cases there were not enough well persons to take care of the sick and bury the dead" (Power, 1876, p. 137).

By late 1832, Asiatic cholera and its often fatal symptoms of severe diarrhea and excruciating abdominal pain entered central Illinois. The years of 1833–1834 appear to have been horrific. The disease was of such high prevalence that few would venture to Springfield and risk infection. A second outbreak of cholera struck in 1849–1850.

Equally as problematic was endemic malaria. Parasitic infection spread by mosquitoes induced the well-documented pattern of severe chills followed by a high, cyclical fever. Often referred to as the "pioneer shakes," the disease was so commonplace it was considered simply part of the frontier settlement process. Mortality schedules for the 1850–1860 period indicate that about 10% of deaths, primarily children, resulted from the disease. The chronic anemia accompanying the disease predisposed the individual to more serious conditions (see details in Faragher, 1986, p. 90). The 1850 mortality schedule for Sangamon County, reported that causes of death were due to cholera (5%), typhoid fever (10%), pneumonia (11%), and tuberculosis (11%).

The winter of 1848–1849 was one of the most severe in Sangamon County, leaving few farm households untouched by fevers. A local physician, George Ambrose, attended and prescribed medicine to one of the Cross children on several occasions in December of 1848, and Margaret Cross required the physician's care in mid-February of 1849. Soon after, in early March, Alvin Cross became severely ill. Sensing impending death, a coffin was ordered and made available for his immediate burial (Alvin Cross Probate Record; see Craig & Larsen, 1993).

In addition to these problems, the daily lives and workloads of pioneer families must have been arduous. Based on his review of historical accounts of labor, Faragher noted: "The commitment of energy took its toll. Men's hands hardened from gripping plow handles, their legs bowed from tramping over the clods turned up by the plowshare; women's hands cracked, bled, and developed corns from the hard water of the family wash, their knees grew knobby from years of kneeling to grit corn or scrub puncheon floors" (1986, p. 99). Other activities, such as horseback riding, long-distance walking, field clearing, and other physically demanding behaviors resulted in general physical hardship.

## NINETEENTH CENTURY DEMOGRAPHY

The first mortality schedules for Sangamon County, 1850 and 1860, are inaccurate and somewhat unreliable. However, they suggest that during the initial years of settlement high fertility was achieved despite remarkable levels of maternal, fetal, and infant mortality. In 1830, the ratio of children under the age of 10 to women between 16 and 45 years was almost 2.5 to 1. Only 1 in 10 of first-generation Sangamon County wives had *fewer* than 5 children; 6 in 10 women had between 6 and 9 children, and 3 in 10 women raised 10 children or more (Faragher, 1986). Margaret Cross bore a total of 11 children, six of whom were born in Sangamon County. Her first child was born in 1823 when she was 21, and her last child was born in 1841 when she was 39. Her children included three sets of twins (Power, 1876).

Faragher (1986) has analyzed available records and indicates that women who were born elsewhere (e.g., Kentucky and Tennessee) around 1800 and who later settled in Illinois died at an average age of 67 years. On the other hand, women born between 1800 and 1840 who spent their childbearing years on the Illinois frontier, died at considerably younger ages—on average at 50 years of age. Males show similar patterns of mortality. Males born outside Illinois before 1800 died at an average age of 61 years, while males born after 1800 who raised young families in Illinois died at an average age of 45 years.

Infant and childhood mortality appears to have been higher in Illinois than national trends for the mid-19th century. Unfortunately, prior to 1900, vital statistics, mortality data in particular, are intermittent and unreliable. Published data for Massachusetts in 1850, the first state to establish a death registration system (see Thompson & Whelpton, 1933), indicates that life expectancy for males and females at birth was 38.3 and 40.5 years, respectively (Jenkinson et al., 1949). Certainly on the Illinois frontier, life expectancy for infants was considerably lower. One physician remarked in 1840 that "nearly one half of the children born die before reaching 5 years of age, and nearly one half of those deaths are from bowel troubles" (Rawlings, 1927:87). Moreover, the mortality schedules for the region compiled for 1850 reveal that deaths of children under the age of five accounted for 45–50% of all deaths.

## OSTEOLOGICAL ANALYSIS: INTERPRETING PATTERNS OF HEALTH, DIET, AND LIFEWAY ON THE FRONTIER

### Methods of Study

The above discussion provides an essential backdrop to the study of the skeletal series recovered from the Cross cemetery. In the following, we describe and interpret the human skeletal remains from the Cross cemetery. In order to accomplish this, standard osteological observations were made, including collection of demographic data (sex, age at death), observations of skeletal and dental pathology, analysis of stable isotopes of carbon and nitrogen, and to a lesser extent, metric and nonmetric trait assessment.

*Demography.* Sex was determined on the basis of pelvic morphology and presence or absence of cranial and postcranial characteristics (Ubelaker, 1989). Sex determination was not attempted for juvenile remains. Age was estimated on the basis of three skeletal components: auricular-surface morphology of the ilium (Lovejoy et al., 1985), pubic symphyseal face morphology (Todd, 1920; Meindl et al., 1985), and degree of dental wear and extent of premortem tooth loss. Other age criteria, e.g., cranial suture closure (Meindl & Lovejoy, 1985), were used to confirm estimates based on the iliac, pubic, and dental-wear indicators. Due to the uneven nature of skeletal preservation, it was not possible to use all approaches for every adult in the series. In order to arrive at an age estimate for each individual, an unweighted mean of component values was determined.

Age-at-death estimates for juveniles were determined by use of dental developmental standards (Moorrees et al., 1963a,b; cited in Ubelaker, 1989). Corroborative information for juvenile age at death was provided by length of the grave shaft. Because all individuals were interred in fully extended positions—a standard 19th century format—the length of the burial pit provided an important source of information, particularly with regard to identification of juveniles, where skeletal remains, including teeth, were either not preserved or very poorly preserved.

*Skeletal and Dental Pathology.* The skeletal pathology recorded included the presence of osteoarthritis (marginal lipping, Schmorl's depressions, and other degenerative changes involving articular joints), cribra orbitalia/porotic hyperostosis, periosteal reactions, and fracture and other evidence of trauma. Dental pathology included presence of dental caries, premortem tooth loss, calculus deposits, and extramasticatory alterations.

Incisors and canines were observed for presence of enamel defects (linear enamel hypoplasia) because these teeth provide the most comprehensive information about physiological stress (Goodman & Rose, 1990). Hypoplasias are visible growth arrests of the teeth caused by metabolic disruptions, such as nutritional deficiency, disease, or both (reviewed in Goodman & Rose, 1990, 1991). For this study, hypoplasias were observed using low-power ($\times10$) magnification with a stereozoom microscope. Two types of information are reported here: 1) frequency of individuals affected by all teeth combined and per tooth type; and 2) number of hypoplasias per tooth type.

An analysis of stable isotopes of carbon ($^{13}C$, $^{12}C$) and nitrogen ($^{15}N$, $^{14}N$) in the organic fraction of human bone, known as collagen, has become an important means of reconstruction of specific components of diet in past human populations (see Katzenberg & Pfeiffer, this volume; Schoeninger & Moore, 1992). Bone collagen was extracted from rib samples of 10 Cross adults and analyzed following standard procedures (see Schoeninger et al., 1990).

Osteometric data were also collected. Standard long-bone lengths were recorded in order to estimate adult stature. Although a battery of other measurements have been recorded and summarized, they are not included here (see Craig & Larsen, 1993). Stature, a general measure of health and well-being, was estimated based on formulae provided by Trotter (1970).

Nonmetric features, such as metopism, were recorded for the analysis. The metopic suture normally bifurcates the frontal into right and left halves and completely fuses by the second or third year of life (Hauser & De Stefano, 1989). However, in very rare circumstances, the suture can remain open well into adulthood. When present in adults, it is either complete or partial. Its underlying genetic nature is poorly understood, but it has been variously ascribed to autosomal dominance (Keeler, 1930), dominance with variable penetrance (Torgersen, 1951), or multiple additive genes (Torgersen, 1963).

### Results and Discussion

*Demographic Assessment.*    The Cross adults are represented by six females and five males. The age-at-death (mortality) profile (Table 1) reveals that nearly two-thirds (61%) of the series are juveniles (individuals less than 15 years). The infant sample ($\leq 2$ years) comprises 35.7% of the entire series. The juvenile component, especially

TABLE 1. Distribution of Age at Death at the Cross Homestead

| Age | Number of cases | Percent of total |
|---|---|---|
| 0–2 | 10 | 35.7 |
| 2.1–5 | 3 | 10.7 |
| 5.1–10 | 2 | 7.1 |
| 10.1–15 | 2 | 7.1 |
| 15.1–20 | 4 | 14.3 |
| 20.1–25 | 0 | 0.0 |
| 25.1–30 | 0 | 0.0 |
| 30.1–35 | 0 | 0.0 |
| 35.1–40 | 4 | 14.3 |
| 40.1–45 | 2 | 7.1 |
| 45.1–50 | 1 | 3.6 |
| 50.1+ | 0 | 0.0 |

infants, indicates a remarkably high preadult mortality in this series. The adult component is represented by two groups, including a young adult group (15.1–20 years; $n = 4$) and an old adult group (35.1–45.1+ years; $n = 7$). No individuals are present between 20 and 35 years. Interestingly, all young adults are females. Only two of the older adults are female (both between 35.1–40 years). Finally, based on osteological criteria, there are no individuals exceeding 46 years at death.

These results point to high juvenile mortality. Moreover, these findings are fully consistent with the historical accounts described above. However, it must be emphasized that the data presented based on the osteological assessment of the Cross series are not strictly comparable to life-table data presented from death-registration statistics for the mid-19th century. First, the mid-19th century mortality data are sparse and unreliable. Second, and more important, unlike census data, a cemetery represents a cumulative sample consisting of deaths occurring over a period of years. Moreover, skeletal series are often subject to a variety of factors that will result in unrepresentative demographic profiles (see Wood et al., 1992). For example, with regard to the Cross series, it is probable that not all adults in the family are included in the cemetery population. If this were the case, then life expectancy at birth, as calculated osteologically, would be unrealistically low.

The compendium of early settlers in Sangamon County indicates that the majority of offspring born to Alvin and Margaret Cross were not buried in the family cemetery at the Cross homestead (see Power, 1876). In fact, only five children were likely to have been buried in the cemetery, including three infants (all unnamed) and two young adult women (Mary Ann and Lavina). Other offspring were either buried elsewhere (for example, son Riley died in the Mexican War and was buried in the Rio Grande River valley) or were adults living elsewhere at the time of the volume's publication (see Power, 1876). As mentioned previously, records indicate that the last interment at the Cross cemetery was in 1849. Thus, all adult offspring living at the time of the publication of Power's volume would have eventually been buried elsewhere. Quite clearly, then, the exclusion of individuals surviving to adulthood has lowered values of life expectancy determined from osteological remains, primarily because of the absence of adult offspring of Alvin and Margaret Cross from the skeletal series.

*Indications of Lifestyle and Health Status.* The Cross series has provided insight into a number of aspects of frontier life. First, the Cross series exhibits a number of pathological conditions that are related to activity, including degenerative joint disease (also called osteoarthritis), nonarthritic joint changes resulting from habitual postures, and fractures arising from trauma. Eight of the 11 adults exhibit one or more skeletal pathologies relating to general activity (e.g., osteoarthritis). With the exception of an adolescent female (burial 8), all postcranial degenerative joint pathology is present in the group of older adults (all individuals >35 years). A 40 year old male (burial 18) shows a range of pathological joint changes. These include marginal lipping of the thoracic, lumbar, and first sacral vertebrae, the first rib–manubrium articulation, and the distal ulna. Two joints of this individual exhibit articular modifications that reflect habitual activities: 1) both femoral heads exhibit increased articular surface area, specifically resulting from an extension of the articular surface anteriorly onto the femoral neck and flattening of the head medially and anteriorly; and 2) the proximal end of the right first metacarpal is hypertrophied and the articular surface is eburnated (polished) from degeneration of articular cartilage and bone-on-bone articulation.

The extension of the femoral head articular surface has been described as a "plaque" associated with the "reaction area" of the medioanterior femoral neck (Angel, 1964). Angel (1964) suggested that the modification was caused by extreme extension of the hip, such as in running or walking downhill. Perhaps extreme extension of the hip in the Cross individuals (a characteristic also present in another older adult male, burial 23) may be related to some type of agricultural activity, such as plowing. It is unlikely that it was caused by ambulatory activities on sloped surfaces, especially given the fact that the central Illinois terrain is extraordinarily flat. Regardless of the cause, however, the presence of plaque on the neck-head region of the femora indicates some form of habitual physically demanding activity (see also Kennedy, 1989).

Other degenerative pathology reflecting excessive physical activity includes Schmorl's depressions on the surfaces of vertebral bodies (burials 3 and 8). These features have a cupped appearance and are restricted to the midregion of inter-vertebral body surfaces. Frequently associated with vertebral compression fractures, they result from herniation of the intervertebral disc due to high levels of mechanical loading of the back (see Merbs, 1989).

Some insight into the health status of the Cross group, based on skeletal pathology, is indicated by observation of two primary types of pathological modifications: cribra orbitalia and porotic hyperostosis, and nonspecific periosteal reactions on bone surfaces. Cribra orbitalia and porotic hyperostosis are sieve-like lesions on the superior eye orbits and the flat cranial bones (e.g., parietals, occipital), respectively. Although the etiology is not fully understood, the lesions result from the expansion of the blood-forming tissues in order to increase red blood cell production during episodes of anemia, particularly during the earlier years of childhood (Stuart-Macadam, 1989). Clinical evidence indicates that genetic hemolytic anemias (e.g., sickle-cell anemia) can result in this type of bone pathology. Most examples from archaeological settings, however, suggest that iron-poor foods, contaminated water, parasitic infections, and poor living conditions are generally important considerations in interpreting the presence of pathology in skeletal samples (Larsen, 1987; Stuart-Macadam, 1989). Cribra orbitalia is present in 28.6% (4/14) of the Cross crania (two young adult females and two older children). All lesions are well healed, indicating skeletal response to episodes of anemia occurring much earlier in the lives of the affected individuals.

Periosteal reactions in the Cross series are mostly limited to slight elevations of the outer surface of bone of the left tibia of an older adult male and the left fibula of a young adult female. Burial 18, a 40 year old male, displays a slight periosteal reaction on the right fibula and a swollen diaphysis of the right tibia. Thus, only three of 16 skeletons with at least one of either or both the fibulae and tibiae present exhibit this kind of skeletal remodeling. These bony responses are generally caused by infection or trauma, such as a blow to the lower leg. Burial 18 also has other degenerative pathology (osteoarthritis) as well as five healed rib fractures. Therefore it is possible that the inflammation may be related to trauma.

In analysis of dental pathology, in particular, the presence of caries and premortem tooth loss serves as another clue to the health status of the Cross family. Dental caries are symptomatic of a disease process that is characterized by the focal demineralization of dental hard tissues. It is caused by bacterial fermentation of dietary carbohydrates, especially sugars (Larsen, 1987). Examination of teeth from the Cross homestead reveals a high frequency of carious lesions. With regard to all permanent teeth (from juveniles and adults combined), 19.6% (58/295) are carious. All adults (except two edentulous individuals) have at least one carious tooth.

Consistent with high rates of cariogenesis, the Cross group displayed elevated levels of premortem tooth loss (25.6% in the adults), indicating advanced periodontal disease. Two older adult males (both >40 years old) were completely edentulous. The age-progressive nature of tooth loss is indicated by comparison of younger and older adults. Four adults aged 16–20 years have only one tooth missing premortem (1.7%, mandibular; 0.0% maxillary); older individuals, however, have in excess of one-third tooth loss (41.5%, mandibular; 37.5%, maxillary).

These findings suggest that the Cross group had access to sugar or other refined foods that are cariogenic (e.g., flour and refined grains). Moreover, the presence of heavy deposits of calculus—plaque that becomes calcified—on at least two adults, as well as no evidence of fillings in teeth, indicates that dental hygiene was very poor and that there was limited or no access to professional dental care. Indeed, comparison with other 19th century groups indicates that dental caries and premortem tooth loss frequencies are unusually high in the Cross homestead population, further confirming their relatively poor dental health (see details in Craig & Larsen, 1993).

An examination for the presence of enamel hypoplasia in all adult canines and incisors in the Cross sample yielded a frequency rate of 67% (10/15). Comparison of tooth types shows that the most commonly affected teeth were maxillary right canines [50% (6/11)], and the least commonly affected teeth were mandibular left second incisors [0% (0/9)]. The frequency rate of enamel hypoplasias in all other tooth types was 25% or less. Assessment of the number of hypoplastic episodes per tooth type indicates a greater number of hypoplasia in maxillary teeth than mandibular teeth. The frequency of hypoplasia per tooth type ranged from 0.0 (mandibular left second incisor) to 0.91 (maxillary right canine). These findings show that the majority of Cross individuals exhibited some evidence of growth disruption via observation of linear enamel hypoplasia. However, comparison with other populations such as the Monroe County Poorhouse series from New York State (see Lanphear, 1990; Sirianni & Higgins, this volume) indicates that the Cross family experienced considerably less physiological stress leading to enamel-growth disruption. For instance, 73% of Monroe County Poorhouse mandibular left canines were affected by hypoplastic events. Although the Cross homestead and Monroe County Poorhouse samples represent two different socioeconomic contexts, their comparison is informative since it contrasts populations living during the 19th century, and underscores differing health profiles.

Study of dental wear in the series reveals that the diet, along with being cariogenic, contained significant amounts of abrasives, either from the food itself or from hard objects incorporated into the food during its preparation. That is, virtually all adult permanent teeth show some degree of occlusal surface wear. Moorrees (1957) has noted that in a sample of 20th-century Whites, molars exhibit relatively little wear on occlusal surfaces. In the Cross series, however, all young adults show some dentin exposure on the first molars. By 35–40 years of age most of the dentin is exposed, with little enamel remaining on the occlusal surface of this tooth (e.g., burial 18).

Two older adult males exhibit considerably greater wear on the maxillary anterior teeth than on the mandibular anterior teeth. Although the reasons for this dichoto-mous wear pattern are unknown, it may reflect the use of the front teeth in an extramasticatory capacity. That is, the wear on the upper incisors and canines is so advanced that it suggests that these teeth were used as a "tool"; for instance, to grip or pull leather on a frequent basis. Other evidence in the sample, suggestive of nondietary use of the anterior dentition, is demonstrated by the presence of step fractures on anterior teeth in two adult females and one adult male. Extensive fracturing is present in at least five teeth in one male and one female. The cause of the fractures is not known, but the pattern is highly suggestive of use of the front teeth in activities resulting in severe trauma.

*Analysis of Diet.* In temperate regions of North America where most plants fix carbon by a $C_3$ photosynthetic pathway, the heavier isotope ($^{13}C$) is discriminated against more than in plants fixing carbon by a $C_4$ photosynthetic pathway. Many of the major Old World plants used by Euroamerican populations in North America— including wheat, barley, oats, and rye—are $C_3$ plants. The only major plant that follows a $C_4$ photosynthetic pathway is the tropical grass, maize, although millet and sugar cane are also included in this group. The analysis of ratios of $^{13}C$ to $^{12}C$ in bone samples should, therefore, indicate the extent to which the Cross family grew and habitually consumed maize in the frontier setting.

The ratio of carbon-stable isotopes are expressed as delta ($\delta$) values in parts per thousand (read as parts "per mil" or ‰) determined by comparison of the sample isotope ratio with a standard (see Schoeninger & Moore, 1992). Humans consuming only $C_3$-based plants should have more negative $\delta^{13}C$ values (at or approaching –21 ‰) than humans consuming exclusively $C_4$-based plants (at or approaching –7.5‰) (van der Merwe, 1982).

Schoeninger and DeNiro (1984) have demonstrated that in many areas of the world, ratios of $^{15}N$ to $^{14}N$ (also expressed as $\delta$ values, or $\delta^{15}N$, relative to a standard) are about 10‰ less positive in terrestrial plants and animals than in marine plants and animals. Indeed, like stable isotopes of carbon, these differences are reflected in isotope composition of foods consumed, as well as their trophic level, such that consumers of predominantly terrestrial foods are distinct from consumers of pre-dominantly marine foods (e.g., Schoeninger & DeNiro, 1984). Results of the analysis of carbon- and nitrogen-stable isotopes reveal important characteristics of diet on the Illinois frontier during the early 19th century. With regard to $\delta^{13}C$ data, eight of the 10 values show little variation, ranging from –14.1 to –11.3‰. Two values, –16.2 (burial 3) and –19.4 (burial 8), are well outside this range. We suspect that these values are due to contamination by humic acids in the burial matrix rather than reflecting dietary signatures (see Craig & Larsen, 1993). Therefore, for purposes of this discussion, we have excluded these two individuals from the analysis.

Comparison of the $\delta^{13}C$ values with late prehistoric midwestern Native American populations, who were dependent on maize agriculture, strongly suggests that the Cross adults consumed maize on a regular basis. In particular, the mean value (−12.4‰) is similar to prehistoric maize agriculturalists (Late Woodland and Mississippian periods) from Illinois (e.g., Dickson Mounds = −10.8‰; Schild = −12.3‰; Norris Farms No. 36 = −12.6‰) (Buikstra & Milner, 1991) and other areas of the eastern United States (see summary in Schoeninger & Moore, 1992; Buikstra, 1992). This finding is consistent with other available evidence of dietary practices regarding the specific crops that were raised on the Cross homestead. That is, the appraisal of the personal property of Squire Cross (6 September 1847), brother of Alvin Cross, following his death indicates the presence of "20 acres corn (more or less)" (see Craig & Larsen, 1993, Appendix A). Although this corn was likely used primarily as feed stock for farm animals, it may have also been used as food for the occupants of the homestead. The only other crop mentioned in the probate records was oats, a $C_3$ plant.

The Cross $\delta^{13}C$ values are different from the 19th century Harvie rural pioneer series from Ontario (see Fig. 2). Katzenberg (1991) found that all Harvie values were negative (mean = −18.7‰, range = −20.9 to −16.5‰), thus suggesting a consumption of $C_3$-based foods in rural Ontario. Unlike the comparison of Cross values with late prehistoric Illinois populations, which show little change over time, the Harvie values contrast sharply with late prehistoric maize Ontario agriculturalists (mean = −12‰; Katzenberg, 1991).

The $\delta^{15}N$ values also show very little range of variation (10.3–13.3‰; mean = 12.2‰). These values are more positive than what is typically seen in terrestrial populations from the interior of North America (see Schoeninger & Moore, 1992), suggesting that a major source of protein in rural Illinois was freshwater fish from nearby streams. A nearby source of fish capture would have been Sugar Creek, located less than a mile from the Cross homestead. Similar $\delta^{15}N$ values have been reported from the Great Lakes region (e.g., Schwarcz et al., 1985). In contrast to the stable carbon isotope values, the stable nitrogen values from Cross are in close agreement with values from the Harvie series analyzed by Katzenberg (1991).

The Cross $\delta^{13}C$ and $\delta^{15}N$ values show very little variation by age or sex. Therefore, individuals residing at the homestead seemingly consumed the same foods in similar proportions.

***Osteometric and Nonmetric Analysis.***    Standard measurement and morphological observation of cranial remains indicates that this sample shares characteristics with other Euroamerican series. The skulls, for instance, are relatively long and narrow, the faces are flat and lack facial and alveolar prognathism, and the nasal apertures are narrow with sharp nasal margins. These features are characteristic of European and Euroamerican populations (Stewart, 1979). Moreover, discriminant function analysis [FORDISC, version 1.0 (Jantz & Ousley, 1993)] of adult crania in the series reveals

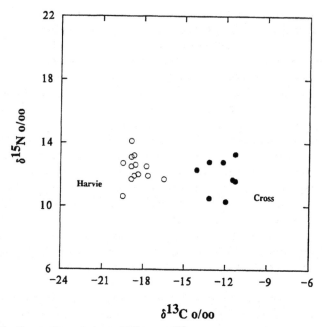

**FIGURE 2.** Comparison of plots of $\delta^{13}C$ and $\delta^{15}N$ values from Cross and Harvie cemeteries.

a pattern fully consistent with these observations, as does the presence of double-rooted mandibular canines in the sample (Turner, 1991; see Craig & Larsen, 1993).

Measurement of length of long bones and calculation of stature shows that males from the Cross cemetery are about 12 cm taller on average than females. Comparison of the meric index, an indicator of flatness of the proximal femur diaphysis, shows that Cross females have relatively flatter proximal femoral diaphyses than Cross males, which is a characteristic of human populations in general (see Ruff, 1987).

Comparisons of the Cross cranial index, meric index, and stature with other pre-20th century U.S. samples reveals no substantial differences in these variables between series (Table 2). Meric index values show that the proximal diaphysis of the femur is relatively round for both males and females. In this regard, the Cross series is similar to other modern U.S. and Canadian skeletal samples, reflecting a temporal trend of reduced activity levels in modern human populations (see Ruff, 1987).

Stature provides an important index of economic and dietary conditions, along with a means to assess the well-being of a human populations (e.g., Komlos, 1987; Steckel, 1979, 1983). Especially noteworthy in stature comparisons made between members of the Cross cemetery and other 19th century U.S. populations is the similarity for both males and females. These findings suggest little evidence of a secular trend from the early 19th to late 20th centuries (see Angel, 1976). Moreover, these findings indicate that despite the hardships and deprivations of pioneer life in the Midwest, genetic growth potential was perhaps reached. This may further indicate

TABLE 2. Comparison of Cranial Index, Meric Index, and Stature between the Cross Homestead and Other Euroamerican Samples

| Sample | Cranial index | Meric index | Stature (cm) |
|---|---|---|---|
| Male | | | |
| Cross[1] | 71.6 | 88.1 | 175 |
| Harvie[2] | 71.8 | 81.4 | 171 |
| Prospect Hill[3] | — | — | 173 |
| Colonial U.S.[4] | 76.0 | 85.3 | 173 |
| Mt. Gilead[5] | — | — | 172 |
| Clifts Plantation[6] | — | — | 169 |
| Belleview[6] | — | — | 170 |
| Ft. Laurens[7] | — | 82.4 | 174 |
| Snake Hill[8] | — | 89.9 | 176 |
| Bradford's Company[8] | — | — | 174 |
| Old Quebec[8,9] | — | 83.8 | 173 |
| West Point cadets[10] | — | — | 172 |
| Modern U.S.[4,11] | — | 87.6 | 174 |
| Female | | | |
| Cross[1] | 76.3 | 82.5 | 163 |
| Harvie[2] | 77.3 | 83.4 | 161 |
| Prospect Hill[3] | — | — | 161 |
| Colonial U.S.[4] | 73.8 | 84.8 | 160 |
| Mt. Gilead[5] | — | — | 162 |
| Modern U.S.[4,11] | — | 86.6 | 161 |

[1]This study.
[2]Saunders & Lazenby, 1991.
[3]Pfeiffer et al., 1989.
[4]Angel, 1976.
[5]Wood et al., 1986.
[6]Rathbun & Scurry, 1991.
[7]Sciulli & Gramly, 1989.
[8]Saunders, 1991.
[9]Cybulski, 1988.
[10]Komlos, 1987; average of 1840s–1870s, 21-year-olds only.
[11]National Center for Health Statistics, 1992.

that nutrition was adequate during the period of initial settlement of central Illinois by Euroamericans.

The examination for the presence of metopism may provide clues to the degree of biological relatedness in this sample of human remains. Although the hereditary basis for metopism is incompletely understood, most workers are confident that the trait has a large genetic component (Hauser & De Stefano, 1989). A long history of observation of this trait in human populations (e.g., Bolk, 1917) is available from many diverse geographic settings worldwide. Virtually all populations with data available on frequency of metopism show less than 10% (Sering & Larsen, 1993). Observation of the Cross series reveals that four full (Fig. 3) and five partial metopic sutures are present among 14 observable crania, representing a frequency of 64.4% with a suture. Given the probable high level of genetic involvement in this trait, this extraordinarily high frequency suggests a nonrandom pattern that is consistent with a family or closely related families being buried in the Cross cemetery.

## SUMMARY AND CONCLUSIONS

The study of the Cross cemetery human remains offers a fund of data on biological characteristics of a pioneer group dating to the initial settlement period of central

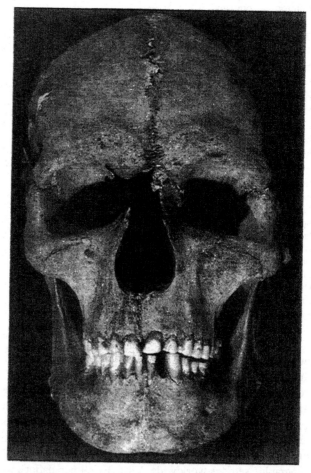

**FIGURE 3.** A full metopic suture from an adult male, Cross cemetery (burial 23).

Illinois and the opening the American Midwest. Based on the presence of three grave markers (belonging to Alvin Cross and two of his daughters), historical documentation, and biological evidence (especially metopism), the majority of interments in the cemetery are believed to be associated with the Cross family, a pioneer family who emigrated to Sangamon County, Illinois, in 1829. Other families, however, may also be represented in the cemetery. The family or families interred in the cemetery were representative of an agrarian-oriented community sharing similar religious beliefs, socioeconomic status, and family relationships. As burial shifted from interment on the family farm to other facilities (e.g., church and town cemeteries) in the mid-19th century, the cemetery was abandoned and eventually forgotten.

Key findings of the study include the following:

1) The Cross family experienced high mortality and low life expectancy at birth ($e_x$ = 18.4 years). However, examination of historical documentation (e.g., Power, 1876) indicates that many children surviving to adulthood left the family farm, eventually being buried elsewhere, reminding us that cemetery populations are fraught with biases that must be accounted for when interpreting population profiles based on archaeologically recovered skeletal series. Nevertheless, historical accounts indicate that life expectancy at birth and childhood was somewhat lower than other 19th century settings.

2) Observation of skeletal pathology suggests that this group led a demanding, harsh existence. For example, presence of cribra orbitalia indicates that iron-deficiency anemia was present. Enamel defects (hypoplasia) resulting from physiological disruption were also present in most individuals. However, the frequency of these conditions is considerably lower than those recorded for the 19th century Monroe County Poorhouse in New York State.

The presence of degenerative joint pathology (osteoarthritis, Schmorl's depressions) shows that the group was physically active and subject to strenuous behaviors characteristic of rural life on the Illinois frontier. On the other hand, there is relatively little evidence of skeletal responses to chronic infection. One difficulty in assessing levels of infectious conditions from skeletal series, however, is that an acute infectious disease leading to rapid death will not be exhibited in skeletal tissues. Nonetheless, abundant morbidity data for the first half of the 19th century in Illinois indicates that a variety of fatal infectious diseases were present in rural Illinois, including tuberculosis, typhoid fever, cholera, and malaria.

3) Study of dental caries and premortem tooth loss reveals extremely poor dental health in the Cross group. The lack of fillings and presence of widespread tooth decay, tooth loss, and calculus deposition strongly suggests that this group had limited knowledge of personal oral hygiene and no access to professional dental care.

4) Study of occlusal surfaces of teeth indicates consumption of hard foods and associated abrasives leading to excessive wear. Unusual patterns of occlusal surface wear and anterior tooth trauma indicate that at least some of the adults—both males and females—used their teeth in extramasticatory capacities, perhaps for gripping and pulling of leather or some other material that would result in loss or fracture of dental enamel and dentin.

5) Analysis of stable carbon and nitrogen isotopes indicates that the Cross group

consumed maize, almost certainly grown on the homestead, and had regular access to fish, probably captured in the nearby Sugar Creek.

6) Cranial and postcranial measurements and morphological observations indicate that this group was similar to other Euroamericans. For example, stature of adult females and males is similar to other 19th century samples reported in the literature, suggesting that despite the presence of a variety of hardships, nutrition was adequate.

7) An extraordinarily high frequency of metopism (64.4%) is consistent with archaeological and historical documentation that the cemetery is likely dominated by the presence of one family or closely related families.

## ACKNOWLEDGMENTS

Support for the excavation and follow-up study of the Cross skeletal series came from Roosevelt National Life Insurance Company, Springfield, Illinois. The authors thank Mr. Joseph H. Metzger and Mr. Ed Grunloh of Roosevelt National Life Insurance for their support and cooperation during all stages of the investigation, and especially for their concern for the history of Sangamon County. The photography for Fig. 3 was completed by Mark C. Griffin. An earlier version of this paper was presented at the 1992 Midwest Archaeological Conference held in Grand Rapids, Michigan. We thank Anne Grauer for her invitation to contribute to this book and for her helpful suggestions for improvement of the manuscript.

## REFERENCES

Angel JL (1964). The reaction area of the femoral neck. Clin Orthop 32:130–142.

Angel JL (1976). Colonial to modern skeletal change in the U.S.A. Am J Phys Anthropol 45:723–735.

Bolk L (1917). On metopism. Am J Anat 22:27–47.

Buikstra JE (1992). Diet and disease in late prehistory. In Verano JW, Ubelaker DH (eds.), Disease and Demography in the Americas, pp. 87–101. Washington: Smithsonian Institution Press.

Buikstra JE, Milner GR (1991). Isotopic and archaeological interpretations of diet in the central Mississippi Valley. J Archaeol Science 18:319–329.

Craig J, Larsen CS (1993). Archaeological and Osteological Investigations at the Cross Cemetery, Sangamon County, Illinois. Contract report prepared for Roosevelt National Life Insurance Company. Springfield: Hanson Engineers Incorporated.

Cybulski JS (1988). Skeletons in the walls of Old Quebec. Northeast Hist Archaeol 17:61–84.

Elia RJ, Wesolowsky AB (eds.) (1991). Archaeological Excavations at the Uxbridge Almshouse Burial Ground in Uxbridge, Massachusetts. Brit Archaeol Rep S564.

Faragher JM (1986). Sugar Creek: Life on the Illinois Prairie. New Haven: Yale University Press.

Finnegan M (1976). Walnut Creek massacre: Identification and analysis. Am J Phys Anthropol 45:737–742.

Goodman AH, Rose JC (1990). Assessment of systemic physiological perturbations from dental enamel hypoplasia and associated histological structures. Yearbook Phys Anthropol 33:59–110.

Goodman AH, Rose JC (1991). Dental enamel hypoplasia as indicators of nutritional status. In Kelley MA, Larsen CS (eds.), Advances in Dental Anthropology, pp. 279–293. New York: Wiley-Liss.

Hauser G, De Stefano GF (1989). Epigenetic Variants of the Human Skull. Stuttgart: E. Schweizerbart'sche Verlagsbuchhandlung.

Jantz RL, Ousley SD (1993). FORDISC 1.0: Computerized Forensic Discriminant Functions. Knoxville: Department of Anthropology, University of Tennessee.

Jenkinson, BL, Handler AB, Lerner W (1949). Historic Statistics of the United States, 1789–1945: A Supplement to the Statistical Abstract of the United States. Washington: U.S. Government Printing Office.

Katzenberg MA (1991). Stable isotope analysis of remains from the Harvie family. In Saunders S, Lazenby R (eds.), The Links that Bind: The Harvie Family Nineteenth Century Burying Ground. Occ Pap Northeastern Archaeol 5:65–69.

Keeler CE (1930). "Parted parietals" in mice. J Hered 21:19–20, 83.

Kennedy KAR (1989). Skeletal markers of occupation stress. In Iscan MY, Kennedy KAR (eds.), Reconstruction of Life from the Skeleton, pp. 129–160. New York: Liss.

Komlos J (1987). The height and weight of West Point cadets: Dietary change in Antebellum America. J Econ Hist 47:897–927.

Lanphear KM (1990). Frequency and distribution of enamel hypoplasia in a historic skeletal sample. Am J Phys Anthropol 81:35–43.

Larsen CS (1987). Bioarchaeological interpretations of subsistence economy and behavior from human skeletal remains. In Schiffer MB (ed.), Advances in Archaeological Method and Theory, vol. 10, pp. 339–445. San Diego: Academic Press.

Little BJ, Lanphear KM, Owsley DW (1992). Mortuary display and status in a 19th-century Anglo-American cemetery in Manassas, Virginia. Am Antiq 57:397–418.

Lovejoy CO, Meindl RS, Pryzbeck TR, Mensforth RP (1985). Chronological metamorphosis of the auricular surface of the ilium: A new method for the determination of adult skeletal age at death. Am J Phys Anthropol 68:15–28.

Meindl RS, Lovejoy CO (1985). Ectocranial suture closure: A revised method for the determination of skeletal age at death based on the lateral-anterior sutures. Am J Phys Anthropol 68:57–66.

Meindl RS, Lovejoy CO, Mensforth RP, Walker RA (1985). A revised method of age determination using the os pubis, with a review and tests of accuracy of other current methods of pubic symphyseal aging. Am J Phys Anthropol 68:29–45.

Merbs CF (1989). Trauma. In Iscan MY, Kennedy KAR (eds.), Reconstruction of Life from the Skeleton, pp. 161–189. New York: Liss.

Moorrees CFA (1957). The Aleut Dentition: A Correlative Study of Dental Characteristics in an Eskimoid People. Cambridge: Harvard University Press.

Moorrees CFA, Fanning EA, Hunt EE Jr. (1963a). Formation and resorption of three deciduous teeth in children. Am J Phys Anthropol 21:205–213.

Moorrees CFA, Fanning EA, Hunt EE Jr. (1963b). Age variation of formation stages for ten permanent teeth. J Dent Res 42:1490–1502.

Nelson LH (1968). Nail chronology as an aid to dating old buildings. Am Assoc State Local Hist Tech Leaf 48, Hist News 24(1).

Owsley DW (1990). The skeletal biology of North American historical populations. In Buikstra JE (ed.), A Life in Science: Papers in Honor of J. Lawrence Angel. Center Am Archaeol Scientific Pap 6:171–190.

Pfeiffer S, Dudar JC, Austin S (1989). Prospect Hill: Skeletal remains from a 19th-century Methodist cemetery, Newmarket, Ontario. Northeast Hist Archaeol 18:29–48.

Pfeiffer S, Williamson RF (eds.) (1991). Snake Hill: An Investigation of a Military Cemetery from the War of 1812. Toronto: Dundurn Press.

Power JC (1876). History of the Early Settlers of Sangamon County, Illinois: "Centennial Record." Springfield: Edwin A. Wilson and Company.

Rathbun TA, Scurry JD (1991). Status and health in colonial South Carolina: Belleview Plantation, 1738–1756. In Powell ML, Bridges PS, Mires AMW (eds.), What Mean These Bones? Studies in Southeastern Bioarchaeology, pp. 148–164. Tuscaloosa: University of Alabama Press.

Rawlings ID (1927). The Rise and Fall of Disease in Illinois. Springfield: State Department of Public Health.

Ruff CB (1987). Sexual dimorphism in human lower limb bone structure: Relationship to subsistence strategy and sexual division of labor. J Hum Evol 16:391–416.

Saunders S (1991). Sex determination, stature and size and shape variation of the limb bones. In Pfeiffer S, Williamson RF (eds.), Snake Hill: An Investigation of a Military Cemetery from the War of 1812, pp. 176–197. Toronto: Dundurn Press.

Saunders S, Katzenberg MA (eds.) (1992). Skeletal Biology of Past Peoples: Research Methods. New York: Wiley-Liss.

Saunders S, Lazenby R (1992). The Links that Bind: The Harvie Family Nineteenth Century Burying Ground. Occ Pap Northeastern Archaeol 5.

Schoeninger MJ, DeNiro MJ (1984). Nitrogen and carbon isotopic composition of bone collagen from marine and terrestrial animals. Geochim Cosmochim Acta 48:625–639.

Schoeninger MJ, Moore K (1992). Bone stable isotope studies in archaeology. J World Prehist 6:247–296.

Schoeninger MJ, van der Merwe NJ, Moore K, Lee-Thorp J, Larsen CS (1990). Decrease in diet quality between the prehistoric and contact periods. In Larsen CS (ed.), The Archaeology of Mission Santa Catalina de Guale: 2. Biocultural Interpretations of Population in Transition. Anthropol Pap Am Mus Nat Hist 68:78-93.

Schwarcz HP, Melbye J, Katzenberg MA, Knyf M (1985). Stable isotopes in human skeletons of southern Ontario: Reconstructing paleodiet. J Archaeol Science 12:187–206.

Sciulli PW, Gramly RM (1989). Analysis of Ft. Laurens, Ohio, Skeletal Sample. Am J Phys Anthropol 80:11–24.

Sering LE, Larsen CS (1993). Metopism in a Euroamerican pioneer series from central Illinois. Poster, American Association of Physical Anthropology annual meeting, Toronto.

Shapiro HL (1930). Old New Yorkers: A series of crania from the Nagel Burying Ground, New York City. Am J Phys Anthropol 14:379–404.

Steckel RH (1979). Slave height profiles from coastwise manifests. Explorations Econ Hist 16:363–380.

Steckel RH (1983). Height and per capita income. Historical Methods 16:1–7.

Stewart TD (1979). Essentials of Forensic Anthropology. Springfield: Charles C Thomas.

Stuart-Macadam PL (1989). Nutritional deficiency diseases: A survey of scurvy, rickets, and iron-deficiency anemia. In Iscan MY, Kennedy KAR (eds.), Reconstruction of Life from the Skeleton, pp. 201–222. New York: Liss.

Thomas DH, South S, Larsen CS (1977). Rich Man, Poor Men: Observations on Three Antebellum Burials from the Georgia Coast. Anthropol Pap Am Mus Nat Hist 53:393–420.

Thompson WS, Whelpton PK (1933). Population Trends in the United States. New York: McGraw-Hill.

Todd TW (1920). Age changes in the pubic bone: I. The White male pubis. Am J Phys Anthropol 9:98–102, 193–210.

Torgersen JH (1951). The developmental genetics and evolutionary meaning of the metopic suture. Am J Phys Anthropol 9:98–102, 193–210.

Torgersen JH (1963). Uber erbfaktoren fur die ausbildung von schadelnahten und deren aussagewert uber den hominisationsblauf. Homo 14:16–29.

Trotter M (1970). Estimation of stature from intact long bones. In Stewart TD (ed.), Personal Identification in Mass Disasters, pp. 71–83. Washington: National Museum of Natural History.

Turner II CG (1991). The Dentition of Arctic Peoples. New York: Garland Publishing.

Ubelaker DH (1989). Human Skeletal Remains: Excavation, Analysis, Interpretation (2nd Edition). Washington, D.C.: Taraxacum.

van der Merwe NJ (1982). Carbon isotopes, photosynthesis, and archaeology. Am Scien 70:596–606.

Wood JW, Milner GR, Harpending HC, Weiss KM (1992). The osteological paradox: Problems of inferring prehistoric health from skeletal samples. Curr Anthropol 33:343–370.

Wood WD, Burns KR, Lee SR (1986). The Mt. Gilead Cemetery Study: An Example of Biocultural Analysis from Western Georgia. Athens, GA: Southeastern Archeological Services, Inc.

# 10 Health and Hard Times: A Case Study From the Middle to Late Nineteenth Century in Eastern Texas

FRANK WINCHELL, JEROME C. ROSE,
and RANDALL W. MOIR

## INTRODUCTION

Bioarchaeologists often regard the study of small skeletal populations to be so fraught with interpretive problems that they warrant only descriptive treatment. In other words, significant trends are not discernable from small samples. On some occasions, however, small skeletal samples can be highly informative and can tell us much about the living conditions of a particular sector of the population. For example, the health and welfare of lower- and middle-class households is not readily documented in historical records of 19th century Texas, but this information *is* encoded in the interred physical remains of its former inhabitants. In this chapter we provide an example of the potential contributions of small historic cemetery studies when excavation is thorough and osteological techniques are comprehensively applied.

One critical component necessary in the study of interred individuals is comprehensive excavation. Comprehensive excavation includes the recovery of not only the denser skeletal remains and major durable artifacts, but also the fragile and extremely small items often present under conditions of poor preservation. The recovery techniques used in the excavation of the cemetery referred to as 41DT105 were designed to retrieve such fragile remains as enamel tooth caps and small pieces of rusted iron or small iron coffin-liner tacks. These field and laboratory methods were the cumulative results of more than a decade of refinements developed by Rose on historic graves (e.g., Rose et al., 1985; Rose, in Lebo, 1988) and are presented in detail in the 41DT105 site report (Winchell et al., 1992, pp. 35–50). While not practical in all

*Bodies of Evidence*, Edited by Anne L. Grauer.
ISBN 0-471-04153-X   © 1995 John Wiley & Sons, Inc.

situations, such as some emergency recoveries, the formally planned disinterment of burials at 41DT105 allowed for the use of methods that were more refined than those implemented by other cemetery-relocation projects. This kind of comprehensive excavation guaranteed the retrieval of practically all contents from each grave.

## THE SITE

Site 41DT105 was a small, unmarked cemetery located in Delta County, Texas approximately 3 miles south of Cooper, the county's largest town and county seat. The cemetery was used in the mid-to-late 19th century (i.e., 1850–1880) to bury local residents from the community known as Granny's Neck. 41DT105 was abandoned as other larger cemeteries gained greater use and acceptance, and by the 1920s it was no longer maintained. Had it not been for the memory of several elderly informants and the efforts of archaeologists, the cemetery would have been submerged by the waters of Cooper Lake, a reservoir under construction by the U.S. Army Corps of Engineers. Instead, cemetery 41DT105 was located in 1986 through a joint effort by the University of North Texas and the U.S. Army Corps of Engineers, Fort Worth District. Careful removal of the A-horizon by machinery relocated the cemetery and revealed rectangular outlines of 16 grave shafts (Lebo, 1988).

In 1989, 16 graves at 41DT105 were disinterred by the Corps of Engineers using the expertise of physical anthropologists and archaeologists under contract with Southern Methodist University (Winchell et al., 1992). Over 2,400 nonskeletal artifacts were removed, including coffin parts (e.g., nails, lining tacks, and screws), clothing-related items (e.g., buttons, shoe parts, jewelry, buckles, dress hooks), and miscellaneous items (e.g., swan shot). Only one rectangular casket was evident—the other graves contained the remains of hexagonal pine coffins. All had minimal decorative trimmings. No metal coffin handles, decorative coffin tacks, name plates, or other commercial metal hardware, typically found with mid-19th century burials, were present other than white-metal screws used to secure the lids and small iron tacks used to attach inner cloth linings.

The absence of decorative coffin hardware, beyond white-metal screws used to fasten lids on simple pine boxes, is a striking trait for all interments. Comparisons with other contemporary cemeteries underscore the impoverished conditions of the interments. The absence of simple iron handles for even the rectangular casket indicates limited economic resources. The recovery of machine-made white-metal coffin screws from seven coffins indicate that specialized coffin trimmings were available for those who could pay the price. Evidently, the families who buried their dead at 41DT105 could not or chose not to spend money on anything but the very simplest coffin.

The economic profile reconstructed for the entire 41DT105 cemetery population ranks the group at the lower end of the socioeconomic scale. No precious-metal or plated-metal effects, coins, or expensive jewelry were present within the burials. In three cases, glass beads and copper-alloy pins or brooches of very inexpensive manufacture were the only decorative grave goods. Even the few clothing remains present revealed little more than unembellished burial shrouds or plain garments. All of these data indicate interment situations where families spared only enough money to secure the simplest coffins and chose not to bestow any other valuable personal possessions with the deceased other than minimal clothing or a shroud.

## BIOLOGICAL PATTERNS

The goal of the biological analysis is to provide evidence of the general living conditions in northeast Texas during the mid-19th century. Demographic data from 41DT105 are compared to similar data from other contemporary cemetery-site analyses (from Texas and Oklahoma) as well as from census data from this area of Texas during the time period in question. Paleopathology provides evidence of general and specific stress. Possible cause(s) of death, pathologies, indications of childhood nutritional/disease stress, and trauma-related osteological anomalies were therefore recorded.

### Demographic Analysis

Demography, the study of birth and death patterning by age and sex, is the most biologically meaningful measure of a population's adaptive success. Although the use of skeletal remains alone cannot produce all of the data necessary for accurate demographic reconstruction (e.g., numbers of births), and the available data are seldom sufficient (e.g., accurate ages at death and large sample size); demographic interpretation using skeletal remains still provides the most meaningful insight into the biological history of a given sample population.

Since the preservation of skeletal material at 41DT105 was extremely poor, determination of age at death relied predominantly on dental development in sub-adults and occlusal enamel-wear patterns in adults. Age determination is, therefore, quite crude for adults.

The demographic analysis identified a total of 16 individuals—ten fully mature adults (three males, three females, one possible male, one possible female, and two indeterminate), one young adult male, one adolescent (sex indeterminate), two young children (one female, and one possible male), and two infants under ten months old (sex indeterminate).

The age-at-death profile constructed for the 41DT105 population (Table 1) consists of the number of individuals per 10-year interval, converted into the percentage of the entire burial population. These data are compared to profiles derived from other cemetery sites, as well as 1800s census data. The percentages of total deaths for Texans east of the Colorado River (Burnett, 1988, p. 103) was chosen because of the geographical location and the similar time period.

The cemetery data used for comparison were also chosen for similarity in dates of interment and geographical proximity. The Tucker Cemetery, for instance, a family cemetery located to the northeast of 41DT105 in Delta County, was used between 1880 and 1942 (Burnett, 1988, p. 108). The Dawson Cemetery, a community cem-

**TABLE 1. Demographic Comparisons for East Texas, 41DT105, and Several Mid-to-Late 19th-Century Cemeteries, by Percentage of Total Deaths per Age Group**

| Age group (in years) | Texas 1870[a] (%) | 41DT105 (%) | Tucker (%) | Dawson (%) | Five Cemeteries (%) | McGee Creek (%) | Morgan Chapel (%) |
|---|---|---|---|---|---|---|---|
| 0–1 | 23.0 | 12.5 | 27.3 | 4.3 | 18.2 | 11.1 | 50.0 |
| 1–10 | 25.3 | 12.5 | 0.0 | 26.1 | 30.3 | 22.2 | 16.7 |
| 10–20 | 11.1 | 12.5 | 0.0 | 0.0 | 12.1 | 22.2 | 11.1 |
| 20–30 | 11.8 | 12.5 | 27.3 | 8.7 | 6.1 | 0.0 | 0.0 |
| 30–40 | 9.1 | 12.5 | 9.1 | 21.7 | 9.1 | 0.0 | 0.0 |
| 40–50 | 6.7 | 12.5 | 9.1 | 13.0 | 12.1 | 0.0 | 0.0 |
| 50+ | 12.8 | 25.0 | 27.3 | 26.1 | 12.1 | 44.4 | 22.2 |
| Total (n) | 9,015 | 16 | 11 | 23 | 33 | 9 | 18 |

Sources: Texas in 1870 (Burnett, 1988, p. 103); Tucker Cemetery (Lebo, 1988); Dawson Cemetery (Burnett, 1988, p. 99); Five Cemeteries (Fox, 1984); McGee Creek (Ferguson, 1983); Morgan Chapel (Taylor et al., 1986).
[a]Percent of total deaths east of the Colorado River.

etery located to the north and slightly east of 41DT105 in the same county, provides tombstone data for the period between 1865 and 1900 (Burnett, 1988, p. 99). The "Five Cemeteries" data are from the grave relocations of five late-19th-century family cemeteries along the Frio River in Live Oak and McMullen counties, in south Texas (Fox, 1984, p. 2). These data have been combined for comparison with 41DT105. The McGee Creek data derive from the relocation of two late-19th-century Atoka County family cemeteries in southeastern Oklahoma (Ferguson, 1983). The Morgan Chapel data derive from the relocation of graves dating between 1891 and 1937 in Bastrop County, Texas (Taylor et al., 1986).

The 1870 east Texas census data show that 59.4% of all deaths occurred prior to 20 years of age and that 23.0% of the births resulted in death prior to completion of the first year of life (see Table 1). These figures suggest high levels of stress associated with birth and development on the frontier, and are consistent with conditions described by historians (Smallwood, 1975, pp. 81–82; West, 1989, pp. 213–244). The 41DT105 mortality profile is approximately 50% lower than the 1870 census rate for the first 10 years of life, but is slightly higher in the ≥30 years categories. When the disparity of sample sizes (16 for 41DT105 and 9,015 for east Texas) is taken into account, the mortality profile of 41DT105 is remarkably similar to that of east Texas in 1870. The Tucker and Dawson cemeteries produce subadult mortality rates slightly lower than 41DT105, while the Five Cemeteries, McGee Creek, and Morgan Chapel localities all display higher rates. The low death rate for children under one year at the Dawson Cemetery may be due to the fact that these data are derived from tombstones, and young children may not have been provided stones, or, when they were, the stones may have been so small that they did not survive the ravages of time. In summary, these comparisons show that 41DT105 is typical of 19th-century rural family cemeteries and that high subadult mortality was common.

## Paleopathological Analysis

The observation of skeletal lesions was greatly hindered by poor skeletal preservation. Only individuals aged 16 years or older are included in the calculation of pathological lesions because the subadults were too poorly preserved for consistent observation, resulting in too small a sample for comparison to other collections (Table 2). The goal of the paleopathological analysis was to assess the patterns of health and disease in this population as a means towards gaining insight into life in 19th-century Texas. Five pathological indicators of stress were focussed upon in this study: the presence of periosteal reactions (an indication of acute or chronic infection); osteoarthritic or degenerative lesions of the joints (an indication of occupational stress); trauma (an indication of hardship and/or violence); dental caries (an indication of the consumption of high-sugar or high-carbohydrate diets and poor dental hygiene); and enamel hypoplasias and Wilson bands (indicators of developmental growth disruption of dental enamel).

The analysis of periosteal reactions indicated that two individuals displayed infectious lesions. Burial 2 exhibited periosteal reactions of the tibia, while Burial 13 showed striations of the femoral shaft possibly indicative of infection. The resultant frequency rate for infection of 20% is probably an underestimation because the tibial shaft surfaces, the most frequent sites of lesions, were all only partially preserved and one adult had none. The infection rates from Tucker, the Five Cemeteries, and Morgan Chapel are probably also underestimated because of poor preservation and limited opportunity for detailed observation.

The rate of degenerative disease (i.e., arthritis of the joints and osteophytosis of the spine) for 41DT105 is 20%. Burial 16 exhibits initial degeneration of the right hip joint and spinal osteoarthritis, while the left hip joint of Burial 11 suggests the initial

**TABLE 2. Paleopathology Comparisons for Individuals over 16 Years of Age from 41DT105 and Several Mid-to-Late 19th-Century Cemeteries**

|  | 41DT105 | | Tucker[a] | | Five Cemeteries | | Morgan Chapel | |
|---|---|---|---|---|---|---|---|---|
|  | % | n | % | n | % | n | % | n |
| Infections | 20.0 | (10) | 0.0 | (4) | 0.0 | (26) | 33.3 | (3) |
| Degenerative | 20.0 | (10) | 66.6 | (3) | 7.7 | (26) | — | (0) |
| Trauma | 30.0 | (10) | 25.0 | (4) | 7.7 | (26) | 50.0 | (2) |
| Caries[b] | 70.0 | (10) | 66.6 | (6) | 16.7 | (12) | 50.0 | (4) |

[a]Burnett (1988, p. 104).
[b]Caries rate calculated from all erupted and observable permanent teeth.

stages of degenerative disease. The presence of sesamoid bones in Burials 9 and 15 indicates some joint stress, and the heavy muscle development of Burials 11 and 16 may imply relatively strenuous vocations for these individuals. It is suspected that if the other skeletons were as well-preserved as Burial 16, then the degenerative disease rates would be higher.

The trauma rate of 30% in the 41DT105 cemetery does not include the possible death, by fire, of Burial 15. Identified traumatic skeletal lesions include damage to the muscle attachments of the femur (Burial 2), a possible blow to the back of the head (Burial 9), and probable death by gunshot (Burial 8). It has been suggested that accidents to both children and adults were common on the frontier, but were not a major cause of death, at least for children (West, 1989, p. 219). Burnings, caused by catching one's clothing on fire, were also frequent (West, 1989, p. 224) and could be used to infer the possible cause of death for Burial 15, which displayed charred bones.

Violent death from gunshot wounds is likewise an expected frontier phenomenon. A feud that resulted in a pair of killings explains two circa 1860 graves that were relocated in McMullen County (Fox, 1984, p. 9). It should be noted, however, that not all gunshot wounds are purposefully inflicted. West (1989, p. 223) reports that 5% of 40 accidental childhood deaths were due to gunshot wounds. Consequently, we do not know whether the older woman occupying Grave 8 died of a purposeful or accidental double discharge of swan shot. Seventeen 8.2 mm mean diameter lead shot fragments were recovered from the cranial and upper torso areas. It is most likely that accidental injury was as common among the Granny's Neck families as elsewhere in the rural United States.

Dental caries or decay was common at 41DT105, with 70% of the population displaying at least one dental lesion. Per individual, however, caries were not numerous (only 1.45 caries per person). The prevalence of caries at 41DT105 is similar to Tucker and Morgan Chapel cemeteries, but much higher than in the Five Cemeteries sample. The caries-per-person rate is lower than the rate noted for prehistoric horticultural Native Americans residing in the Trans-Mississippi South (Rose et al., 1984) and may suggest a limited availability of refined sugars and carbohydrates to the families of 41DT105. The absence of purchased sugars in the diet of these individuals is understandable, considering that their impoverished grave furniture bespeaks impoverished living standards. The lack of spatial patterning of the presence of carious lesions within the cemetery suggests that there was little or no dietary change over time.

## Evidence of Stress

The pattern and severity of childhood stress can be reconstructed using both demography and dental-defect frequencies per individual. The number and ages at death of children interred at 41DT105 measures the difficulty of surviving the rigors of childhood in this environment. The subadult mortality rate at 41DT105 and the census data from east Texas (Burnett, 1988, p. 103) indicate that childhood stress was much higher than in more recent times. The stress pattern from 41DT105 is reconstructed using both histologically verified enamel hypoplasias and Wilson Bands from the teeth of both children and adults. Because the hypoplasia data from 41DT105 have been histologically verified, it must be emphasized that they are probably among the most conservative reported frequencies. Comparisons with other reported data are limited because there are not, as yet, any uniformly applied standards for identifying hypoplasias. For these reasons, only those hypoplasia and Wilson Band data that were collected using criteria similar to that employed in the 41DT105 analysis are referenced in this interpretation.

Of the four 41DT105 subadults, 75% had at least one Wilson Band, 50% had at least one hypoplasia, and 75% had at least one 6-month period with a stress episode (Table 3). Two of the three subadults with deciduous teeth show evidence of stress in the neonatal period (i.e., just before, during, and after birth). Burial 12 had five more stress episodes (i.e., five Wilson Bands and two hypoplasias) before dying at 3–4 years of age. Burial 3 had a continuous stress period (continuous hypoplasia) from 2–5 years of age and eight acute episodes (Wilson Bands) before dying at 12–15 years of age. These data suggest chronic and frequent periods of childhood stress. Goodman et al. (1987) report that 46.7% of 300 Latino children from the Solis Valley of Mexico had at least one enamel defect. El-Najjar et al. (1978) report 26% and 49% hypoplasias from contemporary white and black Cleveland school children, respectively. Although these figures are not exactly comparable because the contemporary samples had survived childhood, the children at 41DT105 appear to have been subjected to the same or higher stress as the Mexican and Cleveland black children.

Of the nine adults at 41DT105, 78% had at least one Wilson Band, 56% had at least one hypoplasia, and 78% experienced at least one 6-month period with a stress episode (Table 3). Of the six adults with teeth from the Tucker Cemetery, 100% had at least one hypoplasia (Burnett, 1988, p. 105). Interestingly, the eight prehistoric adults excavated as part of the Cooper Lake project (i.e., sites 41DT80, 41DT124, and 41HP78) all had at least one hypoplasia (Burnett & Harmon, 1989). These frequencies suggest the possibility that childhood in this part of east Texas had always been stressful.

Another method of reporting stress frequencies (Rose et al., 1985) is to calculate the number of 6-month enamel units that preserve a Wilson Band and/or hypoplasia, standardized by the number of individuals or total 6-month enamel units observed. Using age-specific 6-month enamel units as the denominator in rate calculation,

**TABLE 3. Percentage of 41DT105 Individuals Who Had at Least One Wilson Band and/or Hypoplasia**

| Dental Defect | Adults | | Subadults | | Total | |
|---|---|---|---|---|---|---|
| | % | n | % | n | % | n |
| Wilson Bands | 78 | (9) | 75 | (4) | 77 | (13) |
| Hypoplasias | 56 | (9) | 50 | (4) | 54 | (13) |
| Combined | 78 | (9) | 75 | (4) | 77 | (13) |

rather than the number of individuals, controls for enamel missing due to tooth wear and interrupted dental development. The sample from 41DT105 exhibited 2.8 Wilson Bands per individual and 0.27 per enamel unit (Table 4). As a comparison, 15 adult Mayans dating to the time of Spanish contact had 2.4 Wilson Bands per person (Wright, 1987) and Woodland period Native Americans from the Libben site in Ohio exhibited 0.07 Wilson Bands per person and 0.02 per enamel unit (Boyd, 1978). The frequencies at 41DT105 are slightly higher than the highly stressed Contact period Mayans and significantly higher than those for the well-adapted Libben people. The hypoplasia frequencies at 41DT105 are 2.2 per individual and 0.21 per enamel unit, slightly lower than the 3.5 hypoplasias per person for the Contact period Mayans (Wright, 1987) and significantly higher than the 0.3 hypoplasias per person and 0.1 per enamel unit at the Libben site (Boyd, 1978). These comparisons strongly suggest that the children at 41DT105 experienced high levels of childhood stress.

The percentages of observed 6-month enamel units with an enamel defect (Wilson Band, hypoplasia, or both), indicating a stress episode, provide the following reconstruction of the age-specific pattern of stress (see Table 5). Stress during the neonatal period is high with two of the three subadults with deciduous teeth exhibiting abnormal neonatal lines. Stress is high during the first year (42% of the total population), slowly increases to a high (60% of the population) at 3.75 years, and then gradually declines to a low (12% of the total population) at 6.25 years. Taking into account that some of the fluctuations in the percentages of stress episodes are due to small sample size, this chronological distribution demonstrates that childhood stress at 41DT105 was high and remained consistently high from birth until 5.5 years of age. The legitimacy of this pattern is established by comparison with the Tucker hypoplasia data (Burnett, 1988, p. 105) which are virtually identical. Childhood stress does not appear to have changed significantly between the middle to late 19th century (41DT105 cemetery) and the late 19th to 20th century (Tucker cemetery) in Delta County, Texas.

Analysis of the Texas census data from the decades between 1850 and 1880 (Burnett, 1988, p. 103) reveals that childhood stress in each decade remained roughly the same in the two age categories of birth–1 year and 1–5 years, before declining significantly in the 5–10 year age group. Therefore, the distributions of mortality (census data; Burnett, 1988, p. 103) and stress (dental-defect data, see Table 5) are

**TABLE 4. Number of Wilson Bands and/or Hypoplasias per Individual and 6-Month Enamel Units at 41DT105**

| Dental Defect | Individual | | Enamel Unit | |
|---|---|---|---|---|
| | % | n | % | n |
| Wilson Bands | 2.8 | (13) | 0.27 | (135) |
| Hypoplasias | 2.2 | (13) | 0.21 | (135) |
| Combined | 3.5 | (13) | 0.30 | (135) |

TABLE 5. Percentage Distribution of One or More Wilson Bands, Hypoplasias, and Both, Combined per 6-Month Observed Enamel Units at 41DT105

| Age | Subadults | | | | Adults | | | | Combined | | | |
|---|---|---|---|---|---|---|---|---|---|---|---|---|
| | E (n) | WB (%) | H (%) | B (%) | E (n) | WB (%) | H (%) | B (%) | E (n) | WB (%) | H (%) | B (%) |
| Prenatal | 3 | 67 | 0 | 67 | — | — | — | — | 3 | 67 | 0 | 67 |
| 0.0–0.53 | 3 | 0 | 0 | 0 | 7 | 0 | 0 | 0 | 10 | 0 | 0 | 0 |
| 0.5–1.0 | 3 | 67 | 0 | 67 | 9 | 33 | 0 | 33 | 12 | 42 | 0 | 42 |
| 1.0–1.5 | 3 | 67 | 0 | 67 | 9 | 0 | 0 | 0 | 12 | 17 | 0 | 17 |
| 1.5–2.0 | 3 | 33 | 0 | 33 | 9 | 44 | 33 | 44 | 12 | 42 | 25 | 42 |
| 2.0–2.5 | 3 | 67 | 67 | 67 | 9 | 33 | 22 | 33 | 12 | 42 | 33 | 42 |
| 2.5–3.0 | 2 | 50 | 50 | 50 | 8 | 25 | 38 | 50 | 10 | 30 | 40 | 50 |
| 3.0–3.5 | 2 | 100 | 100 | 100 | 8 | 0 | 12 | 12 | 10 | 20 | 30 | 30 |
| 3.5–4.0 | 2 | 0 | 50 | 50 | 8 | 50 | 38 | 62 | 10 | 40 | 40 | 60 |
| 4.0–4.5 | 1 | 100 | 100 | 100 | 8 | 38 | 50 | 50 | 9 | 44 | 56 | 56 |
| 4.5–5.0 | 1 | 100 | 100 | 100 | 8 | 25 | 38 | 38 | 9 | 33 | 44 | 44 |
| 5.0–5.5 | 1 | 100 | 0 | 100 | 8 | 12 | 12 | 25 | 9 | 22 | 11 | 33 |
| 5.5–6.0 | 1 | 0 | 0 | 0 | 8 | 0 | 0 | 0 | 9 | 0 | 0 | 0 |
| 6.0–6.5 | 1 | 100 | 0 | 100 | 7 | 0 | 0 | 0 | 8 | 12 | 0 | 12 |

Code: E- number of observed age specific 6-month enamel units; WB- Wilson Bands; H-hypoplasias; B- both Wilson Bands and hypoplasias.

similar, with a continuous high level of stress between birth and 5 years. This pattern is unusual in that most populations show a significant decline in mortality between the first year and the fourth year of life (see model life tables in Weiss, 1973). The children at 41DT105, and possibly all children in Delta County, Texas, were subjected to an unusually high level and pattern of stress between birth and 5 years.

## DISCUSSION

An explanation of childhood-stress patterns must consider both the high stress level and the relatively constant pattern of stress between birth and 5 years. Burnett (1988, pp. 95–106) provides such an interpretation in her treatment of the biohistory of the Tucker Cemetery. Using census data for mortality and cause of death, she identifies two distinct disease constellations for east Texas between 1850 and 1900. The first configuration (1850–1870) results from the Old World urban diseases and epidemics (many were pandemic) brought to east Texas by immigrants into the North American frontier. This configuration included unspecified fever, cholera, pneumonia, congestive fever, tuberculosis, typhoid fever, remittent fever, and scarlatina (Burnett, 1988, p. 101). The population of east Texas was too small for these diseases to remain endemic in the population and they would only appear following contact with immigrants or extralocal merchants. This is the disease profile that most likely severely impacted the children interred at 41DT105. The second configuration (1870–1900) is associated with the expansion of cultivated land and increased population density, which encouraged digestive disorders and malaria (Burnett, 1988, p. 96).

Endemic infectious diseases strike susceptible children in a very specific and predictable age pattern. When not endemic, but introduced from the outside, the exposure of children to pathogens would be chronologically random in terms of the age of incidence. This random appearance of childhood diseases would produce an even chronological pattern of illness and death, which appears in both the distribution of enamel defects and mortality at 41DT105.

Burnett (1988, p. 102) cites the poor sanitation measures and deficient diets of rural southern children as a definite source of childhood stress. Nutritional deficiencies would lower resistance to disease and produce more frequent and severe illnesses. Even mild disorders such as diarrhea (associated with unsanitary living conditions) would further exacerbate the poor nutrition and high susceptibility. Although the etiology of enamel defects is still unclear, poor nutrition is one of the most important factors that has been linked to increased frequencies of enamel defects (Rose et al., 1985). The high frequencies of both Wilson Bands and hypoplasias in the teeth from 41DT105, therefore, may indicate that poor nutrition and unsanitary living conditions were present.


## CONCLUSION

The demographic data obtained from the skeletal remains recovered at 41DT105 suggests that this cemetery is typical of small family cemeteries for eastern Texas during the third quarter of the 19th century. The high subadult mortality indicates high childhood stress and relatively low adaptive efficiency. Childhood stress was high for the individuals interred at 41DT105 and comparable to highly stressed contemporary populations. Comparisons with Tucker dental-defect frequencies and Texas mortality data indicates that childhood stress was high throughout eastern Texas in the late 19th century. High stress was probably associated with poor nutrition, unsanitary living conditions, and poverty. The even distribution of stress between birth and 5 years of age suggests that many of the diseases associated with the dental defects were urban and not endemic in the east Texas population.

The adult infection rate calculated for the 41DT105 population is probably a gross underestimation because of poor bone preservation. The presence of degenerative disease and well-developed muscle markings indicate heavy work loads and that life on the frontier was difficult. The trauma rate is evidence for accidents associated with heavy outdoor work and fires. One case of possible death by gunshot may indicate either interpersonal violence or an accidental death. The dental defects, in addition to suggesting high stress levels, suggests that many of the childhood diseases were imported by immigrants and merchants. Moreover, comparison of dental-defect frequencies between 41DT105 and the Tucker Cemetery suggests little change in childhood stress between the mid-19th and early 20th centuries in Delta County, Texas, and by inference, perhaps the rest of the east Texas frontier.

The analysis and interpretation of 41DT105 demonstrates the importance of small historic cemeteries. Throughout much of American history, residential populations were small and widely scattered and the small family cemeteries are representative of the people who lived there. When a number of these small cemeteries are combined for comparative analysis, clear patterns can and do emerge. The skeletal data must then be interpreted in light of the historic records, where each can make a contribution to our understanding of the past.

## ACKNOWLEDGMENTS

This chapter is derived from a report (Winchell et al., 1992) that was made possible through a contract (DACW-63-87-D-0017) provided by the U.S. Army Corps of Engineers, Fort Worth District. The report was produced by the Archaeology Research Program, Department of Anthropology at Southern Methodist University. Individuals at the U.S. Army Corps of Engineers who directly assisted in the planning and excavations for 41DT105 are Ms. Karen Scott and Mr. Erwin Roemer. We also wish to acknowledge the contributions of several individuals at the Archaeology Research Program who assisted in the production of the final report for 41DT105, particularly the efforts of Mr. David R. Pedler, Dr. Dennis C. Dirkmaat, Dr. J. M. Adovasio, Ms. Melissa Green, and Mr. David H. Jurney. We are also very indebted to many other people ranging from field assistants to consultants and administrators at both the U.S. Army Corps of Engineers and Southern Methodist University who were instrumental with the successful completion of the 41DT105 project. To all of them, we are grateful.

## REFERENCES

Boyd LF (1978). Evaluation of Wilson Bands as an Indicator of Childhood Stress: A Case Study of Developmental Enamel Defects in the Libben Skeletal Population. Master's thesis, University of Arkansas at Fayetteville.

Burnett BA (1988). Bioanthropological patterns. In Lebo S (ed.), An Archaeological and Bioarchaeological Perspective: The Tucker (41DT104) and Sinclair (41DT105) Cemeteries of Delta County, Texas. Institute of Applied Sciences, University of North Texas, Denton, Texas. Submitted to the U.S. Department of the Army, Fort Worth District, Corps of Engineers under Delivery Order No. 11, Contract No. DACW63-85-D-0066, pp. 95–114.

Burnett BA, Harmon A (1989). Descriptive osteology of 41DT80, 41DT124, and 41HP78. In Archaeological Investigations at Cooper Lake: 1987 Season. Draft Report. Archaeology Research Program, Institute for the Study of Earth and Man, Southern Methodist University, Dallas.

El-Najjar MY, DeSanti MV, Ozebek L (1978). Prevalence and possible etiology of dental enamel hypoplasia. Am J Phys Anthropol 48(2):185–192.

Ferguson B (1983). Final Report of the McGee Creek Cemetery Relocations, Atoka County, Oklahoma. Submitted to Bureau of Reclamation McGee Creek Project. Farris, Oklahoma.

Fox AA (1984). A Study of Five Historic Cemeteries at Choke Canyon Reservoir, Live Oak and McMullen Counties, Texas. Choke Canyon Series No. 9, Center for Archaeological Research, University of Texas at San Antonio, San Antonio.

Goodman AH, Allen LH, Hernandez GP, Amador A, Arriola LV, Chavez A, Pelto GH (1987). Prevalence and age at development of enamel hypoplasias in Mexican children. Am J Phys Anthropol 72(1):7–19.

Lebo SA (1988). An Archaeological and Bioarchaeological Perspective: The Tucker (41DT104) and Sinclair (41DT105) Cemeteries of Delta County, Texas. Institute of Applied Sciences, University of North Texas, Denton, Texas. Submitted to the U.S. Department of the Army, Fort Worth District, Corps of Engineers under Delivery Order No. 11, Contract No. DACW63-85-D-0066.

Rose JC, Burnett BA, Nassaney MS, Blaeuer MW (1984). Paleopathology and the origins of maize agriculture in the Lower Mississippi Valley and Caddoan Culture areas. In Cohen MN, Armelagos GJ (eds.), Paleopathology at the Origins of Agriculture, pp. 393–424. Orlando: Academic Press.

Rose JC, Condon KW, Goodman AH (1985). Diet and dentition: Developmental disturbances. In Gilbert RI, Mielke JH (eds.), The Analysis of Prehistoric Diets, pp. 281–305. Orlando: Academic Press.

Smallwood MAN (1975). Childhood on the Southern Plains Frontier; 1870–1910. Ph.D. dissertation, History. Texas Tech University, Lubbock.

Taylor AJ, Fox AA, Cox IW (1986). Archaeological Investigations at Morgan Chapel Cemetery (41BP200), A Historic Cemetery in Bastrop County, Texas. Archaeological Survey Report No. 146. Center for Archaeological Research, University of Texas at San Antonio, San Antonio.

Weiss KM (1973). Demographic Models for Anthropology. Society for American Archaeology Memoir 27.

West E (1989). Growing Up with the Country. University of New Mexico Press, Albuquerque, New Mexico.

Winchell F, Rose JC, Moir RW (1992). Bioanthropological Investigations of Nineteenth Century Burials at Site 41DT105. Archaeology Research Program, Department of Anthropology, Southern Methodist University, Dallas, Texas.

Wright LE (1987). Stresses of Conquest: A Scanning Electron Microscope Study of Wilson Bands and Enamel Hypoplasias in the Maya of Lamanai, Belize. Unpublished Bachelors thesis, Trent University, Peterborough, Ontario.

# 11 A Glimpse of Early Nineteenth Century Cincinnati as Viewed from Potter's Field: An Exercise in Problem Solving

ELIZABETH A. MURRAY and ANTHONY J. PERZIGIAN

## INTRODUCTION

Relatively few collections of skeletal material exist representing nonindigenous North American peoples from the 17th through 19th centuries. Though comparatively small in quantity, these collections provide significant clues to the lives of early European and West African inhabitants whose descendants have subsequently spread across and populated much of North America.

This chapter serves to highlight the need to examine and document historic exhumation and reinterment practices, in particular from sites known as "potter's fields." In addition, this study may provide evidence for biases possibly encountered by other researchers. Two potential sources of bias in recovery are discussed: one occurs at the time of initial disinterment and one potentially occurs upon the excavation of the more recent secondary site.

This study involves a quantity of commingled human bone recovered in May of 1988 from a communal cement crypt built in the early 20th century in downtown Cincinnati, Ohio. The discovery was made in the basement level of an elevator shaft in Cincinnati's Music Hall during installation of a new elevator system. A survey of various literature and maps, as well as a title search of the property, revealed more historical details of the site, which were used to enhance information derived from the bones.

*Bodies of Evidence*, Edited by Anne L. Grauer.
ISBN 0471-04153-X  © 1995 John Wiley & Sons, Inc.

## HISTORY OF THE SITE

The "Miami Country" along the Ohio River was explored by Europeans as early as 1751. By January of 1790, General St. Clair, the Governor of the Northwest Territory, had changed the then-named city of Losantiville to Cincinnati (Cincinnati Historical Society, 1988). Historical records indicate that the earliest settlers in Cincinnati came from many locations, but most were native-born Americans from the eastern states, primarily of English and Scottish ancestry. From its inception in 1803, Ohio was a free state, and although African Americans passed through the area frequently, many continued northward (Cincinnati Historical Society, 1988).

As settlement of the Cincinnati area continued, places of burial were established surrounding local places of worship. A map of 1819 reveals "Public Burying Ground" at a location known as "Outlot 53" on the northern edge of downtown Cincinnati. A title search of this property showed that it was transferred from private ownership to the City of Cincinnati in September of 1818. From this date the site served the city as a place of interment for commoners, the indigent, and recent migrants, at least until (and possibly for some time after) the next tenant of the property, the Cincinnati Orphan Asylum, took possession in 1837 (Murray, 1993).

Apparently, between 1818 and 1837, deceased "commoners" were continually filling the "Public Burying Ground." A city map of 1838 denotes no further indication of a burying ground at "Outlot 53." No reference was found to indicate any exhumation or removal of skeletal material when the Orphan Asylum was constructed.

By 1858, the property was used as a public park or square. In 1870, a new structure, Sangerfest Hall, was erected upon the former Public Burying Grounds. At the time of its construction skeletal remains were unearthed, as reported (six years later) in the *Cincinnati Commercial Newspaper.*

> Those bones were simply packed into a barrel and stowed away in a convenient part of the building, apparently much to the discomfort of their invisible owners. For skulls and thigh bones and vertebrae had been hopelessly jumbled up in that barrel, so that no one save a most expert articulator could have sorted them out properly (Hearn, 1876).

In 1876, the citizens of Cincinnati sought to build a more permanent Music Hall structure at the site. This necessitated exhumation of countless unidentifiable individuals once interred in the former cemetery. "This rich yellow soil, fat with the human flesh and bone and brain it has devoured, is being disemboweled by a hundred spades and forced to exhibit its ghastly secrets to the sun" (Hearn, 1876). The description of the excavation recounts large dry-goods boxes being filled with commingled skeletal elements, primarily composed of skulls and long bones. "Few of the smaller bones remain; none of those forming fingers and toes; no complete skeletons are exhumed. Most of the skulls are broken, crushed, crumbled in . . . " (Hearn, 1876).

Crowds formed around the exhumation, and without security guards, there was no means to protect the site from plunder.

Bone after bone as soon as thrown out is turned over with a scientific application of kicks; ragamuffins brandish femora with disgusting exultation; dirty fingers are poked into empty eye sockets . . . ribs crack in pitiful remonstrance to reckless feet . . . and by night there come medical students to steal the poor skulls (Hearn, 1876).

A transfer slip from Cincinnati's Spring Grove Cemetery, dated November of 1876, documents the eventual disposition of the remains from the Music Hall foundation excavation. The skeletons disinterred during the period 1876–1879, and relocated to Spring Grove Cemetery, do not constitute the sample herein studied. Documentation of the relocations, however, provides valuable testimony to the treatment and recovery processes that were carried out.

Remodeling of Cincinnati Music Hall in 1927, in preparation for the golden jubilee, brought further skeletal material to the surface. Between 65 and 70 grave sites were disturbed in at least three separate incidents during renovations. "The remains were given fitting burial in the pit of the new elevator shaft. Carefully cemented in a four-foot vault, the bones were lowered into their new grave, the sides of which were lined with brick and tightly sealed" (Music Hall Association, 1928). This reference substantiates the presence of the communal crypt beneath the elevator shaft which lay undisturbed from 1927 to 1988.

## METHODS AND TECHNIQUES

The skeletal material rediscovered in the crypt beneath the Music Hall in May of 1988 was taken by the Cincinnati Police Department to the Hamilton County Coroner's Office. The bones were first sorted by skeletal element, revealing an abundance of long bones, a number of fragmentary skulls, and various smaller elements. In early Spring of 1989, the remains were released to the custody of the authors for further study. At that time, a plan was developed to clean, catalogue, restore, and preserve the skeletal material. Guidelines for cleaning, labeling, reconstruction, and conservation were followed as described in Bass (1987) and Brothwell (1981).

The state of preservation ranged from poor to good; many bones were fragmentary, and all fresh breaks that were apparent were reconstructed. A majority of the fragmentary elements could not be reconstructed. It was evident that the skeletal material had suffered from poor handling during the 1927 excavation, as well as in 1988.

Working with a commingled collection, a general catalogue system was developed, so that all elements could be recorded and entered into a database. A seven-part coding system was devised to facilitate data entry and retrieval as follows: A three-digit number, beginning in ascending order with 001, for each identifiable piece of bone to be labeled; a two-letter designation for the type of bone (e.g., Hu = humerus, Fe = femur, Pe = pelvic element); a single-letter designation for side (e.g., R = right, L = left, N = side not applicable); followed by a single-letter code for state of preservation (e.g., C = relatively complete and measurable, D = distal portion measurable, F = identifiable fragment not applicable to any other preservation category).

A resulting catalog number of 001FeRC, for example, would indicate a right femur, reasonably complete for measurement purposes, with an identification code number of 001. Only the University of Cincinnati accession number and the three-digit identification code were applied to each bone with indelible ink, in standard archaeological format. In addition, the computer database and printout included columns in which other related information could be recorded, such as whether a bone was X-rayed and on which of the numbered radiographs it appeared, whether a bone was submitted for chemical analysis and its chemistry sample number, and whether a bone received mention in the pathology catalogue. (For a complete description of the database system and codes used, as well as a complete inventory, see Murray, 1993.)

Pursuant to cleaning, reconstruction, and cataloguing, a formal inventory was taken for each bony element. It was immediately apparent that not a single complete individual was present in the sample. Including both right and left sides, a cursory inventory of the relatively complete long bones included 68 femora, 30 tibiae, 22 humeri, 20 ulnae, 18 radii, and 11 fibulae. In addition, there were only 11 metatarsals and 4 metacarpals in the total sample; and not a single phalanx of the hand or foot was identified in the collection. There were 16 crania moderately intact, along with numerous skull fragments.

The simplest explanation for this inventory phenomenon lies in faulty or partial recovery; in other words, construction workers in 1927 likely picked up only larger pieces of bone. A direct correlation was apparent in our sample between the size of a bony element and its frequency of occurrence. Similarly, the completeness of the sample was adversely affected by the deliberate removal of some elements from the collection during the 1927 excavation. "The bones were carefully laid aside on the lot Wednesday night, and the watchmen were told to see that they remained undisturbed. But despite this precaution four or five of the skulls were stolen during the night" (Ludwig, 1927). A further complication occurred in 1988, when the communal grave was opened during construction at Music Hall. Formal archaeological techniques were neither invited nor performed by the Cincinnati Police Department. Consequently, complete recovery was not likely. Finally, taphonomic processes would have undoubtedly taken a greater toll on the smaller bones of the skeleton. No soil samples were available from either the original grave sites or from the communal crypt to ascertain the acidity, permeability, or chemical composition of these environments.

Due to the poor state of preservation of much of this sample, and the inability to isolate multiple elements of the same individual, problems arose in finding standard anthropometric methods that could be adequately applied. This necessitated treating the collection as groups of skeletal elements, rather than individuals. Minimally, information on age at time of death, sex, racial or ethnic affinity, and estimates of stature was sought. Standard techniques for these features may be found in Krogman (1962), El-Najjar and McWilliams (1978), Stewart (1979), Bass (1987), and Steele and Bramblett (1988), among others.

Although reliable, many of these methods are frequently based on skeletal parts that are fragile or frequently damaged, such as the pubic symphysis or the craniofacial area. Some methods require intact and measurable crania, articulated pelves, or multiple measurements from the same individual. These ideal circumstances are extremely unlikely to be encountered when dealing with commingled or ossuary material. Methods of evaluation, using more durable parts of the skeleton, must be carefully chosen. Biased samples of human remains, such as the case here, underscore the importance of developing and expanding methods for analyzing fragmentary human remains, especially since these cases are frequently encountered in historical and forensic situations (Finnegan, 1976; McKern, 1958; Snow & Folk, 1970; Ubelaker, 1974).

Techniques to be employed on fragmentary and commingled samples are available (see Giles, 1964; Kelley, 1979; Lovejoy et al., 1985; Holland, 1986a, 1986b). In particular, due to a relative abundance and good preservation, the femora in the Music Hall collection provided a basis for assessment of sex (Krogman, 1962; Black, 1978; Stewart, 1979; Jantz & Ousley, nd) and race (Iscan & Cotton, 1990). Stature estimates were easily obtained using Trotter and Gleser's (1952, 1958, 1977) standard formulae on the reasonably intact femora. In addition, reliable, although subjective, anthroposcopic criteria were heavily utilized for sex determination on pelves (Bass, 1987; Steele & Bramblett, 1988) and skulls (Bass, 1987); similar approaches were used for race (Rhine, 1990).

It should be noted that single measurements must be used with caution, and accumulated data from any particular individual greatly enhances the reliability of assessments. In addition, many methods have been developed on one ethnic or racial group and are not readily applicable to others. Further, the racial affinity or sex of an individual frequently must be ascertained before some techniques can be utilized. These features make analyses of commingled and partial remains particularly difficult. Owing to the nature of this sample, precise and accurate demographic assessments were largely unattainable, and estimates varied considerably among subsets of skeletal elements. In summary, many anthropological methods have limited utility in commingled or fragmentary remains; consequently, demographic or stature reconstructions gleaned from this sample undoubtedly reflect these limitations.

## RESULTS AND DISCUSSION

### Demographic and Pathological Evaluation

With the above caveats in mind, the results of the analysis of the commingled Music Hall skeletal sample can be presented. The minimum number of individuals was established at 30 adults, based upon the presence of 20 complete and 10 proximal ends of adult left femora in the sample. A very limited amount of subadult material was contained in the collection. Some nonhuman bone was present, though not analyzed in this study. Due to the incomplete and commingled nature of the sample, there is no absolutely reliable means by which to determine the maximum number of individuals.

In theory, it is likely that as many as 65–70 individuals (the number of burials reported disturbed in 1927) could be present in this sample, many of whom are represented by only a few bones. The large variance among skeletal elements suggests a higher minimum number of individuals. For example, the sex ratios obtained from measuring various elements provide very diverse results and could result from recovery processes where only a few elements from each individual were included in the sample. In addition, very few substantive matches between right and left long bones could be made. These features render the probability of reconstructing individual skeletons highly unlikely, although future advances, perhaps in chemical analyses, multivariate morphometric analyses, or other highly technical histologic or molecular methods, may render articulations possible among such a commingled and incomplete sample.

Based on metric analyses of the femoral sample (Krogman, 1962; Black, 1978; Stewart, 1979; Jantz & Ousley, nd), two-thirds (66.7%) of the individuals were likely male and one-third (33.3%) female. This skeletal sample, representing individuals interred between 1817 and 1838, may be compared to historical references from the City of Cincinnati. The literature documents living populations of 55% male and 45% female in 1810 (Drake, 1815), and 56% male and 44% female by 1840 (Cist, 1841). Chi-square analyses of these sets of ratios revealed no statistically significant differences between the skeletal sample and the historical data.

Cist (1841) provides an explanation for the presence of a greater number of males than females within Cincinnati at this time. Family men traditionally set out for the West prior to their dependents in an attempt to establish themselves before sending for their family. In addition, many young, unmarried men came seeking employment in Cincinnati, more so than women. Although not statistically significant, the skeletal collection does exhibit a slightly disproportionate sex distribution than would be suggested by the historical census data. It is possible that this could be the result of an increased likelihood for males to be interred in a Public Burying Ground if they were transient or new to the area and without kin.

It appears that the majority of individuals in the skeletal sample were over 40 years old at death, with several being beyond their fifth decade of life. Mild and infrequent expressions of osteoarthritis corroborate an overall age assessment of the group to be in the range of approximately 40–45 years. Due to its questionable reliability, little weight was ascribed to observations of ectocranial suture closure (Meindl & Lovejoy, 1985), although a majority of the skulls exhibited a moderate to significant degree of closure. Dental wear was also mild in most cases, although this can vary substantially between cultures depending on diet and biomechanical dental stresses.

Age records of living adult whites taken from the census data of 1840 in Cincinnati (Cist, 1841), may be utilized for illustrative purposes (although actual statistical comparisons cannot be entertained). A majority of the living Cincinnatians, in fact 51%, were in their third decade of life (their 20s); while 27% were in their fourth decade of life (their 30s); 12% in their fifth decade (their 40s); and 10% were in their sixth decade or beyond (over 50). The marked decline in numbers is obviously related to increasing age-related mortality rates but may also reflect the continued immigration of younger adults into the area.

Regarding racial or ethnic affinities represented in the Music Hall skeletal collection, the more established criteria for assessment relate primarily to morphologic differences in the craniofacial region. The poor state of preservation of many of the skulls rendered them useless for anthropometric techniques. The use of Rhine's (1990) visual indicators of the skull and Iscan and Cotton's (1990) metric analysis of the femora suggested that as many as 40% to 60% of the sample was of African American ancestry.

Data on Cincinnati's racial distribution in 1810 (Drake, 1815) indicate that only 3% of the recorded population was African American, a number that increased slightly to 5% by 1840 (Cist, 1841). These proportions are significantly lower than the proportion of African Americans in the skeletal analysis. It is possible that the Public Burying Grounds of 1818–1837 was segregated, and that the Music Hall renovations of 1927 disturbed a primarily African American section of the earlier cemetery. It is also likely that, owing to prevailing social conditions, African Americans were more often buried in the Public Burying Ground than in other church-affiliated cemeteries that surrounded the general area. It is further possible that osteologic racial assessments based on 20th century samples are not wholly applicable to this early 19th century sample. Any number of these factors could explain the apparent overrepresentation of African American individuals in the Music Hall skeletal collection when compared to 19th century historic data.

Stature estimates were performed on the femora using long-bone lengths (Trotter & Gleser, 1952; 1958; 1977). Given the assumption that individuals of both African American and European ancestry were present in the sample, the average male stature is estimated at 169.5 cm (66.7 in) for the right femora ($n = 12$), and 172.1 cm (67.8 in) for the left femora ($n = 13$). (This reasonably large discrepancy between right and left estimates further illustrates the likelihood that the sample does not reflect a high number of paired right and left elements.) The two tallest males were approximately 175.5 cm (69.0 in) (based on two left femora), while the shortest male was estimated at 159.3 cm (62.7 in).

The females of the Music Hall skeletal collection had an average stature of 158.1 cm (62.2 in) using the right femora ($n = 6$), and 157.6 cm (62.0 in) if the left femora ($n = 4$) were used. The tallest female is estimated at 162.4 cm (63.9 in), and the shortest approximately 149.3 cm (58.8 in).

In addition to basic demographics and stature estimates for the sample, a survey of pathologies present was undertaken. In general, this study revealed little significant or advanced pathology in the Music Hall skeletal collection. Dental disease and attrition were mild, with only infrequent manifestations of moderate disease among the bones. A slight degree of nutritional and metabolic insult with recovery and survivorship was evident in the form of a limited number of Harris lines and linear enamel hypoplasias. Only 3 of 22 right femora (13.6%) exhibited Harris lines radiographically, each femur displaying a single band of density. Harris lines were more frequent in the tibiae, with 6 of 14 right tibiae (42.9%) X-rayed demonstrating density banding, but again, a single band was the most frequent pattern displayed. Gross hypoplastic defects in tooth enamel were observed in only three teeth (all from different individuals), and all occurrences were mild, involving only slight striations without significant mottling or pitting of the enamel.

There were some mild degenerative conditions noted, including a limited amount of osteoarthritis and dental attrition. Arthritic changes were most frequent at the knee, hip, and elbow joints, although these pathologies were never severe, and usually reflected only slight lipping of the articular regions. Occurrences by surface ranged from 0% at nonweight-bearing regions with little contribution to joint function (such as distal ulna and proximal radius), to 62.5% at the proximal ulna and 57.1% at the distal femur. Pregnancy changes were seen in three of four right female ilia (75.0%) and three of six left female ilia (50.0%). All of these cases demonstrated a marked preauricular sulcus, possibly indicative of a reproductive history.

Regarding dental attrition, 41 of 53 (77.4%) mandibular teeth exhibited some degree of wear, while the maxillary dentition had a slightly higher incidence rate of 39 of 47 (83.0%). The degree of wear was most often mild, and consisted of slightly worn enamel with cusps remaining and no dentin exposed. It should be considered, however, that badly worn and painful teeth may have been extracted during an individual's lifetime.

These mild degenerative expressions may reflect the relatively young nature of this group, with bone and dental changes suggesting that biomechanical stress was moderate. It appears that a very normal amount of activity-induced pathology was present in the Music Hall skeletal sample.

The relative absence of trauma in these remains was remarkable, with only one macroscopically observable healed fracture and subsequent bony fusion of a distal tibia and fibula noted. Other expressions of trauma included a few Schmorl herniations in vertebrae, and several exostoses of muscle-attachment sites.

Present in the Music Hall skeletal remains were widespread and common osseous changes due to microbial pathogens, although these were nearly always of a mild and healed nature. Many long bones examined displayed expressions of infection ranging from mild (limited pitting, possibly infectious in nature) to moderate (substantial evidence of chronic infection with lifted cortex and increased nutrient foramina). Approximately 45% of the femora and 40% of the tibiae were affected to some degree, although only one long bone (a left tibia) presented severe osteitis (gross suppurative lesions with major morphological changes).

Also related to microbial pathogen exposure, but additionally related to diet, are dental pathologies. Caries and periodontal disease were evident but generally not severe in the Music Hall skeletal collection. In the maxillary arcades examined, 12.8% of the teeth (6 of 47) were affected with carious lesions, while 18.9% of the mandibular teeth (10 of 53) exhibited caries. By tooth type, molars were most frequently affected, but also more often present due to their multiple roots and more protected location within the dental arcade. As previously mentioned, it should be considered that severely carious and painful teeth would likely have been extracted, therefore these occurrences represent a minimal amount of pathologic expression. In addition, many teeth appeared to have been lost post-mortem.

The relative lack of pathology may point to the hardiness of these 19th-century pioneers, and attest to their high rates of survivorship, despite an inhospitable, unsanitary, and preantibiotic environment. However, it could also be hypothesized that documented cases of theft of skeletal remains, particularly by medical students as previously mentioned, preferentially removed pathologic or anomalous bones for study or interest. Conversely, as indicated by Wood et al. (1992) (see also Goodman 1993), these relatively infrequent expressions of disease in the Music Hall individuals may actually infer frailty of constitution (the "osteologic paradox"), wherein lack of expression of chronic disease processes might imply they were unable to survive acute microbial infections.

In summary, it is possible that the deaths of these individuals were often due to acute infectious disease processes that their immunologic defenses could not withstand. The frequency of low-grade and healed infections in these remains allows a variety of interpretations and insights, including: the relative hardiness of these people, the ubiquity of exposure to microbial pathogens, their immunologic capacity to cope with infection, and the sufficiency of their diet (Murray, 1993).

### Chemical Analysis

Many prehistoric and historic analyses of archaeological skeletal material are currently supplementing traditional osteologic data with bone-chemistry studies. A chemical analysis was undertaken using cortical bone samples from ten left humeri of the Music Hall collection. Although soil samples were not available to use as controls, there did not appear to be gross evidence for diagenesis within the study. Pointing to elemental stability in the samples were calcium-to-phosphorus ratios that appeared appropriate, an absence of yttrium in excess of 2 parts per million, and no traces of zirconium (Katzenberg, 1984).

The results demonstrate low lead levels (mean of 29 parts per million, range of 7.5–54.7), potentially suggestive of persons having very limited access or exposure to leaded goods, whether through ingestion or occupational exposure. This has been interpreted as diagnostic of a low socioeconomic status (Aufderheide et al., 1981, 1985), and indicative of persons with little access to pewter and lead-glazed ceramics, items that were the province of the wealthy in colonial and pioneer times.

Small coefficients of variation for strontium/1000 calcium ratios (17.8%) and strontium (19.6%) suggest a dietary homogeneity in this sample, and presumably an omnivorous diet. This homogeneity relative to bone strontium (Schoeninger, 1979), potentially points to common geographic backgrounds or a reasonably long habitation in Cincinnati for the persons sampled.

One individual displayed significant deviation in a related set of metals (zinc, copper, and cadmium), potentially suggesting a combined toxicity of these elements. This sample exhibited a six-fold greater zinc level, a 10-fold increase in copper, and 26 times the cadmium when compared to the corresponding means of the other nine samples analyzed. It could be possible that this individual had been originally interred in a brass coffin, although no coffin materials were recovered in 1988. It may also be a result of an unusual, but likely tragic, occupational exposure to cadmium fumes, such as would occur in zinc refining, brass production, and metalworking (Murray, 1993). The metals industry was secondary only to pork production in early 19th century Cincinnati (Cincinnati Historical Society, 1988). Although obviously limited in its utility, the chemical analysis provided some interesting hypotheses.

## SUMMARY

The paucity of nonindigenous skeletal material from the Colonial and early historic eras has been noted by several researchers (e.g. Rathbun, 1987; Thomas et al., 1977; Owsley et al., 1987; and Sciulli & Gramly, 1989) as a hindrance to our understanding of the human biology of North America. In summary, the Music Hall skeletal collection is one of a limited number of samples of 19th-century populations available for bioanthropological study.

The single greatest obstacle in this particular analysis was the commingled and fragmentary nature of this collection. Since ossuary samples and commingled materials present many problems, it is essential that new methods of sorting, as well as analyzing the most durable elements of the skeleton be developed.

As construction and remodeling of urban areas continue, primary as well as secondary interments will be disturbed and frequently encountered. Only with methodological advances in studying and analyzing commingled remains will ossuary samples yield the potential wealth of information they contain.

## ACKNOWLEDGMENTS

The authors wish to thank Dr. Frank Cleveland and the staff at the Hamilton County Coroner's Office, particularly Bernie Kersker for his radiographic assistance. We also would like to thank personnel from the offices of Cincinnati Music Hall, especially David Curry and John Engst. The authors acknowledge the helpful assistance of Patricia Tench, Nancy Stephens, Lea Huckaby, Angela Earley, Sharon Grohs, and Kathy Phebus in the analysis of the skeletal material.

## REFERENCES

Aufderheide AC, Neiman FD, Wittmers LE Jr., Rapp G (1981). Lead in bone II: Skeletal-lead content as an indicator of lifetime lead ingestion and the social correlates in an archaeological population. Am J Phys Anthropol 55:285–291.

Aufderheide AC, Angel JL, Kelley JO, Outlaw AC, Outlaw MA, Rapp G Jr., Wittmers LE Jr. (1985). Lead in bone III: Prediction of social correlates from skeletal lead content in four Colonial American populations (Catoctin Furnace, College Landing, Governor's Land and Irene Mound). Am J Phys Anthropol 66:353–361.

Bass WM (1987). Human Osteology: A Laboratory and Field Manual (3rd ed.). Columbia: Missouri Archaeological Society.

Black III TK (1978). A new method for assessing the sex of fragmentary skeletal remains: Femoral shaft circumference. Am J Phys Anthropol 48:227–232.

Brothwell DR (1981). Digging Up Bones (3rd ed.). London: British Museum.

Cincinnati Historical Society (1988). Cincinnati: The Queen City (Bicentennial Ed.). Cincinnati: The Cincinnati Historical Society.

Cist C (1841). Cincinnati in 1841: Its Early Annals and Future Prospects. Cincinnati: Charles Cist.

Drake D (1815). Natural and Statistical View, or Picture of Cincinnati and the Miami Country, Illustrated by Maps. Cincinnati: Robert A. Cline, Inc.

El-Najjar MY, McWilliams KR (1978). Forensic Anthropology: The Structure, Morphology, and Variation of Human Bone and Dentition. Springfield, IL: Charles C Thomas.

Finnegan M (1976). Walnut Creek massacre: Identification and analysis. Am J Phys Anthropol 45:737–742.

Giles E (1964). Sex determination by discriminant function analysis of the mandible. Am J Phys Anthropol 22:129–136.

Goodman AH (1993). On the interpretation of health from skeletal remains. Curr Anthropol 34(3):281–288.

Hearn L (1876). Gossip about city ghosts. Cincinnati: The Cincinnati Commercial Newspaper, October 22.

Holland TD (1986a). Race determination of fragmentary crania by analysis of the cranial base. J Forensic Sci 31:719–725.

Holland TD (1986b). Sex determination of fragmentary crania by analysis of the cranial base. Am J Phys Anthropol 70:203–208.

Iscan MY, Cotton TS (1990). Osteometric assessment of racial affinity from multiple sites in the postcranial skeleton. In Gill G, Rhine S (eds.), Skeletal Attribution of Race. Anthropological Papers No. 4, pp 83–90. Albuquerque: Maxwell Museum of Anthropology.

Jantz R, Ousley S (nd). Unpublished. Discriminant functions from the Forensic Data Bank, University of Tennessee, Knoxville. A handout distributed at the 1992 meeting of the American Academy of Forensic Sciences.

Katzenberg MA (1984). Chemical analysis of prehistoric human bone from five temporally distinct populations in southern Ontario. National Museum of Man, Mercury Series. Archaeological Survey of Canada, Paper 129.

Kelley MA (1979). Sex determination with fragmented skeletal remains. J Forensic Sci 24:154–158.

Krogman WM (1962). The Human Skeleton in Forensic Medicine. Springfield, IL: Charles C Thomas.

Lovejoy CO, Meindl RS, Pryzbeck TR, Mensforth RP (1985). Chronological metamorphosis of the auricular surface of the ilium: A new method for determination of adult skeletal age at death. Am J Phys Anthropol 68:15–28.

Ludwig C (1927). Skulls, dug from under Music Hall disappear strangely during night, workmen invade veritable "Valley of Death." 65 old graves, location of one of Cincinnati's oldest cemeteries. Cincinnati: The Daily Times Star, June 30, p. 19.

McKern TW (1958). The use of short wave ultra-violet rays for the segregation of commingled skeletal remains. Environmental Protection Res Div (Quartermaster Res & Dev Center, US Army, Natick, Mass). Tech Report EP-98.

Meindl RS, Lovejoy CO (1985). Ectocranial suture closure: A revised method for the determination of skeletal age at death based on the lateral-anterior sutures. Am J Phys Anthropol 68:57–66.

Murray, EA (1993). An Osteobiography of Early Cincinnati: The Music Hall Skeletal Collection. PhD Dissertation, University of Cincinnati. Ann Arbor: University Microfilms International.

Music Hall Association (1928). Golden Jubilee, Cincinnati Music Hall, 1878–1928. Cincinnati: Cincinnati Music Hall Association.

Owsley DW, Orser Jr., CE, Mann RW, Moore-Jansen PH, Montgomery RL (1987). Demography and pathology of an urban slave population from New Orleans. Am J Phys Anthropol 74:185–197.

Rathbun TA (1987). Health and disease at a South Carolina plantation: 1840-1870. Am J Phys Anthropol 74:239–253.

Rhine S (1990). Non-metric skull racing. In Gill G, Rhine S (eds.), Skeletal Attribution of Race. Anthropological Papers No. 4, pp. 9–20. Albuquerque: Maxwell Museum of Anthropology.

Schoeninger MJ (1979). Diet and status at Chalcatzingo: Some empirical and technical aspects of strontium analysis. Am J Phys Anthropol 51:295–310.

Sciulli PW, Gramly RM (1989). Analysis of the Ft. Laurens, Ohio, skeletal sample. Am J Phys Anthropol 80:11–24.

Snow CC, Folk ED (1970). Statistical assessment of commingled skeletal remains. Am J Phys Anthropol 32:423–427.

Steele DG, Bramblett CA (1988). The Anatomy and Biology of the Human Skeleton. College Station: Texas A&M University Press.

Stewart TD (1979). Essentials of Forensic Anthropology. Springfield, IL: Charles C Thomas.

Thomas DH, South S, Larsen CS (1977). Rich man, poor men: Observations on three antebellum burials from the Georgia coast. Anthropological Papers of the American Museum of Natural History 54(3):393–420.

Trotter M, Gleser GC (1952). Estimation of stature from long bones of American Whites and Negroes. Am J Phys Anthropol 10:463–514.

Trotter M, Gleser GC (1958). A re-evaluation of stature based on measurements taken during life and of long bones after death. Am J Phys Anthropol 16:79–123.

Trotter M, Gleser GC (1977). Corrigenda to "Estimation of stature from long limb bones of American Whites and Negroes," Am J Phys Anthropol (1952). Am J Phys Anthropol 47:355– 356.

Ubelaker DH (1974). Reconstruction of Demographic Profiles from Ossuary Skeletal Samples: A Case Study from the Tidewater Potomac. Smithsonian Contributions to Anthropology No. 18. Washington, DC: Smithsonian Institution Press.

Wood JW, Milner GR, Harpending HC, Weiss KM (1992). The osteological paradox. Curr Anthropol 33(4):343–370.

# 12 Dental Pathologies among Inmates of the Monroe County Poorhouse

RICHARD C. SUTTER

## INTRODUCTION

Bioarchaeologists often reconstruct lifeways for nondocumented cultures by using skeletal and cultural material remains encountered during excavations. The presence and patterns of dental pathologies in particular have been used to infer diet, dietary change, and social status among prehistoric people (e.g. Kelley et al., 1991; Larsen et al., 1991; Powell, 1985; Schneider, 1986; Sutter, 1993; Turner, 1979; Walker & Hewlett, 1990). These interpretations and inferences are contingent, in part, upon the quantity and quality of archaeological preservation. The analysis of historic populations, on the other hand, potentially allows for another body of data, documentary sources, to be incorporated into the research.

Taking this into account, the intent of this project was to explore the dental health of the Highland Park Cemetery population from the 19th century Monroe County Poorhouse using both skeletal and historical data. Four steps are taken in this chapter. First, the frequency of caries in the population is calculated. Second, patterns of dental health according sex and age are assessed. Third, the results are compared with other archaeological populations, and fourth, historical research is undertaken as a further means of garnering information.

## MATERIALS AND METHODS

The Highland Park Cemetery (HPC) collection consists of 305 skeletons from the Monroe County Poorhouse (established in 1826), Rochester, New York. The exact

*Bodies of Evidence*, Edited by Anne L. Grauer.
ISBN 0-471-04153-X  © 1995 John Wiley & Sons, Inc.

identities of the inmates recovered from the cemetery are unknown because tombstones were not present and death records were kept for only 3 years during the use of the cemetery. The cemetery was used from 1826 to 1863 (Oskvig, 1977).

The dental pathologies examined for this study include caries (or cavities) and premortem tooth loss. Dental caries are a disease process that results from the demineralization of a tooth's enamel surface by acids created by bacteria (*Lactobacillus acidophilus, Streptococcus mutans,* and many others). These bacteria inhabit the plaque that covers tooth surfaces and ferment dietary sugars (Menaker, 1980; Newbrun, 1978, 1982).

The dentition of 181 adults (individuals estimated to be over 18 years old at death) from the HPC were examined for this study. Within the adult sample there were 92 dentition (1618 teeth) from females and 89 (1611 teeth) from males. Sex was determined using standard osteological procedures described by Buikstra and Mielke (1985), Kelley (1979), and Phenice (1969). Age at death was determined for each individual by average age estimates from the auricular surface (Lovejoy et al., 1985), pubic symphysis (Meindl et al., 1985), and dental wear (Sutter, 1991). Ectocranial sutures (Meindl & Lovejoy, 1985) were used when no other age indicator was available.

For this study, tooth surfaces were visually inspected for caries and a Caries Index was calculated for each individual using the following equation, as suggested by Moore and Corbett (1971):

$$\text{Caries Index} = \text{Total Number of Carious Teeth} \times 100/\text{Total Number of Teeth}$$

This index provides a ratio of carious teeth to the total number of observed teeth. The number is a simple percentage; the larger the number for the Caries Index, the larger the percentage of teeth that are affected by caries. A number of recent studies have successfully applied this index (Corbett & Moore, 1976; Kelley et al., 1991; Moore & Corbett, 1971, 1973; Powell, 1985; Sutter, 1993).

One shortcoming of the Caries Index, nonetheless, is that it potentially underrepresents the number of teeth that have been affected by caries. This is due to the fact that severely cariogenic teeth often fall out during the individual's life, leaving no positive record after death. Because of this discrepancy an additional ratio, the Diseased–Missing Index (DM Index), was calculated for each individual (Moore & Corbett, 1971). This index uses the ratio of carious teeth and teeth missing before death, relative to the total number of teeth and toothless sockets observed for each individual's dentition. The DM Index is calculated for each individual using the following equation:

$$\text{DM Index} = (\text{Total Number of Carious Teeth and Number of Resorbed Sockets})$$
$$\times 100/\text{Total Number of Teeth and Sockets Observed}$$

An implicit assumption made when using this index is that premortem tooth loss results from caries. There are certainly other factors that may cause premortem tooth loss, such as tooth wear, periodontal disease, and tooth extraction. The presence and potential for these conditions must be examined in the specimens alongside the presence of caries.

Statistical analysis was conducted using the mean Caries Index and the DM Index by sex, tooth type (incisor, canine, premolar, and molar), and arcade (maxillary and mandibular). Two-Way Analysis of Covariance (MANCOVA) statistical procedures were conducted on the Caries Index and DM Index, using age at death as the covariate variable. This statistic permits the researcher to control for differences in age relationship and allows independent variables to be investigated. In this case, we were interested in seeing if there are any differences between frequencies of pathologies in males and females while removing any effects that dental wear or age of the individual might have. The 0.05 level of significance was used for all statistical analyses.

During the course of the present investigation, a variety of historic sources were consulted in an attempt to gain insight into the diet of the Monroe County Poorhouse residents and general trends in the U.S. Most documents provided only broad generalizations and anecdotes (Cummings, 1941; Mesick, 1970; Shryock, 1931). While there are brief descriptions of the diet among poorhouse residents (New York Select Committee, 1857; Rosenberg-Naparsteck 1983), there are no records of food purchases or crops grown on the poorhouse farm. In general, however, it appears that during the 19th century the diet in the United States underwent a dramatic shift as increasingly more fruits and vegetables and highly processed, high-carbohydrate foods were introduced into the diet. These changes were largely due to technological improvements that permitted better storage, rail transportation, and processing of foods (Cummings, 1941).

## RESULTS

Data for adult HCP females and males are summarized in Table 1. As the table indicates, the mean age at death of the 92 adult females is 32.5 years, whereas the average age of the 89 adult HPC males was 35.1. Of the 1618 female teeth examined, 155 teeth demonstrated caries. There were also 714 resorbed sockets in the dental arcades of females. In males, 168 of the 1611 teeth present had caries and 565 resorbed sockets were present. For all teeth and sockets observed, females had a mean Caries Index of 9.59 and a mean DM Index of 37.27, whereas HPC males had a mean Caries Index of 10.44 and a mean DM Index of 33.69. The large discrepancy between these two indicators of caries may suggest an underrepresentation of caries by the Caries Index (or percentage of teeth effected by caries). It may also suggest an overrepresentation of caries by the DM Index. In spite of this, there is substantial clinical evidence supporting the use of the DM index as an indication of caries (Harris, 1968; Menaker, 1980). For this reason, the remainder of this study focuses on differences in the DM Index.

The assessment of the DM Index means, by tooth type and sex, indicates that for all tooth types males display a lower DM Index than females (Table 1). These differences were not found to be statistically significant. However, for both females and males, the anterior dentition (i.e., incisors and canines) demonstrate less disease

**TABLE 1. Summary Data for Highland Park Cemetery Adult Females and Males**

|  | Females | Males |
|---|---|---|
| Number of individuals | 92 | 89 |
| Mean skeletal age at death | 32.5 | 35.1 |
| Number of teeth | 1618 | 1611 |
| Number of carious teeth | 155 | 168 |
| Number of resorbed sockets | 714 | 565 |
| Overall caries index | 9.59 (S.E. = 1.3) | 10.44 (S.E. = 1.7) |
| Overall diseased–missing index | 37.27 (S.E. = 3.5) | 33.69 (S.E. = 3.1) |
| Diseased–missing index by tooth type |  |  |
| Incisors | 15.73 (S.E. = 2.6) | 13.48 (S.E. = 2.4) |
| Canines | 10.60 (S.E. = 1.9) | 8.99 (S.E. = 1.8) |
| Premolars | 31.25 (S.E. = 2.8) | 28.69 (S.E. = 2.6) |
| Molars | 40.22 (S.E. = 3.1) | 38.86 (S.E. = 3.1) |
| Diseased–missing index by arcade |  |  |
| Maxillary arcade | 20.71 (S.E. = 2.9) | 22.17 (S.E. = 3.0) |
| Mandibular arcade | 35.18 (S.E. = 2.9) | 25.44 (S.E. = 3.0) |

and antemortem tooth loss than do teeth of the posterior arcade (i.e., premolars and molars). In addition, molars are diseased and missing more often than premolars. These patterns were found to be statistically significant.

Results for ANCOVA analysis of the DM Index are presented in Table 2. Here age was used as the covariate variable. A covariate variable is one whose "masking" effect is removed. In other words, if a difference exists between the DM Index for males and females, we want to know that this difference isn't simply due to the fact that, on average, one of the sexes is older, and therefore more likely to have more dental disease.

Age at death was found to be significantly related to diseased teeth and teeth missing before death. This result comes as no surprise because a great number of studies have already demonstrated a clear relationship between the age of an in-

**TABLE 2. ANCOVA for the Diseased–Missing Index among Females and Males from the Highland Park Collection: Sex is the Independent Variable and Age is the Covariate**

| Source | Sum of Squares | DF | Mean square | F Ratio | p Value |
|---|---|---|---|---|---|
| Sex | 1591.55 | 1 | 1591.55 | 1.86 | 0.17 |
| Age | 15638.89 | 1 | 15638.89 | 18.31 | 0.00 |
| Error | 152022.34 | 178 | 854 |  |  |

dividual and their susceptibility to caries and dental disease (Corbett & Moore, 1976; Larsen et al., 1991; Menaker, 1980; Moore & Corbett, 1971, 1973; Powell, 1985; Schneider, 1986; Sutter, 1993; Turner, 1979; Walker & Hewlett, 1990, to name a few). However, when age is accounted for (its masking effect removed) there is no significant difference between the DM Index of males and females ($p = 0.17$).

The results of Two-Way ANCOVA analysis of the DM Index by tooth type and sex is displayed in Table 3. In this case we are interested in removing the effects of age in order to see whether dental pathologies differ by sex and tooth type (i.e., detecting whether the mean DM Index for female incisors, for instance, is statistically different than the DM Index for female premolars. The results indicate that significant differences in the DM Index exist among different tooth types and by sex when age is controlled for. In both females and males, the anterior teeth display significantly less disease and antemortem loss than posterior teeth. In addition, molars are diseased and missing significantly more often than premolars. No significant difference exits between male and female tooth loss and disease patterns within each tooth type.

## DISCUSSION

While individual identities of the skeletons are unknown in the HPC population, a general characterization of the residents of the Monroe County Poorhouse can be constructed using historical records. According to Oskvig (1977), many of the early poorhouse inmates were not born within the Rochester area. "The directory of Rochesterville (which eventually became Rochester) states that of the population of 8000 in 1827, not one adult was native born. Thirty-five of the residents are listed at the poorfarm" (Oskvig, 1977, p. 7). Later records indicate that many of the mid-19th century poorhouse residents were native-born U.S. citizens and Irish and German immigrants (Brighton Town Records, 1850). Poorhouse death records for the years 1847, 1850, and 1851 indicate that a majority of poorhouse residents were employed laborers or skilled workers (Brighton Town Records, 1850).

Recent paleopathological research has described the HPC population as having

**TABLE 3. Two-Way ANCOVA for the Diseased–Missing Index within the Highland Park Collection: Tooth Type and Sex are the Independent Variables and Age is the Covariate**

| Source | Sum of Squares | DF | Mean square | F Ratio | p Value |
| --- | --- | --- | --- | --- | --- |
| Tooth type | 102883.25 | 3 | 34294.42 | 60.69 | 0.00 |
| Sex | 2164.02 | 1 | 2164.02 | 3.83 | 0.05 |
| Tooth Type/Sex | 36.24 | 3 | 12.08 | 0.02 | 1.00 |
| Age | 27462.15 | 1 | 27462.15 | 48.60 | 0.00 |
| Error | 402887.41 | 713 | 565.06 | | |

suffered from chronic illness, poor living conditions, and nutritional stress (Lanphear, 1990; Sirianni & Higgins, this volume), but a recent study of stature among these remains indicates the mean stature estimate for poorhouse adults was actually greater than mean estimates on remains of the same period (Steegmann, 1991). Steegmann (1991) concluded that the poorhouse residents' poverty did not result in stunted growth. Steegmann's results, and the general robusticity of many of the remains, both male and female, suggest that many of the poorhouse residents represented in this sample may have led a productive life prior their stay at the poorhouse. Indeed, prior to the mid-19th century, many individuals were only temporary or seasonal inmates (Oskvig, 1977).

According to Oskvig (1977, p. 12), it was not until after 1850 that "a progressively larger proportion of the Almshouse residents were disabled and chronically or acutely ill." Many of the poorhouse residents were individuals who turned to the poorhouse after becoming acutely ill and died shortly after. This assertion is supported by records that show an influx of inmates during epidemics. Oskvig (1977) claims that from 1848 through 1850 as many as 1532 different people per year received shelter within the poorhouse because of the 1849 cholera epidemic. A similar increase in poorhouse residents occurred following the cholera epidemic of 1852.

## Diet and Dental Care

Understanding the results of the above dental analysis requires an examination of the potential diet and dental care available to the residents of the poorhouse. According to Cummings (1941), historical sources indicate that during the late 18th and early 19th century bread and meat were common staples in the United States and molasses was the most common sweetener. Early in the 19th century the American diet has been described as mainly consisting of meat and potatoes (Cummings, 1941; Hoff & Fulton, 1937; Mesick, 1970; Shryock, 1931). Urban residents of the period generally lacked access to fresh milk, fruits, and vegetables. Few perishable items were available during this time. Even when fruits and vegetables were in season, they rarely survived long enough to make it to urban markets unless they were obtained from farms located on the outskirts of town. Improved methods of milling and refining brought flour and sugar into greater use; these items became staples, while cornmeal and homemade sweeteners, such as molasses and maple sugar, became less widely used (Cummings, 1941). Indeed, during the period from 1830 to 1869 the per-capita yearly consumption of processed sugar doubled (Kolodny, 1976 cited in Sledzik & Moore-Jansen, 1991).

As previously mentioned, there are only a few reports concerning the diet of the Monroe County Poorhouse residents. The diet of the children is reported to have been wholesome, consisting of meat and whole grains, while adult inmates reportedly were fed cornmeal mush three times a week as their main meal (New York Select Committee 1857, Rosenberg-Naparsteck 1983). Reconstructing the diet of the inmates before they entered the poorhouse is impossible. It is assumed that most individuals had a refined, highly cariogenic diet typical of most preindustrial populations of the period (Cummings, 1941; Lanphear, 1990; Sledzik & Moore-Jansen, 1991).

Dental care during the mid-19th century was nearly nonexistent. During the second half of the 19th century, badly diseased teeth were often extracted and gum abscesses were lanced (Dammann, 1984). Tooth powders often consisted of powdered white and red chalk, powdered orris root, and myrrh (Paris, 1964, cited in Dammann, 1984). One recipe for a mouth rinse consisted of castile soap, alcohol, honey, and perfume (Dammann, 1984). Dammann further states that the need for dentistry during the Civil War was the impetus for the development of modern dentistry. Not surprisingly, none of the HPC dentition exhibited evidence of dental work.

Given the highly refined carbohydrate diet and lack of dental care during the early and mid-19th century, the results from this study are not surprising. Burials from the Highland Park Cemetery exhibit high levels of dental pathologies as indicated by the high number of diseased and missing teeth (37.27% of all teeth from females and 33.69% of all teeth from males). In all analyses within this investigation, the amount of diseased and missing teeth is related to the age of the specimen.

Within the context of this study it is assumed that dental wear itself does not account for differences that exist in the frequency of dental pathologies. In a previous study, the rate of dental wear was found to be relatively low (Sutter, 1991). The same study revealed that the rate of wear among males and females from this sample is virtually identical.

In all, differences between dental health in males and females appears negligible in this population. While males exhibit slightly fewer diseased and missing teeth than do females, this difference is not statistically significant. While other 19th-century populations display similar patterns between males and females (Corbett & Moore, 1976), this result appears contrary to the significant differences found in prehistoric agricultural populations (Kelley et al., 1991; Larsen et al., 1991; Sutter, 1993; Turner, 1979) and cultures where gender or status-based differences in diet existed (Walker & Hewlett, 1990).

While negligible differences in dental health exist between males and females, this is not the case when differences between tooth type and disease are examined. Tooth-by-tooth comparisons for both males and females within this population indicate that incisors and canines are significantly less diseased and less often missing than premolars and molars. In addition, molars exhibit significantly more disease and are more often missing than premolars. The same pattern of caries by tooth type was noted among both early and late 19th-century British dentition (Corbett & Moore, 1976) and dentition from Civil War soldiers (Sledzik & Moore-Jansen, 1991). Tooth-type differences in the DM Index most likely reflect differences in occlusal morphology and size. Molars and premolars are larger and have more complex chewing surfaces than canines and incisors, thereby increasing the surface susceptible to attack by carious bacteria (Klatsky, 1953).

## Comparative Historical Populations

Comparing the results of the HPC dental analysis with other populations is another means of highlighting the condition and lives of the poorhouse residents. A comparison for values obtained for carious teeth, teeth missing before death, and the DM Index is presented in Fig. 1 for the Highland Park Cemetery remains and from other 19th-century populations. The British I sample is a pre-1850 sample of both males and females from the Ashton-under-Lyne Graveyard, whereas the British II sample consists of both sexes from the post-1850 Ashton-under-Lyne Cemetery (Corbett & Moore, 1976). Data from the mid-19th century (1840–1870) South Carolina Plantation (SCP) cemetery are derived from African American females and males (Rathbun, 1987). Civil War values are derived from data presented by Sledzik and Moore-Jansen (1991).

Corbett and Moore (1976) demonstrated that dentition from 19th-century British populations had an exceptionally high degree of dental pathologies. While the percentage of antemortem tooth loss and the DM Index is unavailable for these samples, the percentage of caries among both British I and British II samples are higher than the percentage of caries or DM Index exhibited among any United States sample. Processed foods were consumed at an earlier time in Britain than in the United States (Moore & Corbett, 1971, 1973). While processed sugar consumption doubled in both the United States and Great Britain during the mid-19th century (Deerr, 1950; Kolodny, 1976 cited in Sledzik & Moore-Jansen, 1991), the British are reported to have consumed nearly twice the amount of this cariogenic item than their American counterparts (Deerr, 1950).

A more cariogenic diet may account for the rate of caries among British samples, however, it is difficult to evaluate this information because mean age-at-death figures are not available for the British samples. Corbett and Moore (1976) present Ashton-

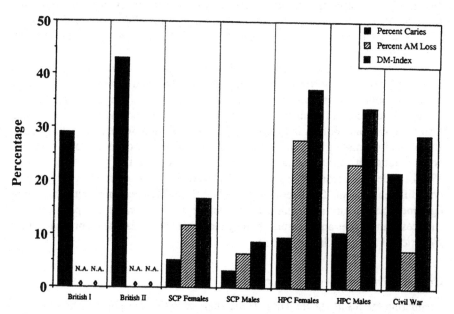

**FIGURE 1.** Comparison of dental pathologies among 19th-century skeletal samples.

under-Lyne caries information using four undefined age classes. Approximately 30% of all dentitions come from the oldest age class within these British samples. Therefore, age differences may also account for the higher percentage of caries among the British sample dentition.

The analysis of dentition from male and female black slaves from the mid-19th century South Carolina Plantation (SCP) suggests that this population suffered fewer caries and missing teeth than did HPC males and females. Other slave samples from the 19th century also demonstrate a lower percentage of teeth affected by dental disease than whites from the same time (Angel et al., 1987). Mean age-at-death values for South Carolina Plantation females (40 years) and males (35 years) are older (for females) or equal (for males) to the values for the HPC sample. Therefore, age does not appear to account for these differences. This may indicate that slaves had less access to the highly processed cariogenic food items available to mid-19th century whites. Others have suggested that African Americans from this period may have had an anticaries factor (Angel et al., 1987), however, these authors did not specify exactly what this "factor" might be.

While mid-19th century Highland Park Cemetery males have a lower percentage of dental caries than those reported for Civil War soldiers, HPC males exhibit a greater number of teeth missing before death. It is difficult to determine whether these differences are due to improved dental hygiene, age differences between the samples, or military-selection criteria. Sledzik and Moore-Jansen (1991) discuss how many potential soldiers were often rejected on the basis of excessive cavities or tooth loss. However, HPC males have a mean age at death of 35.1 years, whereas the mean for the Civil War sample is 27.1 years. Obviously, the older the mean age at death for the population, the more likely that tooth loss will increase. The differences between the DM Index for HPC males and Civil War soldiers do not appear to be very different when age of the sample is taken into account. The greater percentage of antemortem tooth loss among HPC males most likely reflects the loss of teeth due to a longer exposure to carious processes.

## CONCLUSION

This study has suggested, not surprisingly, that a strong relationship exists in the HPC population between age of an individual and the degree of dental disease. The high value of the DM Index for both males and females, coupled with information derived from historical records, might lead us to propose that their diet was highly cariogenic. This might be a reflection of a larger trend in the 19th century toward diets containing increasing amounts of complex carbohydrates. The lack of gender-based differences among dental pathologies in the HPC is a result that is similar to those reported for contemporaneous populations (Corbett & Moore, 1976; Sledzik & Moore-Jansen, 1991) and may indicate that males and females shared similar diets or had diets that consisted of similarly cariogenic substances. While comparisons made between the presence and patterns of dental disease in the HPC population and other 19th-century samples provides intriguing results, they are also confounded by a lack of standardized methods of presenting dental and skeletal information. It is hoped that future research will begin to ameliorate these problems and provide, through the use of skeletal material and historical accounts, a rich and provoking insight into the past.

## ACKNOWLEDGMENTS

I would like to express my thanks to Charles Hays III of the Rochester Museum and Science Center, and the State University of New York at Buffalo's Department of Anthropology for making the Highland Park Collection available for this study. I am indebted to Lauraine Saunders and Brian Nagel for sharing historical information they have gathered during their research on the Highland Park Cemetery. I am also grateful for the help and advice of my former academic advisor, Joyce E. Sirianni, who helped cultivate my research interests and provided valuable advice on earlier stages of this investigation. My current advisor, Robert A. Benfer, also provided many substantive comments on the later stages of this chapter. Many thanks to him as well.

## REFERENCES

Angel JL, Kelly JO, Parrington M, Pinter S (1987). Life stresses of the free Black community as represented by the First African Baptist Church, Philadelphia, 1823–1841. Am J Phys Anthropol 74:213–229.

Brighton Town Records (1850). Vital Records for the Town of Brighton, New York and the Monroe County Poorhouse, 1847–1850.

Buikstra JE, Mielke JH (1985). Demography, diet, and health. In Gilbert RI, Mielke JH (eds.), The Analysis of Prehistoric Diets, pp. 360–422. New York: Academic Press.

Corbett ME, Moore WJ (1976). Distribution of dental caries in ancient British populations: IV. The 19th Century. Caries Res 10:401–414.

Cummings RO (1941). The American and His Food: A History of Food Habits in the United States. Chicago: The University of Chicago Press.

Dammann GE (1984). Dental care during the Civil War. Ill Dent J January–February:12–17.

Deerr N (1950). The History of Sugar. London: Chapman & Hall.

Harris RS (1968). Art and Science of Dental Caries Research. New York: Academic Press.

Hoff H, Fulton J (1937). The centenary of the first American Physiological Society founded at Boston by William A. Alcott and Sylvester Graham. Bulletin of the Institute of the History of Medicine V:714.

Kelley MA (1979). Parturition and pelvic changes. Am J Phys Anthropol 51:541–546.

Kelley MA, Levesque DR, Weidl E (1991). Contrasting patterns of dental disease in five early northern Chilean groups. In Kelley MA, Larsen CS (eds.), Advances in Dental Anthropology, pp. 203–213. New York: Wiley-Liss.

Klatsky M, Fisher RL (1953). The Human Masticatory Apparatus: An Introduction to Dental Anthropology. Brooklyn: Dental Items of Interest Publication Co.

Lanphear KM (1988). Health and Mortality in a Nineteenth Century Poorhouse Skeletal Sample. Ph.D. dissertation: State University of New York at Albany.

Lanphear KM (1990). Frequency and distribution of enamel hypoplasias in a historic skeletal sample. Am J Phys Anthropol 81:35–43.

Larsen CS, Shavit R, Griffin MC (1991). Dental caries evidence for dietary change: An archaeological context. In Kelly MA, Larsen CS (eds.), Advances in Dental Anthropology, pp. 179–202. New York: Wiley-Liss.

Lovejoy CO, Meindl RS, Pryzbeck TR, Mensforth RP (1985). Chronological metamorphosis of the auricular surface of the ilium: A new method for the determination of adult skeletal age at death. Am J Phys Anthropol 68:15–28.

Meindl RS, Lovejoy CO (1985). Ectocranial suture closure: A revised method for the determination of skeletal age at death based on the lateral anterior sutures. Am J Phys Anthropol 68:57–66.

Meindl RS, Lovejoy CO, Mensforth RP, Walker RA (1985). A revised method of age determination using the os pubis, with a review and test of accuracy of other current methods of pubic symphyseal aging. Am J Phys Anthropol 68:29–45.

Menaker L (1980). Biological Basis of Dental Caries, An Oral Biology Textbook. New York: Harper and Row.

Mesick JL (1970). The English Traveler in America, 1785–1835. Westport, CT: Greenwood Press.

Moore WJ, Corbett ME (1971). The distribution of dental caries in ancient British populations: I. Anglo-Saxon Period. Caries Res 5:151–168.

Moore WJ, Corbett ME (1973). The distribution of dental caries in ancient British populations: II. Iron Age, Romano-British and Mediaeval Periods. Caries Res 7:139–153.

Newburn E (1978). Cariology. Baltimore: Williams and Wilkins.

Newburn E (1982). Sugar and dental caries: A review of human studies. Science 217:418–423.

New York State Select Committee (1857). Report of the Select Committee. Albany: New York State, Document VI, No. 8.

Oskvig RM (1977). A Lombardic Edifice with Gargoylism. Rochester, NY: The Landmark Society.

Phenice TW (1969). A newly developed visual method of sexing the os pubis. Am J Phys Anthropol 30:297–30.

Powell ML (1985). The analysis of dental wear and caries for dietary reconstruction. In Gilbert RI, Mielke JH (eds.), The Analysis of Prehistoric Diets, pp. 307–338. New York: Academic Press.

Rathbun TA (1987). Health and disease at a South Carolina plantation: 1840–1870. Am J Phys Anthropol 74:239–253.

Rosenberg-Naparsteck R (1983). Life and death in nineteenth century Rochester. Rochester History 45:1–24.

Schneider KN (1986). Dental caries, enamel composition, and subsistence among pre-historic Amerindians of Ohio. Am J Phys Anthropol 71:95–102.

Shryock RH (1931). Sylvester Graham and the popular health movement. Mississippi Valley Historical Review XVIII:172–183.

Sledzik PS, Moore-Jansen PH (1991). Dental disease in nineteenth century military skeletal samples. In Kelly M, Larsen CS (eds.), Advances in Dental Anthropology, pp. 215–224. New York: Liss.

Steegmann Jr. AT (1991). Stature in an early mid-19th century poorhouse population: Highland Park, Rochester, New York. Am J Phys Anthropol 85:261–268.

Sutter RC (1991). Dental Wear in the Highland Park Collection: A New Technique for Dental Aging. Masters Project: The State University of New York at Buffalo.

Sutter RC (1993). Resource Distribution and Social Stratification as Inferred from Dental Pathologies: A Preliminary Report from Chiribaya Alta. Unpublished.

Turner II CG (1979). Dental anthropological indications of agriculture among the Jomon People of Central Japan. Am J Phys Anthropol 51:619–636.

Walker PL, Hewlett BS (1990). Dental health diet and social status among Central African foragers and farmers. Amer Anthropol 92:383–395.

Wilkinson L, Hill M, Vang E (1992). SYSTAT: Statistics, Version 5.2 Edition. Evanston, IL: SYSTAT, Inc.

# 13 Bone Chemistry Analysis and Documentary Archaeology: Dietary Patterns of Enslaved African Americans in the South Carolina Low Country

THOMAS A. J. CRIST

## INTRODUCTION

Of the many contributions physical anthropologists and historical archaeologists have made to current interpretations of American history, none have been more important than the inclusion of ethnic minorities in the study of the American past. Ethnic minorities, so often overlooked or ignored in the documentary record, have been the focus of numerous archaeological projects since the inception of American historical archaeology in 1967 (Schuyler, 1980). In that year, Charles H. Fairbanks and his students at the University of Florida initiated the first archaeological investigations of enslaved African Americans, launching plantation archaeology in the Southeast.

In concert with historical archaeologists, physical anthropologists have been able to provide unique information about the past through the analysis of human skeletal remains. Human bone provides a dynamic and durable record of biological responses made by past peoples to social, economic, and environmental conditions. By analyzing human remains from a variety of mortuary contexts, physical anthropologists not only answer questions about the biological history of the human species, but also generate new interpretations of how particular groups adapted to specific socio-economic and physical stresses.

Nowhere has this multidisciplinary approach been more important and more successful than in the study of slavery in the New World (Handler & Corruccini, 1983; Khudabux, 1991; Kelley & Angel, 1987; Owsley et al., 1987; Rathbun, 1987).

*Bodies of Evidence*, Edited by Anne L. Grauer.
ISBN 0-471-04153-X © 1995 John Wiley & Sons, Inc.

Although skeletal remains of former slaves have been limited in number, comparative analyses of the available osteological material have provided important information about the diets, levels of biomechanical stress, patterns of activity and occupation, disease loads, differential mortality, and quality of life for a variety of African-American groups. Much of this information had been unavailable from documentary sources, and only inferred from archaeological evidence. As a result, researchers have used the results of skeletal and dental studies not only to interpret past human behavior but also evaluate the reliability of historic records and written accounts.

Various methods of studying human bone have become important in seeking answers about the past. One of the most promising techniques is the analysis of chemical elements found in archaeological bone. These studies attempt to reconstruct the subsistence patterns of past peoples and the nutritional adequacy of their diets.

Like many other technical methods borrowed by anthropologists, bone-chemistry analysis has passed through phases of acceptance, use, refinement, and reconsideration since its first anthropological applications in the 1970s. Since then, several edited volumes (Grupe & Herrmann, 1988; Lambert & Grupe, 1993; Price, 1989a; Sandford, 1993) and numerous articles have discussed applications of bone-chemistry analysis in the reconstruction of prehistoric diets. Although complex in terms of methodological concerns and confounding factors, multielement studies of human bone offer the potential to investigate the diets and diseases of past societies in ways unavailable even 20 years ago. To researchers concerned with the African experience in the diaspora, bone-chemistry analysis affords the opportunity to enhance current interpretations of slavery, the "peculiar institution," and its impact on generations of African Americans.

In seeking an understanding of the biocultural impacts that slavery made on its victims, scholars have engaged in a considerable debate about the nature of this most exploitative of economic systems. At the center of this debate has been the ongoing attempt to gauge the quality of life of the enslaved African Americans. Some scholars have taken the position that slavery became more humane through the antebellum period (Genovese, 1974), while others have portrayed the enslaved as constantly resisting exploitation by their masters (Ferguson, 1990; Mullin, 1992). Regardless of position, many scholars make reference to the diets of enslaved African Americans to support their arguments. This is largely because diets provide quantifiable measures of adequacy in terms of calories ingested versus energy expenditures, and can be assessed in light of current knowledge regarding human nutritional requirements. Cliometric examinations of slavery are divided regarding the adequacy of slave diet: Fogel and Engerman (1974) demonstrated that slave subsistence exceeded modern recommended daily nutritional requirements while Kiple and King (1981) and Sutch (1975) argued that, in general, plantation diets were not balanced and were in fact deficient.

At the core of these opposing arguments lies the composition of the slave diet. It is in this regard that archaeologists provide important information typically unavailable from documentary sources. Recovery of food remains and other artifacts from slave quarters provides primary evidence of living conditions and daily domestic activities that were often disregarded or censored by writers of the period, many of whom were plantation owners attempting to justify slavery.

Prior to the excavation of slave quarters most researchers who depended on historical documentation assumed that the diets of the enslaved were limited and homogeneous across the South (Reitz et al., 1985). However, archaeological evidence and ethnographic reconstructions of slave life (Blassingame, 1979; Gutman, 1976; Joyner, 1984) have shown that diet was a varied and multifarious component of slave society, a portrayal very different than that depicted in written accounts from the antebellum period.

This chapter presents the results of the bone-chemistry analysis of 26 African American adults recovered from the slave cemetery at the former Remley Plantation near Charleston, South Carolina. Combined with historical and archaeological data from other plantation sites in the South Carolina Low Country, the results of the chemical analysis of these individuals provide fresh insights into the diversity of diets within the society of enslaved African Americans on one peribellum plantation.

## BONE-CHEMISTRY ANALYSIS

Human bone is composed of organic and mineral components. It is in the mineral fraction, mostly composed of calcium and phosphate, where most of the elements of relevance to dietary reconstruction are deposited. The mineral phase of living bone also contains sodium, magnesium, various trace elements, fluorides, and carbonates. As ions are exchanged in the living bone, trace elements from food and environmental sources replace other ions in the hydroxyapatite of the mineral phase (see Sandford, 1992, 1993; Mertz, 1986; and Urist, 1980 for excellent discussions of human skeletal biochemistry). The basic premise underlying bone-chemistry studies is that the elements found in human bone reflect the types of foods ingested during life, since elemental levels vary widely among different classes of foods. While no single element is indicative of an individual's diet, multielemental analysis can reveal trends suggesting dietary preferences or limitations.

Elements in the human body are classified as either major or trace elements, based on the quantity each comprises. Almost 98% of the human body is composed of oxygen, carbon, hydrogen, nitrogen, calcium, and phosphorus, in descending order (Gilbert, 1985). Elements in lesser concentrations include potassium, chloride (in ion form), sodium, and magnesium. Trace elements are defined as making up less than 0.01% of the total body mass, and include dietary essentials, possible essentials, nonessentials, and toxic elements (Mertz, 1986). The function of essential trace elements is to promote catalytic reactions. Since virtually all trace elements are toxic at high levels, elements that are toxic at relatively lower concentrations, like lead, mercury, and cadmium, are generally included in bone-chemistry analyses as indicators of exposure to various industrial or occupational activities (Aufderheide et al., 1981, 1985; Corruccini et al., 1987; Ericson & Coughlin, 1981).

Fifteen trace elements have been identified as dietary essentials among higher animals (Mertz, 1986; Passwater & Cranton, 1983). These elements are: arsenic, chromium, cobalt, copper, fluorine, iodine, iron, manganese, molybdenum, nickel, selenium, silicon, tin, vanadium, and zinc. Several other possible essential trace elements have also been used in dietary reconstructions, including boron, aluminum, barium, and, in particular, strontium.

The use of skeletal strontium levels and strontium/calcium ratios is based on the physiological phenomenon that strontium quantities among organisms vary inversely to their positions on the trophic pyramid (Brown, 1973; Sandford, 1992; Schoeninger, 1979). That is, foods of plant origin display significantly higher levels of strontium than do animal products. In theory, herbivores should present the highest strontium levels and carnivores the lowest, with omnivores like humans exhibiting intermediate concentrations. If dichotomous dietary patterns exist within a given society, whereby meat is eaten by a privileged subgroup (based on gender, age, economic position, etc.), then those individuals should display lower average strontium levels than do members of other subgroups (Sillen & Kavanagh, 1982).

The most common applications of archaeological bone-chemistry analysis have focused on discriminating between diets based on animal and vegetable products (see Beck, 1985; Gilbert, 1975, 1985; and Lambert et al., 1979). Since concentrations of chemical elements vary significantly between different food sources, comparisons of specific elements and elemental groups can allow the relative amounts of foods from different categories to be ascertained. In general, animal products contain higher concentrations of zinc, copper, molybdenum, and selenium than do food resources from plants. Other elements, including strontium, magnesium, manganese, vanadium, cobalt, and calcium, are usually found in higher levels in vegetables and legumes. Table 1 provides data on the mean concentrations of several

**TABLE 1. Mean Elemental Concentrations of Various Food Groups (in ppm)**

|  | Grains and cereals | Vegetables[a] | Meats[b] | Nuts | Seawater |
|---|---|---|---|---|---|
| Cobalt | 0.43 | 0.14 | 0.22 | 0.47 | .000001 |
| Copper | 2.00 | 1.20 | 3.90 | 14.80 | .0001 |
| Magnesium | 805.00 | 307.00 | 267.00 | 1970.00 | — |
| Manganese | 7.00 | 2.50 | 0.20 | 17.00 | .00001 |
| Molybdenum | 1.79 | 0.51 | 4.82 | — | .00014 |
| Nickel | 0.15–0.35 | 1.5–3.0 | 0.13 | — | — |
| Selenium | 0.15 | 0.01[c] | 0.92 | — | .00004 |
| Strontium | 3.00 | 1.90 | 2.00 | 60.00 | .08 |
| Vanadium | 1.10 | 1.60 | 0.05[d] | 0.71 | .00005 |
| Zinc | 17.70 | 6.00 | 30.60 | 24.00 | .00015 |

[a]Includes leafy material, legumes, and tubers.
[b]Excludes marine resources.
Sources: Gilbert 1985; Buikstra et al. 1989 citing [c]Morris and Levander 1970, [d]Schroeder et al. 1963.

chemical elements in leguminous and leafy plants, grains and cereals, meats, and nuts. Seafood, not included in Table 1, typically contains high levels of barium, cadmium, calcium, copper, and magnesium (Whitmer et al., 1989). Iron is found almost equally in meats, poultry, fish, and grains, but human adults aged 20–34 years receive twice the iron intake from meats and fish than from grains and cereals (Passwater & Cranton, 1983).

The consumption of nuts has been noted to confound interpretations of bone-chemistry levels by providing a convenient explanation for unusually high levels of certain elements (Buikstra et al., 1989). Although technically part of a plant, nuts contain extremely high levels of magnesium and several trace elements, including copper, manganese, and zinc (Furr et al., 1979), and strontium levels that are almost as low as in animal products. Cadmium and vanadium, however, both occurring in low concentrations in nuts, may aid in distinguishing whether nuts were a major constituent in past diets. The archaeological and historical contexts may also provide a means to assess the relative contribution of nuts in the diets of particular groups.

While many of the bone-chemistry studies conducted on prehistoric skeletal remains apparently demonstrated significant differences in dietary patterns among population subgroups, many concerns abound regarding the use of bone-chemistry analysis to reconstruct past diets. Whether bone-chemistry results indicate distinctions in the availability and preferences of food resources, or physiological differences between males and females, or the old versus the young, is currently a topic of considerable debate. Factoring in the effects of food preparation and cooking on elemental concentrations is also difficult, as is attempting to identify the elemental levels of resources used in the past. Sampling choices, sample preparation techniques, and the selection of statistical methods used to analyze the numerical results are also areas of extensive deliberation. Yet, most critiques of bone-chemistry analysis conclude that the technique has the potential to inform us about the diets, stresses, and social organization of past societies, despite the methodological problems noted in previous studies. It appears that most researchers are nonbelievers when it comes to bone-chemistry analysis, but are wishing and indeed hoping that the technique fulfills its potential. The present study, while suffering from many of the faults found with other efforts, provides information that can be used to augment the current understanding of the diversity of diets among the enslaved in the South Carolina Low Country, even if future refinement of bone-chemistry techniques leads to different interpretations of the data collected from the Remley Plantation remains.

## DIAGENESIS

Diagenesis is the postmortem alteration of elemental levels after bone is deposited in soil. It occurs in much the same manner as ion exchange does in living bone, particularly due to the crystalline structure of hydroxyapatite, the most prevalent component of the mineral phase of bone (Sillen, 1989). Elements can be lost and gained from the bone depending on local soil conditions, particularly soil pH and water-table levels. Numerous other factors are also involved, and their variability makes diagenesis a significantly confounding factor in the interpretation of elemental levels in archaeological bone (Price, 1989b; Radosevich, 1993).

The determination of which elements were altered during interment has been traditionally evaluated by comparing antemortem concentrations of modern humans with those observed in archaeological bone samples. Deviations have been presumed to demonstrate diagenesis, while stability was indicated by the correspondence of levels in both samples. Most studies of diagenesis have utilized diffusion theory to assess the postmortem movements of chemical elements. Diffusion is a chemical activity whereby elements move from areas of greater concentration to areas of lesser concentration until an equilibrium is established. In order to assess the degree of diffusion in a given burial environment, soil and bone samples are independently evaluated. In theory, observation of concentration gradients indicates the direction of element movement during the period the body was in contact with its surrounding soil matrix.

Like most other features of bone-chemistry analysis, the use of concentration gradients as a means of controlling for diagenesis has been brought into question (Radosevich, 1993; Sandford, 1992). Some researchers have demonstrated that postmortem elemental distributions may behave in a manner opposite to the actions predicted by diffusion theory, so that lower elemental levels in soil relative to bone levels may indicate previous movement of elements into the skeletal material (Lambert et al., 1984). With diffusion theory, postmortem contamination of skeletal material is suggested when higher levels of an element are found in the soil surrounding a bone then in the bone itself.

As a means to control for diagenesis, comparisons were made between soil samples taken from various positions within each coffin. In 1984, when the remains from the Remley Cemetery were relocated, the use of diffusion theory for controlling diagenesis represented a valid methodology, and, while in dispute, the technique has yet to be proven ineffective.

## MATERIALS AND METHODS

### Skeletal Sample

The present study was conducted on a group of 26 adult skeletons relocated from an unmarked cemetery located east of Charleston in Mt. Pleasant, South Carolina (Fig. 1). Discovered during construction activities in 1984, the former cemetery yielded the remains of 36 individuals, including eight subadults (Rathbun, 1987). Historic records and maps indicated that the cemetery was part of a small plantation owned by Paul Remley until the end of the Civil War and thereafter by free African-American tenant farmers, many of whom were enslaved on the very lands they continued to farm (Crist, 1991). Based on stylistic evidence from the coffin furniture and burial artifacts, estimates for the use of the cemetery ranged between ca. 1840 and 1870, with none of the burials postdating 1920 (Trinkley & Hacker-Norton, 1984). The recovery of a legible memorial plate listing 1863 as the date of death for a 49 year old male supported these estimates.

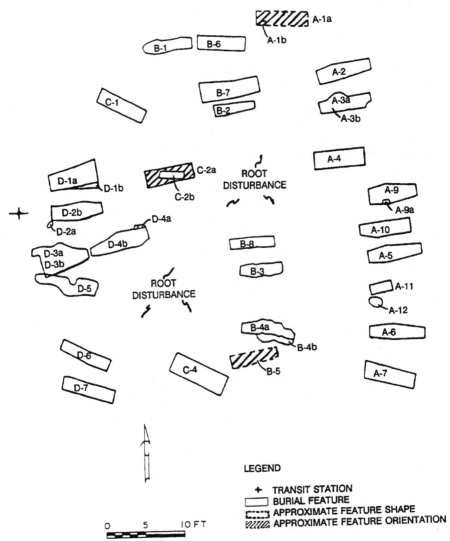

**FIGURE 1.** Site plan of the African-American Cemetery at the former Remley Plantation property, Mt. Pleasant, South Carolina; in use ca. 1840–1870.

Samples for bone-chemistry analysis were taken from 26 of the best-preserved adults (13 males and 13 females). The average age at death was 40 years for the females and 35 years for the males. Sixty-four percent of the adults presented evidence of generalized systemic infection and 36% exhibited cribra orbitalia, pin-point lesions in the orbital roofs that have been linked with genetic or iron-deficiency anemia (Stuart-Macadam & Kent, 1990; Stuart-Macadam, 1992). Thirty percent of the adults displayed diploic expansion, also suggestive of anemia. The prevalence of these lesions was not sex-specific. No lesions with specific nutritional etiologies were observed.

## Chemical Elements and Sample Preparation

A battery of 14 macro and trace elements shown in previous studies to vary by diet and occupational exposure was selected to assess dietary diversity among age and sex subgroups at the former Remley Plantation cemetery. These elements are listed in Table 2. All of the elements selected had been included in previous studies of diagenesis (Whitmer et al., 1989).

Bone samples were removed from the left femora of 26 well-preserved adult skeletons. Cross-sectional bone cores of approximately 1 gram each were taken from the mid-shaft of each femur, in order to include a representative portion of cortical bone from periosteal to endosteal surfaces. The bone cores were ground and dried at 100°C, then wet-ashed by a cool perchloric–nitric acid digest. Gentle heating drove off the nitric acid, and each sample was brought up to 20 ml in volume and 1 $N$ in acidity with deionized water.

The samples were analyzed by inductively coupled plasma emission spectrometry (ICP) using a Jarrell-Ash 9000 spectrometer at the University of Georgia Plasma Emission Laboratory. This technique involves the injection of the bone sample in solution into an argon plasma at approximately 15,000°C (Fassel, 1978). The resulting light is dispersed and the various wavelengths recorded by photocells. Since each chemical element emits a specific wavelength, the concentration of the element in the sample can be directly measured. Inductive plasma spectrometry is sensitive to most of the elements in the periodic table, and can distinguish concentrations as low as a few parts per billion in solution (Klepinger et al., 1986). Results are reported as parts per million (ppm) per ashed weight of bone except for calcium and phosphorus, which are reported as percent bone ash.

**TABLE 2. Elements Included in Chemical Analysis of Remley Plantation Skeletal Remains**

| Essential trace elements | Macro elements |
|---|---|
| Arsenic (As) | Calcium (Ca) |
| Copper (Cu) | Magnesium (Mg) |
| Iron (Fe) | Phosphorus (P) |
| Manganese (Mn) | Toxic elements |
| Selenium (Se) | Cadmium (Cd) |
| Silicon (Si) | Lead (Pb) |
| Strontium (Sr) | |
| Vanadium (V) | |
| Zinc (Zn) | |

## Subgroup Comparisons

Historical documentation regarding the diets of the enslaved in South Carolina indicated that most slave groups ate a homogenous diet served from a centralized kitchen. In order to test this historical statement, comparisons were made between the average levels of 14 elements in the skeletal remains of 1) males and females; 2) all individuals over and under age 40; 3) males over and under age 40; and 4) females over and under age 40. The breakpoint at 40 years of age was selected because it was the older of the two mean ages for the males and females from the Remley Cemetery and allowed almost equal sample sizes to be compared. Biologically, it represents the end of the reproductive years for women, and marks the beginning of the final third of the average lifespan for the individuals buried at the cemetery. Differences between clusters of average elemental concentrations among the selected subgroups would be taken to suggest dietary differences and varying occupational exposures among the members of each age and sex cohort.

## Statistical Analysis

In order to assess statistically whether bone-chemistry levels varied significantly among age and sex subgroups at the Remley Plantation Cemetery, the Student's *t*-test was performed univariately on the average concentrations of the 14 elements listed in Table 2. Recent discussion has focused on whether elemental concentrations are normally distributed and whether parametric or nonparametric statistics are more appropriate for analyzing bone-chemistry results (Buikstra, et al. 1989; Sandford, 1992). The *t*-test assumes that the sample variates are randomly selected from a normally distributed population, exhibit independent errors, and are homoscedastic, that is, exhibit homogenous variances. Some degree of violation, however, is permissible when employing the *t*-test on data that may not be normally distributed, as long as the hypotheses being tested are nondirectional (Thomas, 1986).

While the 0.05 level is usually taken to indicate the significance of observed differences, many researchers stress the importance of relationships between elements and expectations based on contextual data rather than on a strict adherence to statistical protocol (Gilbert, 1985, p. 355). Disregarding the results of *t*-tests not meeting the 0.05 confidence interval may obscure important relationships between chemical elements reflecting dietary trends. Therefore, several of the *t*-tests conducted on the Remley Plantation remains are included in the overall interpretation of the data, even if the test results approached but did not exceed the 95% confidence level.

## Controlling for Diagenesis

The sampling methodology for investigating the potential diagenetic changes in the remains from the Remley Cemetery was designed to measure the levels of elemental concentrations along a diffusion gradient. Soil samples were removed at progressively greater distances from the remains sampled for bone-chemistry analysis. Soil designated as "body" samples was removed from between the femora of each individual. The next interval of soil samples, designated "coffin" samples, was taken from 11 burials whose coffin outlines were clearly discernable. Soil was removed from within each coffin, near the inner wall of the sideboard. Each sample was approximately 30 cm from the skeleton. Six control samples were also taken from the approximate corners of the cemetery. The "control" samples were chosen to provide baseline concentration levels for the ambient soil at the site. One limitation in using the control samples was that they were taken from the graded levels at the site, rather than from the depth of the burials. However, the control samples were removed from within 30 cm of the burials. Soil pH levels were also assessed following the concentration gradient model.

## RESULTS

Archaeological and ethnographic evidence strongly suggests that enslaved African Americans supplemented their masters' rations by growing their own vegetables and raising domesticated livestock. Further evidence indicates that many of the enslaved exploited local maritime resources and hunted wild game, even using firearms whose parts have been recovered from slave living quarters (Fairbanks & Mullins-Moore, 1980; Singleton, 1991). This data contradicts much of the historical documentation that indicates the enslaved shared the same diet from a central kitchen supplied by the plantation master. The hypothesis tested in the current study stated that if the enslaved at the Remley Plantation shared a similar core diet their bone-chemistry levels would not differ among the age and sex subgroups of the assemblage. If, however, the diets of the subgroups were different, due to occupations, the African-American social structure, or individual cooking practices, then bone-chemistry levels would vary significantly among age and sex cohorts. This hypothesis does not entertain the possibility that sex- and age-related physiological differences could also lead to similar trends in bone-chemistry levels, since analysis by age and sex subgroups more likely reflects intergroup dietary patterns rather than intragroup physiological phenomena.

### Sex: Males Compared to Females

Comparisons between males and females (Table 3) indicated that only the strontium concentrations differed significantly (reaching the 0.01 level), with the females exhibiting a higher average value. The females also presented a higher average copper level, although the statistical significance of the difference with the males only approached the 0.05 confidence level (p value of 0.08). Higher strontium levels among the female sample suggests a greater dependence on vegetable and marine resources than that of the males. And even though the other elements used in the comparisons did not differ significantly between the males and females, general trends provided evidence that the males ate more meats, cereals, and nuts than did the females. For instance, the average concentration of selenium, an essential trace

**TABLE 3. Mean Elemental Concentrations[a] in Males and Females from the Remley Cemetery Site**

| | Males (n = 13) | | Females (n = 13) | | |
| | Mean | s.d. | Mean | s.d. | p |
|---|---|---|---|---|---|
| As | 24.14 | 22.03 | 26.88 | 21.85 | .7531 |
| Cu | 0.36 | 0.73 | 1.02 | 1.04 | .0770 |
| Fe | 0.38 | 1.03 | 0.48 | 1.18 | .8203 |
| Mn | 0.26 | 0.48 | 0.35 | 0.53 | .6741 |
| Se | 12.07 | 24.53 | 4.59 | 11.98 | .3328 |
| Si | 3289.92 | 1238.00 | 2932.61 | 1307.00 | .4812 |
| Sr | 27.19 | 3.67 | 31.20 | 4.04 | .0142[b] |
| V | 2.41 | 2.81 | 3.79 | 4.23 | .3358 |
| Zn | 27.25 | 33.20 | 51.50 | 34.74 | .5062 |
| Ca | 38.79 | 1.66 | 38.98 | 1.18 | .7447 |
| Mg | 312.75 | 56.24 | 299.56 | 52.16 | .5410 |
| P | 17.66 | 0.80 | 17.56 | 0.56 | .7308 |
| Cd | 0.40 | 0.95 | 0.35 | 0.92 | .9006 |
| Pb | 23.36 | 26.52 | 30.18 | 38.90 | .6061 |

[a]Concentrations reported in parts per million (ppm) except Ca and P, reported in percent bone ash.
[b]Values significant at or below 0.05 confidence level.

element provided through the ingestion of seafood and organ meats, was two and one-half times higher in the males. The low strontium and high selenium levels in the males suggests a diet based predominantly on animal-derived products, while the opposite concentrations of these elements in the females indicates a different diet, one more reliant on leafy and leguminous vegetables.

Copper and zinc were both found in higher average concentrations in the females. Both elements are indicators of animal-dependent diets, but may also reflect the greater use of cereal grains by the males. Cereal grains contain phytate, which inhibits zinc absorption and leads to higher levels of copper. Since both copper and zinc levels were higher in the females by three and two times the concentrations in males, respectively, the males may have been eating more cereal grains, as suggested by higher levels of magnesium and silicon among the male sample. Magnesium is very highly concentrated in cereal grains and in nuts, while silicon is suggestive of unpolished rice and grains. Cadmium, another element highly concentrated in wheat and rice, was also higher in the males. Cadmium is found in very low levels in nuts, so the higher levels in the males may reflect a greater prevalence of nuts in the diets of the men.

The females from the Remley Cemetery presented higher lead levels than did the males, perhaps indicating that females on this plantation were more likely to be assigned domestic chores than the enslaved males. These women would have been more susceptible to lead contamination as a result of their proximity to lead-glazed serving wares and foods stored in lead-glazed containers. The male slaves, whose daily work in the field limited their access to the master's food supplies, would have exhibited a reduced overall lead intake. Lead-glazed wares recovered from slave cabins also suggest that women cooking in their own quarters after the regular workday had a greater exposure to lead than did the males.

## Age and Sex: Males and Females over and under 40 Years

In order to evaluate whether sex-related differences in diet were also influenced by age, the adults were separated into two age groups with 40 years as the break-point, since it is the older of the two mean ages for the males and females (35 and 40 years respectively). Combined by sex, 15 adults were under 40 and 11 over 40 (Table 4).

Three elements, manganese, strontium, and cadmium, varied significantly (at or below the 0.05 level) between the two age groups, with all three elements in higher average concentrations in the males and females over 40. Manganese was more than seven times lower in the younger adults, while cadmium was almost ten times higher in the older adults. These values suggest that older adults primarily subsisted on leafy vegetables, grains, and cereals. Selenium, representative of animal-based diets, was 46 times higher in the younger adults, also strongly suggesting that younger adults

TABLE 4. Mean Elemental Concentrations[a] in Females and Males over and under age 40 from the Remley Cemetery Site

| | Females and males over 40 ($n = 11$) | | Females and males under 40 ($n = 15$) | | |
|-----|-----|-----|-----|-----|-----|
| | Mean | s.d. | Mean | s.d. | $p$ |
| As | 17.55 | 21.38 | 31.35 | 20.39 | .1078 |
| Cu | 0.73 | 0.96 | 0.66 | 0.97 | .8618 |
| Fe | 0.65 | 1.46 | 0.26 | 0.73 | .3720 |
| Mn | 0.61 | 0.64 | 0.08 | 0.04 | .0049[b] |
| Se | 0.31 | 1.03 | 14.21 | 24.01 | .0684 |
| Si | 2749.36 | 1313.00 | 3376.67 | 1195.00 | .2167 |
| Sr | 31.23 | 4.51 | 27.71 | 3.59 | .0363[b] |
| V | 3.70 | 4.03 | 2.66 | 3.31 | .4770 |
| Zn | 28.85 | 36.27 | 47.09 | 116.50 | .6219 |
| Ca | 38.57 | 1.30 | 39.12 | 1.49 | .3396 |
| Mg | 284.61 | 45.43 | 321.96 | 54.93 | .0784 |
| P | 17.46 | 0.56 | 17.72 | 0.75 | .3453 |
| Cd | 0.78 | 1.28 | 0.08 | 0.31 | .0508[b] |
| Pb | 24.45 | 23.20 | 28.48 | 39.11 | .7636 |

[a]Concentrations reported in parts per million (ppm) except Ca and P, reported in percent bone ash.
[b]Values significant at or below 0.05 confidence level.

had access to more animal-derived products. Zinc was one and one-half times higher in the younger adults, and although not statistically significant, supports the interpretation that older adults ate more vegetables and less meat products.

Lead levels, which typically accumulate in human bone through years of exposure, were higher in the younger adults. This result may reflect a reduced exposure to lead in older age among both sexes, as well as a greater exposure by younger female adults who performed domestic chores including cooking. Additionally, if older members of the Remley Plantation ate more grains, vegetables, and seafood than the younger slaves, they may have had less exposure to foods that had been stored in lead-glazed containers. Arsenic was almost two times higher in the younger adults, and, as arsenic-deprivation indicators are similar to zinc-deficiency symptoms, may reflect the distribution of zinc between the two groups.

### Age: Males over and under 40

To assess whether dietary trends based on age differences independent of sex existed within the African-American community at the Remley Plantation, males and females were analyzed separately according to age. Two elements, arsenic and manganese, varied significantly between five males over 40 years and eight males under 40 (Table 5). The level of manganese was 12 times greater in males over 40, while

**TABLE 5. Mean Elemental Concentrations[a] in Males over and under age 40 from the Remley Cemetery Site**

|  | Males over 40 (n = 5) | | Males under 40 (n = 8) | | |
|---|---|---|---|---|---|
|  | Mean | s.d. | Mean | s.d. | p |
| As | 9.40 | 15.14 | 33.35 | 21.19 | .0513[b] |
| Cu | 0.40 | 0.69 | 0.34 | 0.81 | .8888 |
| Fe | 0.72 | 1.61 | 0.16 | 0.46 | .3663 |
| Mn | 0.60 | 0.66 | 0.05 | 0.14 | .0396[b] |
| Se | 0.68 | 1.52 | 19.19 | 29.66 | .1976 |
| Si | 2886.40 | 1374.00 | 3542.13 | 1166.00 | .3758 |
| Sr | 29.26 | 4.74 | 25.90 | 2.30 | .1107 |
| V | 2.66 | 2.88 | 2.25 | 2.96 | .8106 |
| Zn | 41.64 | 53.52 | 18.25 | 3.60 | .2316 |
| Ca | 38.29 | 1.30 | 39.11 | 1.87 | .4148 |
| Mg | 286.00 | 43.42 | 329.48 | 59.28 | .1859 |
| P | 17.63 | 0.45 | 17.68 | 0.99 | .9229 |
| Cd | 0.80 | 1.43 | 0.15 | 0.42 | .2441 |
| Pb | 27.36 | 23.70 | 20.86 | 29.43 | .6864 |

[a]Concentrations reported in parts per million (ppm) except Ca and P, reported in percent bone ash.
[b]Values significant at or below 0.05 confidence level.

arsenic concentrations were three and one-half times greater in the younger males. Although not statistically significant, the average selenium level was 28 times greater in younger males, while zinc was a little over two times higher in older males. Cadmium was almost five and one-half times higher in older males. Strontium was also higher in the older males. The levels of these elements suggest that older males ate more leafy and leguminous vegetables, and the high selenium level among the younger males indicates that the younger males subsisted on a diet predominantly based on animal products.

Lead levels were higher in the older males, likely reflective of longer average lifetime exposures. The difference may also reflect the reassignment of older males to more domestic chores, bringing them into closer contact with lead-glazed wares and contaminated foodstuffs.

## Age: Females over and under 40

No elements varied significantly among the older and younger groups of women (Table 6). However, even though not varying significantly, the trends among the elements under investigation suggest that older women relied more heavily on plant foods. Strontium, vanadium, and cadmium levels were all greater in the women over 40. Women under 40 exhibited no cadmium in their skeletal remains, while no

**TABLE 6. Mean Elemental Concentrations[a] in Females over and under age 40 from the Remley Cemetery Site**

|  | Females over 40 ($n = 6$) | | Females under 40 ($n = 7$) | | |
|  | Mean | s.d. | Mean | s.d. | $p$ |
|---|---|---|---|---|---|
| As | 24.33 | 24.68 | 29.06 | 20.86 | .7152 |
| Cu | 1.00 | 1.12 | 1.03 | 1.07 | .9632 |
| Fe | 0.60 | 1.47 | 0.37 | 0.98 | .7443 |
| Mn | 0.62 | 0.68 | 0.11 | 0.20 | .0868 |
| Se | 0.00 | 0.00 | 8.51 | 15.75 | .2152 |
| Si | 2635.17 | 1380.00 | 3187.57 | 1290.00 | .4717 |
| Sr | 32.87 | 3.95 | 29.77 | 3.81 | .1791 |
| V | 4.57 | 4.89 | 3.13 | 3.85 | .5647 |
| Zn | 18.18 | 6.28 | 80.06 | 171.11 | .3979 |
| Ca | 38.80 | 1.38 | 39.13 | 1.07 | .6347 |
| Mg | 283.45 | 51.14 | 313.37 | 52.72 | .3233 |
| P | 17.32 | 0.65 | 17.77 | 0.40 | .1554 |
| Cd | 0.77 | 1.28 | 0.00 | 0.00 | .1391 |
| Pb | 22.02 | 24.73 | 37.19 | 48.91 | .5074 |

[a]Concentrations reported in parts per million (ppm) except Ca and P, reported in percent bone ash.
[b]Values significant at or below 0.05 confidence level.

selenium was present in the bones of the older females. Zinc levels were almost four and one-half times lower in the older females.

In contrast to the pattern observed among the males, the average lead level was over one and one-half times higher in the younger women, probably reflecting a more intense exposure to lead through occupational activities. Women under 40 exhibited the highest lead levels among all sex and age subgroups from the Remley Cemetery.

### Diagenesis

Comparisons between elemental levels of soil samples taken from inside the coffins, at the coffin sideboards, and outside of the cemetery were made to assess the degree of movement of the elements used to reconstruct dietary trends at the Remley Cemetery. Table 7 provides the results of the soils analysis and comparisons with the average elemental levels in the adult bone samples.

Student's $t$-tests performed on the soil samples indicated that most elements used in dietary reconstructions were significantly higher in soil samples taken near the skeletal remains than in either the coffin or control samples (Table 8). The pH levels and strontium, zinc, and calcium concentrations were significantly higher in the body samples when compared with both the coffin and control samples. When comparing the body samples to the control samples, iron and silicon were both significantly

**TABLE 7. Mean Elemental Concentrations[a] in Bone and Soil Samples Taken at the Remley Cemetery Site**

| | Bone | | Body ($n$ = 25) | | Coffin ($n$ = 11) | | Control ($n$ = 6) | |
|---|---|---|---|---|---|---|---|---|
| | Males | Females | Mean | s.d. | Mean | s.d. | Mean | s.d. |
| pH | — | — | 4.54 | 0.48 | 4.14 | 0.62 | 3.88 | 0.39 |
| As[b] | 24.24 | 26.88 | — | — | — | — | — | — |
| Cu | 0.36 | 1.02 | 7.57 | 8.22 | 4.43 | 9.55 | 1.27 | 2.22 |
| Fe | 0.38 | 0.48 | 262.81 | 86.08 | 207.38 | 71.49 | 113.48 | 30.93 |
| Mn | 0.26 | 0.35 | 3.13 | 3.67 | 3.43 | 2.67 | 3.46 | 2.62 |
| Se[b] | 12.07 | 4.59 | — | — | — | — | — | — |
| Si | 3289.92 | 2932.61 | 146.53 | 67.77 | 182.02 | 86.00 | 370.72 | 147.53 |
| Sr | 27.19 | 31.20 | 3.04 | 2.17 | 1.35 | 1.46 | 0.21 | 0.07 |
| V[b] | 2.41 | 3.79 | — | — | — | — | — | — |
| Zn | 27.25 | 51.50 | 7.74 | 6.95 | 2.11 | 1.84 | 1.23 | 1.08 |
| Ca | 38.79 | 38.98 | 10.06 | 8.66 | 4.06 | 5.19 | 0.41 | 0.09 |
| Mg | 312.75 | 299.56 | 90.65 | 107.69 | 33.75 | 34.58 | 11.33 | 5.19 |
| P | 17.66 | 17.56 | 8.63 | 4.62 | 3.74 | 3.79 | 9.50 | 5.78 |
| Cd | 0.40 | 0.35 | 0.14 | 0.06 | 0.11 | 0.04 | 0.12 | 0.03 |
| Pb | 23.56 | 30.18 | 30.23 | 46.86 | 23.95 | 36.65 | 34.20 | 47.53 |

[a]Concentrations reported in parts per million (ppm) except Ca and P, reported in percent bone ash.
[b]Element not included in sampling.

**TABLE 8. Results of Student's *t*-Tests on Soil Samples[a] from the Remley Cemetery Site**

| | Samples[b] | | |
| --- | --- | --- | --- |
| | Body compared to coffin (*p* value) | Coffin compared to control (*p* value) | Body compared to control (*p* value) |
| pH | .0556[c] | .3768 | .0041[c] |
| Cu | .3205 | .4440 | .0761 |
| Fe | .0706 | .0084[c] | .0003[c] |
| Mn | .8049 | .9824 | .8342 |
| Si | .1913 | .0042[c] | .0001[c] |
| Sr | .0250[c] | .0784 | .0038[c] |
| Zn | .0129[c] | .3023 | .0316[c] |
| Ca | .0408[c] | .1105 | .0116[c] |
| Mg | .0979 | .1406 | .0855 |
| P | .0041[c] | .0248[c] | .6956 |
| Cd | .1504 | .7104 | .3397 |
| Pb | .6963 | .6263 | .8541 |

[a]Concentrations reported in parts per million (ppm).
[b]$n = 25$ for body samples; $n = 11$ for coffin samples; $n = 6$ for control samples.
[c]Values significant at or below 0.05 confidence level.

higher in the control samples, indicating the presence of these elements in the ambient sandy soil matrix. Iron and silicon were also significantly higher in the control samples when compared with the coffin samples.

Following diffusion-gradient theory, it appears that at the Remley Cemetery site, if any of the elements of importance in dietary reconstructions were transported, their direction was from the skeletal remains into the surrounding soil. Comparing the elemental levels of the skeletal samples to those in the soil samples suggests stability of some of the most important elements in dietary reconstructions. Strontium, zinc, calcium, magnesium, phosphorus, and cadmium were in significantly highest concentrations in the skeletal samples. Copper and iron were significantly higher in the body and coffin samples, perhaps reflecting the decay of coffin hardware attached to the coffin sideboards. Based on the large differences between the average concentrations of most elements tested in the skeletal and soil samples, it appears that diagenetic processes did not significantly alter the chemical composition of the remains of the individuals buried at the Remley Cemetery site. Therefore, the results of the bone-chemistry analyses can be accepted with a high degree of confidence.

## DISCUSSION

Foodways are an integral part of any social group, and as such partly shape the culture of the group, becoming one of the symbols of group identity (Joyner, 1984). This phenomenon is particularly important in the lives of disenfranchised groups like the enslaved African Americans of the Old South, who sought empowerment within a society in which they were absolutely exploited. Foodways consist of an interrelated system of procurement, distribution, preparation, and consumption. Within the slave community the master maintained control of most aspects of this system, but not as completely as the historical documentation usually suggests. Sutch (1976) distinguished between the *ration* and *diet* of the enslaved, wherein the rations supplied by the slavemasters were monotonous and perhaps inadequate and the diet was more richly supplemented by foods procured by the enslaved themselves. The true heterogeneity of slave diets has only recently been appreciated (Reitz et al., 1985; Singleton, 1991).

Archaeological and ethnographic evidence clearly indicates that the enslaved in the South Carolina Low Country did not always share a central kitchen, and that many of the enslaved prepared and ate most of their meals in their own quarters. Although well-documented in plantation records, no archaeological evidence of the centralized kitchens has thus far been recovered (Singleton, 1991). Evidence from plantation account books also indicates that the rations provided to the enslaved were based on the occupations, work assignments, ages, and sexes of the slave complement.

Primary historical sources indicate that enslaved African Americans were typically provided a core diet of beef, salt pork, bacon, salt fish, cornmeal, rice or peas, and occasionally molasses (Gibbs et al., 1980; Hilliard, 1972; Olmsted, 1856). Rice was a staple crop in the Low Country, distributed almost every working day throughout the year and often boiled with salt pork, fish, and vegetables (Joyner, 1984). While exslave narratives differ in regards to the composition of the slave diet, probably the result of regional variety and plantation masters' preferences, it is generally agreed that the core diet was consistent, if not monotonous.

Zooarchaeological evidence from numerous sites in the southeast strongly suggests that the diet of the enslaved was considerably more varied than is inferred by historical sources. Vegetables and other seasonal foods may not have been recorded in travellers' accounts, and many slaveholders did not want to acknowledge the amount of food stolen by slaves as acts of empowerment and resistance. Some plantation masters allowed their slaves to tend their own vegetable gardens near their quarters (Flanders, 1933; Joyner, 1984; Olmsted, 1856; Stampp, 1956; Yetman, 1970), increasing the variety of their diets. Joyner (1984) noted that the basic ingredients in the diets of the enslaved were vegetables, which were sometimes grown in a large communal garden for the whole plantation. The more typical pattern was for the enslaved to have small garden plots near their own quarters, which they tended after the regular workday was completed (Vlach, 1993). These gardens allowed the enslaved an opportunity for autonomy, leading to an extensive market economy and occasionally freedom for some of the enslaved (Rawick, 1972).

Between the 1830s and 1860s, treatment of the enslaved in the South apparently improved as slaveholders attempted to convince the enslaved that emancipation would not improve their socioeconomic conditions (Genovese, 1974; Koger, 1985). This included improvements to the physical structures intended for the welfare of the enslaved (Anonymous, 1858). Dining halls were constructed on many plantations in which all the adult slaves ate a common diet. Food for the children was often prepared and provided separately. On the larger plantations field slaves and house slaves often had their own kitchens and mess halls, with fares specific to each. These meals, however, did not preclude the enslaved from supplementing their rations with their own foodstuffs prepared in their quarters. In fact, many slaves resisted their masters' attempts to provide communal kitchens, preferring to receive rations they could cook themselves.

While on many plantations centralized kitchens were used for the early meals, the last meal of the day was usually prepared individually in the family quarters (Fox-Genovese, 1988). Many slave quarters were hall-and-parlor houses or two-unit buildings, each type of which included chimneys on the gabled ends or the center of the structures for cooking and heating (Vlach, 1993). It is from within these cabins that archaeological evidence of African-American foodways provides the most revealing portraits of daily slave subsistence.

In general, African-American women were commonly the cooks on the southern plantations, preparing meals for the slaveholders' families as well as for the enslaved themselves. While elderly men who could no longer work in the fields sometimes worked as cooks, female slaves were typically given the absolute responsibility to oversee the operations of the plantation kitchens (Fox-Genovese, 1988).

Along the southern coast the enslaved had numerous ecological niches to exploit in supplementing their plantation rations. A combination of forests, saltwater tidal marshes, and freshwater creeks and rivers provided an abundance of species that could be fished, trapped, or hunted throughout the year. One estimate is that wild game may have comprised 40% of the meat in diets of the enslaved along the South Carolina coast (Reitz et al., 1985). Mammals like sheep and goats that could be raised easily on modest plots of land were also important sources of food. Chickens, more valued for their eggs, comprised only a minor proportion of the overall diet (Singleton, 1991). The remains of marine animals and numerous fishing hooks recovered from slave quarters attests to the importance that marine resources had in the diets the enslaved chose for themselves. Pork products were also essential to the diet of the enslaved, partially because pigs were easier than cattle to raise near the slave quarters and pork preserved better than beef (Bowen, 1988; Hilliard, 1969; Otto, 1984).

Bone-chemical analysis of the skeletal remains from the Remley Cemetery resulted in some dietary trends becoming evident through the distribution of elemental concentrations in age and sex subgroups. As a group, it appeared that males ate more animal-derived products, grains, and nuts than did the females. Men working in the fields often received only grits and rice for lunch and at breaks, whereas women working in closer proximity to the master's provisions may have had greater access to more vegetables. However, as indicated by plantation records and ethnographic accounts, meat may have been reserved for the male fieldworkers rather than the female domestic servants, who typically received more vegetables in their rations. Meat may have represented a dietary item of low preference in the diets of the enslaved, and may have been fed to the fieldworkers in their capacity as lower-status slaves.

Regardless of sex, older adults at the Remley Plantation apparently relied on diets predominantly comprised of more vegetables and less meat products. This is consistent with historical accounts of the older slaves being reassigned to domestic chores that brought them into closer proximity to fresh vegetables in the master's house. Also, the older adults were often given the responsibility to care for the children of both the master and the enslaved, most of whom ate more vegetables than animal products. A cultural reason may also account for these results. Most of the enslaved in South Carolina originated in West Africa, where the diets consisted of very little meat and large quantities of vegetables and rice, often dipped in relishes and then eaten. Older African Americans may have developed a preference in childhood for vegetable foods, based in part on African dietary traditions that survived the middle passage and became rooted in African-American society. The forms and styles of many of the wares made by African Americans (called colono-wares) found within slave quarters suggests that many of the foods the enslaved ate were prepared and served in much the same fashion as were traditional foods in the West African homeland (Ferguson, 1990).

When analyzed separately, the elemental concentrations of both males and females over 40 years of age suggested that both groups subsisted on diets primarily based on vegetable products. It appears that age and sex as social factors operated independently of each other at the Remley Plantation, so that age rather than sex was the primary factor in determining the diet of an individual. Conversely, exposure to lead, probably as a result of occupational activities, appears to have been based on sex rather than age, in that as a group younger females exhibited the highest average lead levels among the Remley Cemetery remains. Again, historical documentation strongly indicates that female slaves primarily performed domestic chores often focused in the kitchens, where access to lead-glazed wares and contaminated food-stuffs and water were common. Fieldworkers were less likely to come into contact with such items and therefore exhibited lower average lead concentrations. Lead levels among the Remley Cemetery remains were highest among the younger females and lowest among the younger males, the latter of whom were most likely to be field slaves.

## CONCLUSION

Whether the results of the bone-chemistry analysis of this or any other skeletal series actually reflects dietary trends in the past remains at least as debatable as the effects of diagenesis on archaeological bone samples. Elemental bone levels most likely reflect very complicated and interwoven aspects of human physiology, nutrition, skeletal biochemistry, and taphonomic processes and are surely not simply the results of ingestion, digestion, and distribution of foodstuffs and their chemical constituents. In order to understand even a fraction of the complexities of human biochemistry, the researcher must attempt to derive from an entangled web of possibilities a few basic expectations and subject them to scientific scrutiny in order to begin to unravel the mysteries of the whole interrelated system.

The results of the bone-chemistry analysis of the Remley Cemetery remains were consistent with evidence provided by archaeological, ethnographic, and historical documentation, and provided no contradictory data regarding the diets of the enslaved in the Old South. In essence, these results supported the findings of previous studies and demonstrated a testable, repeatable technique through which the diets and internal social dynamics of past groups can be investigated. The importance of the present effort is that dietary differences between age and sex subgroups were demonstrated at least grossly within the enslaved community at the Remley Plantation. As the precision of bone-chemistry studies becomes increasingly better defined, a more accurate reconstruction of the foodways of enslaved African Americans will be realized, as will a truer appreciation of the African-American social identity within that most peculiar of human institutions.

## ACKNOWLEDGMENTS

I would like to express my appreciation to Anne Grauer for the opportunity to contribute this chapter to this important volume. I would also like to acknowledge the support of Ted A. Rathbun, who played an instrumental role in my research. I thank Leland G. Ferguson, Greta D. Little, and John L. Seidel for their review of this chapter in its earlier incarnation as my master's thesis and for their very helpful suggestions. More recent comments were provided by Arthur Washburn and Molly A. Hickey. I stand solely responsible for the interpretations and any errors or omissions in this research and this chapter. This research was supported in part by NIH Biomedical Research Support Grant Award 507 RR07160.

## REFERENCES

Anonymous (1858). Notes on the management of a southern rice plantation. DeBows Review 24:324–326.

Aufderheide AC, Neiman FD, Wittmers, Jr. LE, Rapp, Jr. G (1981). Lead in bone. II: Skeletal-lead content as an indicator of lifetime lead ingestion and the social correlates in an archaeological population. Am J Phys Anthropol 55:285–291.

Aufderheide AC, Angel JL, Kelley JO, Outlaw AC, Outlaw MA, Rapp, Jr. G, Wittmers LE (1985). Lead in bone. III: Prediction of social correlates from skeletal lead content in four colonial American populations (Catoctin Furnace, College Landing, Governor's Land, and Irene Mound). Am J Phys Anthropol 66:353–361.

Beck LA (1985). Bivariate analysis of trace elements in bone. J Hum Evol 14:493–502.

Blassingame JW (1979). The Slave Community: Plantation Life in the Antebellum South. New York: Oxford University Press.

Bowen J (1988). Seasonality: An agricultural construct. In Beaudry MC (ed.), Documentary Archaeology in the New World, pp. 161–171. Cambridge: Cambridge University Press.

Brown A (1973). Bone strontium content as a dietary indicator in human skeletal populations. PhD dissertation, University of Michigan. Ann Arbor: University Microfilms.

Buikstra JE, Frankenberg S, Lambert JB, Xue L (1989). Multiple elements: Multiple expectations. In Price TD (ed.), The Chemistry of Prehistoric Human Bone, pp. 155–210. Cambridge: Cambridge University Press.

Corruccini RS, Aufderheide AC, Handler JS, Wittmers LE (1987). Patterns of skeletal lead content in Barbados slaves. Archaeometry 29:233–239.

Crist TAJ (1991). The Bone Chemical Analysis and Bioarchaeology of an Historic South Carolina African-American Cemetery. Volumes in Historical Archaeology No. 18. Columbia: South Carolina Institute of Archaeology and Anthropology.

Ericson JE, Coughlin EA (1981). Archaeological toxicology. Ann New York Acad Sci 376:393–403.

Fairbanks CH, Mullins-Moore SA (1980). How did slaves live? Early Man 2:2–6.

Fassel VA (1978). Quantitative elemental analyses by plasma emission spectroscopy. Science 202:183–191.

Ferguson LG (1990). Uncommon Ground: Archaeology and Early African America, 1650–1800. Washington, DC: Smithsonian Institution Press.

Flanders RB (1933). Plantation Slavery in Georgia. Chapel Hill: University of North Carolina Press.

Fogel RW, Engerman SL (1974). Time on the Cross: The Economics of American Negro Slavery. Boston: Little, Brown.

Fox-Genovese E (1988). Within the Plantation Household: Black and White Women of the Old South. Chapel Hill: University of North Carolina Press.

Furr AK, MacDaniels LH, St. John, Jr. LE, Gutenmann WH, Pakkala IS, Lisk DJ (1979). Elemental composition of tree nuts. Bull Env Contam Tox 21:392–396.

Genovese ED (1974). Roll, Jordan, Roll: The World the Slaves Made. New York: Random House.

Gibbs T, Cargill K, Lieberman LS, Reitz EJ (1980). Nutrition in a slave population: An anthropological examination. Med Anthropol 4:175–262.

Gilbert RI (1975). Trace element analysis of three skeletal Amerindian populations at Dickson Mounds. PhD dissertation, University of Massachusetts at Amherst. Ann Arbor: University Microfilms.

Gilbert RI (1985). Stress, paleonutrition, and trace elements. In Gilbert RI, Mielke JH (eds.), The Analysis of Prehistoric Human Diets, pp. 339–358. Orlando: Academic Press.

Grupe G, Herrmann B (eds.) (1988). Trace Elements in Environmental History. Heidelberg: Springer-Verlag.

Gutman H (1976). The Black Family in Slavery and Freedom, 1750–1925. New York: Pantheon Books.

Handler JS, Corruccini RS (1983). Plantation slave life in Barbados: A physical anthropological analysis. J Interdisc Hist 14:65–90.

Hilliard SB (1972). Hog Meat and Hoe Cake: Food Supply in the Old South, 1840–1860. Carbondale: Southern Illinois University Press.

Hilliard SB (1969). Pork in the antebellum south: The geography of self-sufficiency. Ann Assoc Amer Geographers 59:461–480.

Joyner C (1984). Down By the Riverside: A South Carolina Slave Community. Urbana: University of Illinois Press.

Kelley JO, Angel JL (1987). Life stresses of slavery. Am J Phys Anthropol 74:199–211.

Khudabux MR (1991). Effects of life conditions on the health of a Negro slave community in

Suriname. PhD dissertation, Leiden University, Netherlands. The Hague: Pasmans Offset-drukkerij BV.

Kiple KF, King VH (1981). Another Dimension to the Black Diaspora: Diet, Disease, and Racism. Cambridge: Cambridge University Press.

Klepinger LL, Kuhn JK, Williams WS (1986). An elemental analysis of archaeological bone from Sicily as a test of predictability of diagenetic change. Am J Phys Anthropol 70:325–331.

Koger (1985). Black Slaveholders: Free Black Slave Masters in South Carolina, 1790–1860. Jefferson, NC: McFarland.

Lambert JB, Szpunar CB, Buikstra JE (1979). Chemical analysis of excavated human bone from middle and late Woodland sites. Archaeometry 21:403–416.

Lambert JB, Simpson SV, Szpunar CB, Buikstra JE (1984). Copper and barium as dietary discriminants: The effects of diagenesis. Archaeometry 26:131–138.

Lambert JB, Grupe G (1993). Prehistoric Human Bone: Archaeology at the Molecular Level. New York: Springer-Verlag.

Mertz W (ed.) (1986). Trace Elements in Human and Animal Nutrition (5th ed.). New York: Academic Press.

Morris VC, Levander AO (1970). Selenium content of foods. Nutrition 100:1383–1388.

Mullin M (1992). Africa in America: Slave Acculturation and Resistance in the American South and British Caribbean, 1736–1831. Urbana: University of Illinois Press.

Olmsted FL (1856). A Journey in the Seaboard Slave States: With Remarks on Their Economy. New York: Dix and Edwards.

Otto JS (1984). Cannon's Point Plantation, 1794–1860: Living Conditions and Status Patterns in the Old South. Orlando: Academic Press.

Owsley DW, Orser CE, Mann RW, Moore-Jansen PH, Montgomery RL (1987). Demography and pathology of an urban slave population from New Orleans. Am J Phys Anthropol 74:185–197.

Passwater RA, Cranton EM (1983). Trace Elements, Hair Analysis, and Nutrition. New Canaan, CT: Keats.

Price TD (ed.) (1989a). The Chemistry of Prehistoric Human Bone. Cambridge: Cambridge University Press.

Price TD (1989b). Multi-element studies of diagenesis in prehistoric bone. In Price TD (ed.), The Chemistry of Prehistoric Human Bone, pp. 126–154. Cambridge: Cambridge University Press.

Radosevich SC (1989). Diet or diagenesis: An evaluation of the trace element analysis of bone. PhD. dissertation, University of Oregon.

Radosevich SC (1993). The six deadly sins of trace element analysis: A case of wishful thinking in science. In Sandford MK (ed.), Investigations of Ancient Human Tissue, pp. 269–332. Langhorne, PA: Gordon and Breach.

Rathbun TA (1987). Health and disease at a South Carolina plantation: 1840-1870. Am J Phys Anthropol 74:239–253.

Rawick GP (ed.) (1972). The American Slave: A Composite Autobiography. 19 vols. Westport, CT: Greenwood Press.

Reitz EJ, Gibbs T, Rathbun TA (1985). Archaeological evidence for subsistence on coastal plantations. In Singleton TA (ed.), The Archaeology of Slavery and Plantation Life, pp. 163–191. Orlando: Academic Press.

Sandford MK (1992). A reconsideration of trace element analysis in prehistoric bone. In Saunders SR, Katzenberg MA (eds.), Skeletal Biology of Past Peoples: Research Methods, pp. 79–103. New York: Wiley-Liss.

Sandford MK (ed.) (1993). Investigations of Ancient Human Tissue. Langhorne, PA: Gordon and Breach.

Schoeninger MJ (1979). Diet and status at Chalcatzingo: Some empirical and technical aspects of strontium analysis. Am J Phys Anthropol 51:295–310.

Schroeder HA, Balassa JJ, Tipton IH (1963). Abnormal trace elements in man: Vanadium. Chron Diseases 16:1047–1071.

Schuyler RL (ed.) (1980). Archaeological Perspectives on Ethnicity in America. Farmingdale, NY: Baywood.

Sillen A (1989). Diagenesis of the inorganic phase of cortical bone. In Price TD (ed.), The Chemistry of Prehistoric Human Bone, pp. 211–229. Cambridge: Cambridge University Press.

Sillen A, Kavanagh M (1982). Strontium and paleodietary research: A review. Yearbk Phys Anthropol 25:67–90.

Singleton TA (1991). The archaeology of slave life. In Campbell, Jr. EDC (ed.), Before Freedom Came: African-American Life in the Antebellum South, pp. 155–175. Richmond: The Museum of the Confederacy.

Stampp K (1956). The Peculiar Institution: Slavery in the Antebellum South. New York: Alfred A. Knopf.

Stuart-Macadam PL, Kent S (eds.) (1990). Diet, Demography, and Disease: Changing Perspectives on Anemia. New York: Aldine de Gruyter.

Stuart-Macadam PL (1992). Porotic hyperostosis: A new perspective. Am J Phys Anthropol 87:39–47.

Sutch R (1976). The care and feeding of slaves. In David PA, Gutman HG, Sutch R, Temin P, Wright G (eds.), Reckoning with Slavery: A Critical Study of the Quantitative History of American Negro Slavery, pp. 231–301. New York: Oxford University Press.

Sutch R (1975). The treatment received by American slaves: A critical review of the evidence presented in "Time on the Cross." Explor Econ Hist 12:386–394.

Thomas DH (1986). Refiguring Anthropology. Chicago: Waveland.

Trinkley MB, Hacker-Norton D (1984). Analysis of Coffin Hardware from 38CH778, Charleston County, South Carolina. Research Series 3. Columbia, SC: Chicora Foundation.

Urist MR (1980). Fundamental and Clinical Bone Physiology. Philadelphia: Lippincott.

Vlach JM (1993). Back of the Big House: The Architecture of Plantation Slavery. Chapel Hill: University of North Carolina Press.

Whitmer AM, Ramenofsky AF, Thomas J, Thibodeaux LJ, Field SD, Miller BJ (1989). Stability or instability: The role of diffusion in trace element studies. In Schiffer MB (ed.), Archaeological Method and Theory (Vol. 1), pp. 205–273. Tucson: University of Arizona Press.

Yetman N (ed.) (1970). Life Under the "Peculiar Institution": Selections from the Slave Narrative Collection. New York: Holt, Rinehart, and Winston.

# 14 Nitrogen Isotope Evidence for Weaning Age in a Nineteenth Century Canadian Skeletal Sample

M. ANNE KATZENBERG and SUSAN PFEIFFER

## INTRODUCTION

The study of skeletal remains from the historic era can offer numerous rewards. Studies of samples, such as the old church cemetery discussed here, can yield information about the life and times of our recent ancestors, thus contributing to social history. Such studies can help us validate methods that we may wish to apply to prehistoric samples, and they can even contribute to our understanding of the mechanisms of human evolution. Evolutionary processes are fueled by patterns of fertility and mortality, with the highest mortality occurring soon after birth. Breast feeding and weaning are crucial behavioral variables influencing both human fertility and mortality patterns.

In well-nourished mothers, breast milk is a complete food for at least the first 6 months of life (Jelliffe & Jelliffe, 1978). Among earlier peoples, only when a mother died during childbirth, or was otherwise unable to nurse, was the infant deprived of this food. Mother's milk contains T and B lymphocytes, immunoglobins and antistaphylococcal factor, as well as other resistance factors (Popkin et al., 1986). Weaning is a potentially dangerous time for infants and young children since they lose the benefit of passive immunity from mother's milk. The foods onto which children are weaned, such as grain gruel, may be difficult to digest and may not meet all nutritional requirements. The weaning foods may introduce new infectious agents. Thus, the

*Bodies of Evidence*, Edited by Anne L. Grauer.
ISBN 0-471-04153-X  © 1995 John Wiley & Sons, Inc.

culturally defined timing of weaning can be critical to the survival of a population's offspring generation. Further, weaning age reveals information about birth spacing and population regulation; a longer interval between births results in lower total fertility.

In studies of prehistoric human skeletal remains, several skeletal and dental indicators of nonspecific stress, such as Harris lines and enamel hypoplasia, occur in higher frequencies during late infancy and early childhood, ages that are consistent with possible weaning ages (Cook, 1979; Buikstra & Cook, 1980). While these have been interpreted as resulting from stress during weaning, until recently it has not been possible to estimate weaning age directly from skeletal remains.

Sillen and Smith (1984) attempted to estimate weaning age directly using the ratio of strontium to calcium in bone mineral. They reasoned that since strontium (Sr) is discriminated against in favor of calcium (Ca) in the mammary gland during the production of milk, the Sr/Ca ratio will be very low in milk. Strontium is also discriminated against at the placenta, so the newborn Sr/Ca ratio should be low. In comparison, the Sr/Ca ratio in plants is high and weaning diets are mainly cereal based. Further, discrimination against Sr in favor of Ca in the infant gut is poorly developed. Therefore, the shift from milk to cereal should be reflected by an increased Sr/Ca ratio in bones. Results from a sample of Middle Eastern prehistoric skeletons showed very low Sr/Ca ratios in newborns, as expected. There was a gradual increase in the Sr/Ca ratio with a peak between 1.5–3.5 years of age.

More recently, another new tool, stable nitrogen isotope analysis, has become available for determining diet and weaning age. DeNiro and Epstein (1981) established that the nitrogen stable isotope values (expressed as $\delta^{15}N$) of an organism's diet are related to the stable isotope values of its tissues. Schoeninger and DeNiro (1984) demonstrated a trophic-level effect of nitrogen isotope ratios in animals within an ecosystem. For example, the nitrogen isotope ratio of a carnivore's tissue is approximately 3‰ higher than that of its prey. This has subsequently been verified by others (e.g., Schoeninger, 1985; Ambrose, 1986; Katzenberg, 1989). Fogel and colleagues (1989) applied this information to mothers and nursing infants. In effect, the baby is feeding from the mother's tissues in the form of milk, and therefore exhibits a trophic-level shift. Newborns would be expected to have $\delta^{15}N$ values similar to those of adults in a population. Nursing infants will have higher $\delta^{15}N$ values (by 2–4 ‰), and at weaning age the values will return to levels in line with the adults in the sample. Subsequently, others have found an age relationship in nitrogen isotope ratios similar to that described by Fogel and colleagues (Katzenberg et al., 1993; Katzenberg, 1993; White & Schwarcz, 1994).

In this study we analyzed stable carbon ($\delta^{13}C$) and nitrogen isotopes in bone collagen from 76 individuals who were buried between 1824 and 1879 in a Methodist cemetery in Newmarket, Ontario. The sample contains many subadults (49% of all individuals in the sample died at 16 years of age or younger) and 20% of the total sample died in the first year of life. The large size and the skewed age distribution of the sample make it suitable for testing the hypothesis that weaning age can be determined in skeletal samples using stable nitrogen isotope values of collagen.

Furthermore, it is an early historic cemetery, so there is some information about infant feeding practices available.

## THE SITE

### History of the Cemetery

The skeletal remains analyzed in this study are from a historic Methodist Church cemetery, known as Prospect Hill, in Newmarket, Ontario (Fig. 1). The cemetery was in use from approximately 1824 to 1879. In 1879, when the cemetery was closed, family members were asked to remove remains for reinterment in the Newmarket Cemetery. Some individuals were moved, but many remained in the cemetery. A school was later built on the site. Following demolition of the school, a retirement home was erected on the site in 1989. It was at this time that the remaining burials were discovered (Pfeiffer et al., 1992).

Conditions of the salvage excavation included minimal accommodation for scientific analysis. No remains other than small tissue samples were allowed off-site, and all individuals were reinterred within a few weeks of disinterment. Because of the closure of the cemetery and subsequent multiple uses of the land, there were no grave markers to positively identify individuals. Church burial records no longer exist for this congregation, and attempts to contact possible descendants were unsuccessful. So, while there is some historic information about the region and the town at this time, there is no historic information on this specific group of individuals. Nevertheless, this study supplies biohistoric information only obtainable from the physical remains of Ontario's early European immigrant communities.

### The Excavated Sample

In total, 77 skeletons or partial skeletons were excavated. The age profile of the sample (Fig. 2), shows 49% juveniles and only four adults over 60 years of age. Juvenile age assessments are based on dental formation and eruption (Moorrees et al., 1963; Ubelaker, 1978). Adult age estimates are based on the morphology of the pubic symphyses, iliac auricular surfaces, sternal rib ends, and closure of the cranial vault sutures. The specific methods are those described by Moore-Jansen and Jantz (1986). Sex determination is based on pelvic and cranial criteria.

Historic documents indicate that the population of Newmarket was 1,388 in 1861. The Wesleyan Methodist Church, valued at $1300, could accommodate 300 worshippers. It appeared to excavators, as coffins were exposed, that members of the congregation were poor, because there was no coffin hardware or other funerary paraphernalia. Cemetery sites from other denominations in this time period are characterized by ornate Victorian styles (Woodley, 1992). Subsequent historic research established that the Wesleyan Methodists of Newmarket gave generously to the Missionary Society and were relatively high-status shopkeepers and crafts people.

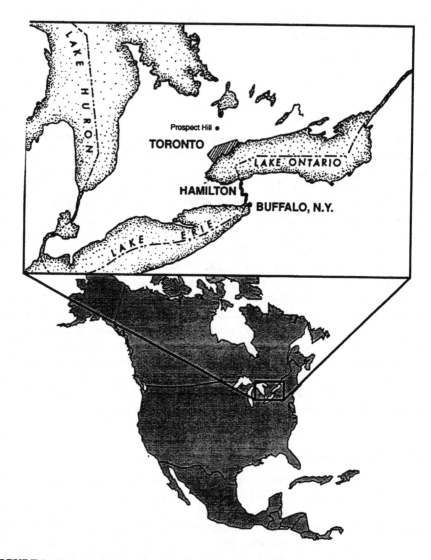

**FIGURE 1.** Map showing the location of the Prospect Hill Cemetery in Newmarket, Ontario, Canada.

The mothers, who are the focus of this study, were likely the wives of bakers, innkeepers, masons, shoemakers, teachers, or perhaps the one Newmarket melodeon maker of the 1871 census. Health care was available to them. The 1861 census lists five physicians, the 1871 census records the names of eight physicians and one dentist. Methodist teachings of this era urged that burials of the faithful should

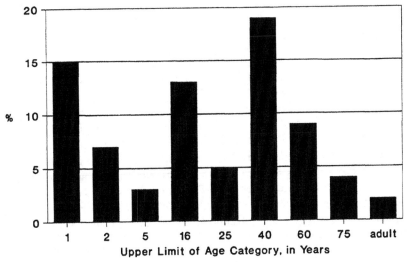

**FIGURE 2.** Age distribution of the cemetery sample.

include "no pomp, no equipage, no escutcheon," hence the very simple coffins (Whiteley et al., 1993).

### Historical Sources on Infant Feeding

General writings from this time and from the preceding century, in both Canada and Great Britain, suggest that women usually weaned their infants gradually, beginning as early as 6 months, but more often between 8 and 14 months (Apple, 1987; Thompson, 1984; Yeung, 1981). While wealthier women in Britain frequently sent their children to a wet nurse, this was less common among rural people (McLaren, 1979). Cows were kept in Newmarket at this time, but feeding cow's milk to infants was considered dangerous due to the high incidence of infection associated with the practice. Infant formulas were promoted beginning in the 1890s, so this sample precedes the early use of such formulas. We assume that the infant-feeding practices for this population generally conform to the British practice of breast feeding until at least 6 months and as long as 14 months, with gradual weaning onto solid foods.

## METHOD OF ANALYSIS

Ribs were selected from 65 burials and were cleaned ultrasonically, then crushed. Collagen, the structural protein of bone, was extracted from 1–3 grams of bone following the method described by Schoeninger and DeNiro (1984). Collagen samples were analyzed for carbon-to-nitrogen ratios (C/N ratios) and stable isotopes of carbon ($\delta^{13}C$ ‰$_{PDB}$)[1] and nitrogen ($\delta^{15}N$ ‰$_{AIR}$)[2] using a Carlo Erba gas analyzer and a Micromass Prism mass spectrometer, respectively, in the department of Physics, the University of Calgary, under the direction of H.R. Krouse. The C/N ratios are an indication of the quality of preservation of the bone protein. Protein degrades over time and contaminants from the burial environment can be introduced. The C/N ratio of fresh bone collagen is approximately 3.2. Ratios between 2.9 and 3.6 (suggested by DeNiro, 1985) are generally accepted as suitable for stable isotope analysis (see Ambrose, 1993). Departures from this range suggest either degradation of the original protein or the addition of extraneous organic matter from the burial environment. Either of these can alter the $\delta^{13}C$ and $\delta^{15}N$ ratios and affect their interpretation.

The use of stable isotope analysis in reconstructing prehistoric diets has become more common in the last few years since its introduction as an analytical tool in the late 1970s (Vogel & van der Merwe, 1977; van der Merwe & Vogel, 1978; DeNiro & Epstein, 1978). A number of recent reviews of the methods and applications are available (Ambrose, 1993; Katzenberg, 1992; Schoeninger & Moore, 1992; Schwarcz & Schoeninger, 1991).

## RESULTS

Results of C/N analysis (Table 1) indicate that all samples are typical of well-preserved collagen, with C/N ratios ranging from 2.9 to 3.6. Results of stable carbon and nitrogen isotope analysis are presented by Katzenberg (1993) and are reproduced here in Table 1. The range of $\delta^{13}C$ values is $-21.1‰$ to $-17.4‰$ with a mean of $-19.5‰$ and a standard deviation of 0.8. These values are typical of people subsisting primarily on $C_3$ grains such as wheat and oats. People eating only $C_3$ plants and animals feeding on $C_3$ plants would be expected to have $\delta^{13}C$ values around $-21.4‰$ (Vogel & van der Merwe, 1977), so the mean of $-19.5‰$ for Prospect Hill indicates that there was a small input of $C_4$ plants such as maize and cane sugar. The Methodists had a prohibition against alcohol, so it is unlikely that the latter was in the form of rum. Research on 19th century Canadian diet indicates that maize and sugar were called for in small quantities in some recipes such as cornbread and shortbread (Abonyi, 1993).

Results of stable nitrogen isotopes show a range of 10.4‰ to 16.6‰ with a mean of 12.7‰ and a standard deviation of 1.1. The highest values are found in infants. These values are typical of individuals subsisting on a terrestrial omnivorous diet (DeNiro, 1987). The wide range of values is the result of higher $\delta^{15}N$ among infants and young children.

In order to investigate the relationship between age and stable isotope values, several statistical analyses were carried out on the age and stable isotope data. In earlier studies (Katzenberg et al., 1993; Katzenberg, 1993), it was found that there is a significant negative correlation between $\delta^{15}N$ and age and a very weak negative correlation between $\delta^{13}C$ and age in samples with a large number of infants and subadults. Because it was apparent in other studies that the major difference in $\delta^{15}N$ occurs only in infants and children, and that adults show little variation, we also used

**TABLE 1. Stable Isotope and Age at Death Data from the Skeletal Sample of the Prospect Hill Cemetery**

| Burial # | C/N | $\delta^{13}C$ | $\delta^{15}N$ | Age (years) |
|---|---|---|---|---|
| X | 3.0 | −19.2 | 12.3 | adult |
| 1 | 3.0 | −19.3 | 12.5 | 45 |
| 11A | 3.2 | −20.1 | 13.8 | 30–40 |
| 11B | 3.1 | −18.5 | 14.6 | .5–1.5 |
| 12 | 3.3 | −19.5 | 12.8 | 40–50 |
| 16 | 3.1 | −20.6 | 12.1 | 7.5–8.5 |
| 17 | 3.5 | −20.3 | 12.8 | |
| 19 | 3.4 | −19.4 | 12.4 | 4–6 |
| 32 | 3.2 | −19.7 | 13.6 | 0–.5 |
| 33 | 3.6 | −19.7 | 13.0 | 4–5 |
| 34 | 3.2 | −20.2 | 14.2 | 1.5 |
| 35 | 3.1 | −19.6 | 13.3 | 30–35 |
| 36 | 3.3 | −19.0 | 13.2 | .5–.75 |
| 37 | 3.0 | −20.7 | 11.5 | 4 |
| 38 | 3.1 | −20.6 | 12.2 | 25–30 |
| 39 | 3.0 | −18.4 | 13.1 | .75–1 |
| 40 | 3.0 | −20.4 | 12.1 | 17–20 |
| 41 | 3.0 | −17.4 | 12.5 | 25–35 |
| 42 | 3.1 | −20.2 | 11.0 | 2 |
| 43 | 3.0 | −20.4 | 12.5 | 7 |
| 44 | 3.5 | −19.9 | 12.9 | 14–16 |
| 47 | 2.9 | −19.7 | 12.1 | 1.2–2.5 |
| 48 | 3.0 | −19.1 | 12.0 | 45–50 |
| 49 | 3.0 | −20.0 | 11.8 | 6 |
| 50A | 2.9 | −19.6 | 11.9 | 35–40 |
| 50B | 3.0 | −19.9 | 12.4 | 60+ |
| 51 | 2.9 | −20.2 | 12.0 | 2 |
| 52 | 3.0 | −19.9 | 12.0 | 27–30 |
| 53 | 2.9 | −18.7 | 12.9 | 25–26 |
| 54 | 3.0 | −17.8 | 11.6 | 30–35 |
| 55 | 2.9 | −18.6 | 16.6 | 0.75 |
| 58 | 3.0 | −19.4 | 12.5 | 18–25 |
| 59 | 2.9 | −18.6 | 12.2 | 25–40 |
| 60 | 3.0 | −19.9 | 12.5 | 1.5–2 |
| 61 | 3.0 | −20.0 | 10.4 | 35–40 |
| 62 | 2.9 | −20.7 | 12.3 | 25–26 |
| 63 | 3.0 | −19.8 | 11.6 | 28–30 |
| 65 | 3.1 | −19.0 | 13.4 | 0–.1 |
| 65A | 3.1 | −19.6 | 12.4 | 1.5–2.5 |
| 66 | 3.0 | −18.5 | 11.6 | .5–.75 |
| 67 | 2.9 | −20.0 | 11.6 | 42–46 |
| 69 | 3.0 | −19.7 | 15.5 | .6–1.3 |

(*continued*)

**TABLE 1.** *Continued*

| Burial # | C/N | $\delta^{13}C$ | $\delta^{15}N$ | Age (years) |
|----------|-----|----------------|----------------|-------------|
| 70 | 3.0 | −19.1 | 12.7 | 40–50 |
| 72 | 3.0 | −20.0 | 11.8 | 8.5–9.5 |
| 73 | 2.9 | −19.8 | 11.7 | 9 |
| 74 | 2.9 | −21.1 | 11.3 | 7 |
| 77 | 3.0 | −17.8 | 13.9 | 0.75 |
| 78 | 3.0 | −20.4 | 12.4 | 1.5 |
| 79B | 3.0 | −20.2 | 11.5 | 30–35 |
| 80B | 3.0 | −20.4 | 11.7 | 9 |
| 83 | 2.9 | −20.2 | 12.1 | 40–55 |
| 84 | 3.0 | −20.0 | 11.9 | 12–13 |
| 85 | 2.9 | −20.2 | 12.7 | 20–25 |
| 87 | 2.9 | −19.4 | 15.2 | 1 |
| 89 | 2.9 | −19.5 | 12.6 | 0–.5 |
| 90 | 3.5 | −18.7 | 13.9 | 0–.5 |
| 91 | 3.0 | −19.2 | 12.4 | 38–44 |
| 93 | 2.9 | −19.1 | 12.1 | 25–29 |
| 94A | 3.0 | −20.0 | 11.9 | 33–40 |
| 99 | 3.0 | −19.5 | 13.2 | 0–.1 |
| 100 | 3.0 | −18.1 | 15.0 | .4–.8 |
| 103 | 3.0 | −19.0 | 14.1 | 1.5 |
| 105 | 3.2 | −18.8 | 14.4 | .75–1 |
| 108 | 2.9 | −19.5 | 12.3 | 8 |
| 109 | 3.0 | −19.7 | 11.8 | 42–52 |

statistical analyses for this evaluation, which compared subadults and adults. Finally, because there is some error involved in estimating the age at death from skeletal remains, we used nonparametric, rank-order correlations in addition to parametric correlation analysis.

Carbon isotope ratios relative to age are plotted in Figs. 3 and 4. Figure 3 shows individuals aged only to 40 years, since age-estimation techniques for the skeleton are not accurate beyond this age and the correlation analyses performed are more accurate when older individuals of uncertain age are omitted. Figure 4 shows individuals aged birth to 8 years. Because of the high variability of infant values, it is desirable to view them on a finer scale, allowed by isolating them from older children and adults.

Nitrogen isotope ratios relative to age are plotted in Figs. 5 and 6. Figure 5 shows individuals aged birth to 40 years, while Fig. 6 shows only those individuals birth to 8 years, as was done with the carbon isotope data.

Both correlation and rank-order correlation analysis were done on the carbon and nitrogen isotope results for individuals aged 0–40 years. For $\delta^{13}C$, neither Pearson's $r$ nor Kendall's $\tau$ are significant ($r = -.064$ and $\tau = -.148$). Subadult values, however,

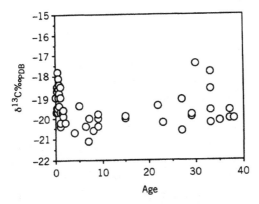

**FIGURE 3.** Carbon isotope values plotted against age at death for individuals aged birth to 40 years. Reproduced from Katzenberg (1993), with permission of the publisher.

are more variable, with some being very high (less negative). For $\delta^{15}N$, both Pearson's r and Kendall's $\tau$ are significant, with $p < .001$ ($r = -.541$ and $\tau = -.585$). $\delta^{15}N$ values decrease with age. It is evident from the figure that this occurs almost entirely among individuals aged 2 years or less. In order to compare individuals 0–2 ($n = 23$) to those older than 2 years ($n = 41$), $t$-tests were performed. For $\delta^{13}C$, $t = 2.57$ and $p = .013$. For $\delta^{15}N$, $t = 5.43$ and $p < .001$.

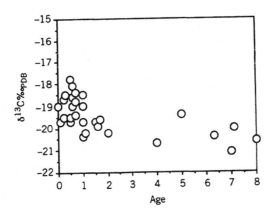

**FIGURE 4.** Carbon isotope values for children aged birth to 8 years plotted against age. Reproduced from Katzenberg (1993), with permission of the publisher.

## DISCUSSION

### Carbon Isotopes

DeNiro and Epstein (1978) established that the stable isotope values of an organism's diet are related to the stable isotope values of its tissues. Numerous controlled feeding studies show that the difference in $\delta^{13}C$ between diet and bone collagen is between 2 and 5‰. Studies of laboratory and free-ranging animals with monotonous diets show that variation within a population is small, on the order of ±1‰. Studies of organisms within food chains suggest a very small trophic level shift for carbon, on the order of +1‰. If there is a trophic level effect for nursing infants, their $\delta^{13}C$ values should be higher than those of adults by approximately 1‰. It is evident in Figs. 3 and 4, and from the results of the *t*-test, that infants do have slightly heavier (higher) $\delta^{13}C$ values than do most of the adults. The mean value for the birth to 2 years old is −19.2 ± 0.7‰, while the mean value for those over 2 years of age is −19.7 ± 0.7‰. High values among some adults are undoubtedly due to dietary differences within the population.

### Nitrogen Isotopes

Nitrogen isotopes distinguish animals feeding at different trophic levels. Among plants, legumes have the lowest $\delta^{15}N$ values, since they fix atmospheric nitrogen via the symbiotic relationship with nitrogen-fixing bacteria in their roots. Other terrestrial plants have slightly higher $\delta^{15}N$ values because they take up nitrogen from decomposition products in the soil. Animals eating these plants have $\delta^{15}N$ values that are approximately 2–3‰ higher than their diet. Animals consuming herbivores are again about 2–3‰ higher than the herbivore tissue. Infants consuming mother's milk should exhibit a further shift of +2–3‰.

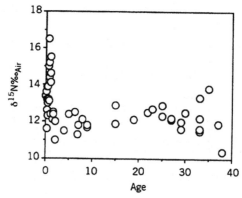

**FIGURE 5.** Nitrogen isotope values plotted against age at death for individuals birth to 40 years. Reproduced from Katzenberg (1993), with permission of the publisher.

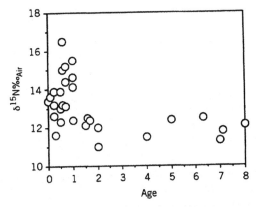

**FIGURE 6.** Nitrogen isotope values for children aged birth to 8 years plotted against age. Reproduced from Katzenberg (1993), with permission of the publisher.

The sample from Prospect Hill shows the elevated $\delta^{15}N$ values in infants relative to children and adults quite clearly. No adults have $\delta^{15}N$ values greater than 13.8‰, while infant $\delta^{15}N$ values range from 13.4–16.5‰. The mean value for those aged birth to 2 years is 13.5 ± 1.4‰, while the mean for those over two years of age is 12.2 ± 0.6‰.

With such a large sample of children, it should be possible to estimate the average age at weaning. Weaning is not a sudden event and infants are generally supplemented with solid foods for up to several months before being completely weaned from the breast. Bone-collagen turnover rates are not known for infants or young children, but logically must be much faster than the 10–20 year turnover rates generally cited for adults (Stenhouse & Baxter, 1976). This sample and others (Fogel et al., 1989; Katzenberg, 1993) illustrate that higher $\delta^{15}N$ values are recorded in the collagen within the first months of life, so it is reasonable to assume that lower $\delta^{15}N$ due to weaning should also occur within a few months. In order to estimate average age at weaning from the Prospect Hill data, we used distance-weighted least squares analysis for individuals aged birth to 3 years (Fig. 7). The curve begins to drop at 1 year of age. This corresponds to the general historic information of the time, which states that infants were normally weaned between 8 and 12 months of age.

## The Sample of Children

Simple methods for estimating childhood health, such as comparing bone-shaft length to dental development, indicate that the Prospect Hill children who died are shorter for their age than North American standards (Maresh, 1970). The Prospect Hill children fall in the 25th percentile. This is in contrast to Saunders and colleagues' (1993) and Saunders and Herring's (this volume) data on another 19th century Ontario sample of European origin, the St. Thomas Church sample from Belleville,

Ontario. The Prospect Hill children have bones that are relatively short compared to dental development, despite the fact that the adults of the population were tall. Slower growth for age may have been caused by poor nutrition, or by illness (Pfeiffer et al., 1992). Two infant skulls showed dramatic diploic thickening and disorganized ecto-cranial bone tissue, suggesting a relatively long bout of ill health prior to death. However, the isotopic values of these two are not distinctive. This may indicate that the mothers continued to breast feed their babies throughout the illnesses. While there is no specific evidence, in the way of bone lesions, that the Prospect Hill children were chronically ill prior to death, we cannot rule out the possibility. In any study of a skeletal sample in which age and stable isotope ratios are compared, the question of cause of death and its effect on bone chemistry must be considered.

Unlike other sites at which it has been possible to differentiate remains of probable stillborn infants through their low $\delta^{15}N$ values (Katzenberg, 1993), even the youngest infants at Prospect Hill (0–1 month) have elevated nitrogen isotope values. This suggests that these infants survived the birth process and further suggests that the rapid metabolic turnover and rapid bone deposition of the newborn infant creates a heavier isotopic signature very soon after breast feeding begins.

## CONCLUSIONS

These data clearly show a trophic-level shift for infants with respect to $\delta^{15}N$ values. They suggest that weaning occurred a few months prior to 1 year of age. The fact that this corresponds with the historic information available for 19th century Canada increases our confidence in the use of stable nitrogen isotopes for determining weaning age in prehistoric skeletal collections. The use of nitrogen isotopes in earlier skeletal samples with a large proportion of infants and children should allow a fairly

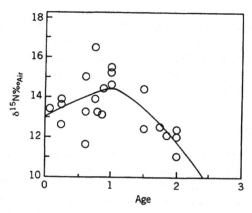

**FIGURE 7.** Distance weighted least squares smoothing of nitrogen isotope values of individuals aged birth to 3 years.

precise estimate of weaning age. A knowledge of the duration of nursing can provide information on birth spacing, population regulation and total fertility among pre-historic and early historic peoples. In addition, weaning age can be compared to skeletal and dental markers of stress, such as Harris lines and enamel hypoplasia, that have traditionally been associated with weaning stress.

This study also illustrates that while the trend is strong, individual values will display a range of isotopic values that probably reflect individual life histories. Nineteenth-century mothers appear to have breast fed their babies for about 1 year, but factors such as socioeconomic status and the child's overall health may have influenced their decisions. This approach to human bone-chemistry interpretation allows us to explore questions that are directly relevant to the survival of infants, a topic of central concern for social historians and researchers interested in human evolution.

## ACKNOWLEDGMENTS

Collagen samples were prepared by Jeannette Smith. Stable isotope and C/N analyses were carried out in the Stable Isotope Laboratory, University of Calgary, under the direction of Dr. H. R. Krouse with technical support by Nenita Lozano and Jesusa Pontoy. Access to the Prospect Hill sample was facilitated by Archaeological Services, Inc., Toronto, Ontario.

## NOTES

1.

$$\delta^{13}C(\text{\textperthousand},\text{PDB}) = \left[ \frac{^{13}C/^{12}C_{\text{sample}}}{^{13}C/^{12}C_{\text{standard}}} - 1 \right] \times 1000$$

The notation refers to the difference between the ratio of atoms of $^{13}C$ and atoms of $^{12}C$ in the sample, relative to that same ratio in a standard. The standard for carbon, abbreviated PDB, is a marine carbonate from the PeeDee formation in South Carolina. The standard is zero and terrestrial plants have less $^{13}C$ in comparison, so are expressed as negative numbers. Plants following the $C_3$ pathway of photosynthesis, including most temperate species, have $^{13}C$ values averaging $-26.5\text{\textperthousand}$, while grasses of tropical origin, such as maize, that use the $C_4$ pathway of photosynthesis have $^{13}C$ values averaging $-12.5\text{\textperthousand}$.

2. Similar to the notation for carbon isotopes, this refers to the difference in the ratio of $^{15}N$ to $^{14}N$ in the sample relative to the same ratio in the standard. For nitrogen, the standard is atmospheric $N_2$.

## REFERENCES

Abonyi S (1993). The effects of processing on stable isotope levels and mineral concentration if foods: Implications for paleodietary reconstruction. M.A. Thesis, Department of Archaeology, University of Calgary.

Ambrose SH (1986). Stable carbon and nitrogen isotope analysis of human and animal diet in Africa. J Hum Evol 15:707–731.

Ambrose SH (1993). Isotopic analysis of paleodiets: Methodological and interpretive considerations. In Sandford MK (ed.), Investigations of Ancient Human Tissue: Chemical Analyses in Anthropology. Food and Nutrition in History and Anthropology Vol. 10, pp. 59–130. Langhorne, PA: Gordon and Breach.

Apple RD (1987). Mothers and Medicine: A Social History of Infant Feeding, 1890–1950. Madison: University of Wisconsin Press.

Buikstra JE, Cook DC (1980). Paleopathology: An American account. Ann Rev Anthropol 9:433–470.

Cook DC (1979). Subsistence base and health in prehistoric Illinois valley: Evidence from the human skeleton. Med Anthropol 4:109–124.

DeNiro MJ (1985). Post-mortem preservation and alteration of in vivo bone collagen isotope ratios in relation to paleodietary reconstruction. Nature 317:806–809.

DeNiro MJ (1987). Stable isotopy and archaeology. Am Scientist 75:182–191.

DeNiro MJ, Epstein S (1978). Influence of diet on the distribution of carbon isotopes in animals. Geochimica et Cosmochimica Acta 42:495–506.

DeNiro MJ, Epstein S (1981). Influence of diet on the distribution of nitrogen isotopes in animals. Geochimica et Cosmochimica Acta 45:341–351.

Fogel M, Tuross N, Owsley DW (1989). Nitrogen isotope tracers of human lactation in modern and archaeological populations. Carnegie Institution, Annual report of the Director: Geophysical Laboratory.

Jelliffe DB, Jelliffe EFP (1978). Human Milk in the Modern World: Psychosocial, Nutritional, and Economic Significance. Oxford: Oxford University Press.

Katzenberg MA (1989). Stable isotope analysis of archaeological faunal remains from southern Ontario. J Archaeol Sci 16:319–329.

Katzenberg MA (1992). Advances in stable isotope analysis of prehistoric bones. In Saunders SR, Katzenberg MA (eds.), Skeletal Biology of Past Peoples: Research Methods, pp. 105–119. New York: Wiley-Liss.

Katzenberg MA (1993). Age differences and population variation in stable isotope values from Ontario, Canada. In Lambert JB, Grupe G (eds.), Prehistoric Human Bone: Archaeology at the Molecular Level, pp. 39–62. Berlin: Springer-Verlag.

Katzenberg MA, Saunders SR, Fitzgerald WR (1993). Age differences in stable carbon and nitrogen isotope ratios in a population of prehistoric maize horticulturists. Am J Phys Anthropol 90:267–281.

Maresh M (1970). Measurements from roentgenograms. In McCammon RW (ed.), Human Growth and Development, pp. 157–199. Springfield, IL: Charles C Thomas.

McLaren D (1979). Nature's Contraceptive. Wet-nursing and prolonged lactation: The case of Chesham, Buckinghamshire, 1578–1601. Medical History 23:426–441.

Moore-Jansen PH, Jantz RL (1986). A computerized skeletal data bank for forensic anthropology. Department of Anthropology, University of Tennessee.

Moorrees CFA, Fanning EA, Hunt EE (1963). Age variation of formation stages for ten permanent teeth. J Dental Res 42:1490–1502.

Pfeiffer S, Dudar JC, Austin S (1992). Prospect Hill: Skeletal remains from a 19th century Methodist cemetery, Newmarket, Ontario. Northeast Historical Archaeology 18(1989):29–48.

Popkin BM, Lasky T, Litvin J, Spicer D, Yamamoto ME (1986). The Infant-Feeding Triad: Infant, Mother and Household. New York: Gordon and Breach.

Saunders SR, Hoppa RD, Southern R (1993). Diaphyseal growth in a 19th century skeletal sample of subadults from St. Thomas' Church, Belleville, Ontario. Int J Osteoarchaeol 3:265–281.

Schoeninger, MJ (1985). Trophic level effects on $^{15}N/^{14}N$ and $^{13}C/^{12}C$ ratios in bone collagen and strontium levels in bone mineral. J Hum Evol 14:515–525.

Schoeninger MJ, DeNiro MJ (1984). Nitrogen and carbon isotopic composition of bone collagen from marine and terrestrial animals. Geochimica et Cosmochimica Acta 48:625–639.

Schoeninger MJ, Moore K (1992). Bone stable isotope studies in archaeology. J World Prehistory 6:2:247–296.

Schwarcz HP, Schoeninger MJ (1991). Stable isotope analyses in human nutritional ecology. Yearbook Phys Anthropol 34:283–322.

Sillen A, Smith P (1984). Weaning patterns are reflected in strontium–calcium ratios of juvenile skeletons. J Archaeol Sci 11:237–245.

Stenhouse MJ, Baxter MS (1976). The uptake of bomb $^{14}C$ in humans. In Berger R Suess HE (eds.), Radiocarbon Dating. Proceedings 9th International Conference on Radiocarbon Dating.

Thompson B (1984). Infant mortality in nineteenth-century Bradford. In Woods R, Woodward J (eds.), Urban Disease and Mortality in Nineteenth Century England. New York: St. Martin's.

Ubelaker DH (1978). Human Skeletal Remains. Chicago: Aldine.

van der Merwe NJ, Vogel JC (1978). $^{13}C$ content of human collagen as a measure of prehistoric diet in Woodland North America. Nature 276:815–816.

Vogel JC, van der Merwe NJ (1977). Isotopic evidence for early maize cultivation in New York State. Am Antiq 42:238–242.

White CD, Schwarcz HP (1994). Temporal trends in stable isotopes for Nubian mummy tissues. Am J Phys Anthropol 93:165–187.

Whiteley MF, Pfeiffer S, Austin S, Dudar JC (1993). Archaeology, biology and history: Research collaboration in the Prospect Hill project. In Semple N (ed.), Canadian Methodist Historical Society Papers, Vol.9, pp. 65–78. Toronto.

Woodley PH (1992). The Stirrup Court Cemetery coffin hardware. Ontario Archaeology 53:45–64.

Yeung DL (1981). Essays on Pediatric Nutrition. Canadian Public Health Association, Ottawa.

# Index

Toxic waste laws, 11
Trace elements, 199–200, 201
*Transylvania Journal of Medicine and the Associate Sciences*, 115
*Transylvania Medical Journal*, 115
Trauma, 149, 150, 166, 170, 180
Tree roots, 51–52, 54
Trevathan, W. R., 109
Trinity Episcopal Church Cemetery (Newark), 22, 23, 30
Trotter, M., 146, 177
Trox beetle, 45
Tuberculosis, 46
  Illinois, 143
  Monroe County Poorhouse, 124, 125
  Rochester area, 133, 134
Tucker Cemetery (Tex.):
  active use of, 163
  dental evidence from, 166, 167, 168, 170
  mortality evidence from, 164
  paleopathological evidence from, 165, 169
Turner, Elvis, 27, 29
Two-Way Analysis of Covariance, 187
Typhoid, 143
Typhus, 126, 128–129, 133, 134

United Empire Loyalists, 71
U.S. Army Corps of Engineers, 162
U.S. Congress, 21
U.S. Federal Census:
  Augusta, 111
  Cook County, 93, 95–96, 97–98, 99, 100
U.S. Federal Highway Administration, 25, 27
U.S. Food and Drug Administration, 46
University of Calgary, 226
University of Cincinnati, 176
University of Florida, 197
University of Georgia, 204
University of Indianapolis, 55
University of North Texas, 162
Urban renewal projects, *see* Construction projects

Vanadium, 201, 210
Vegetables:
  consumption of, 187, 190, 207, 215
  cultivation of, 206, 213
Vertebral bodies, 148
Vertebrate paleontology, 51
Vine Expressway (Philadelphia), 23, 25, 27, 28
Virginia, 39
Visitors, *see* General public
Vital events, 74, 75
Voegtly Evangelical Church (Pittsburgh), 41–42
Von Endt, D. W., 53

Walker, P. L., 62
Warped bones, 52
Washington, Paul, 27
Waste streams, 106–107, 113
Water, *see* Drinking water; Floodwaters; Groundwater
Weaning, 81–82, 83–84, 221–235
Weiss, Carl, 44–45
Weiss, K. M., 58, 91, 96
Wesleyan Methodists, 222–225, 226
West African Americans, 173, 215
Whiskey, 108
White Americans, *see* European Americans
White-metal screws, 162
"White plague", *see* Tuberculosis
White River levee, 54
Williams, Lavina Cross, 140, 147, 155
Williamsburg (Va.), 39
Wilson Bands, 166–167, 168, 169, 170
"Winter of the Deep Snow," 143
Wood, J. W., 92, 181
Working class, 27, 58. *See also* Physical labor
World War II victims, 54, 61
Written records, *see* Documentary records

X-rays, 43–44

Yorktown, Battle of (1781), 39
Yttrium, 181

Zimmerman, L. J., 22
Zinc, 181, 207, 209, 211
Zirconium, 181

CPSIA information can be obtained
at www.ICGtesting.com
Printed in the USA
LVOW04s1356300817
546972LV00009B/184/P